DARK HISTORY OF THE
POPES

DARK HISTORY OF THE POPES

VICE, MURDER, AND CORRUPTION IN THE VATICAN

BRENDA RALPH LEWIS

amber
BOOKS

This edition published in 2011

Reprinted in 2012

ISBN 978-1-907446-71-9

Printed and bound in China

Published by
Amber Books Ltd
74–77 White Lion Street
London N1 9PF
www.amberbooks.co.uk

Project Editor: James Bennett
Design: Zoë Mellors
Picture Research: Terry Forshaw

CONTENTS

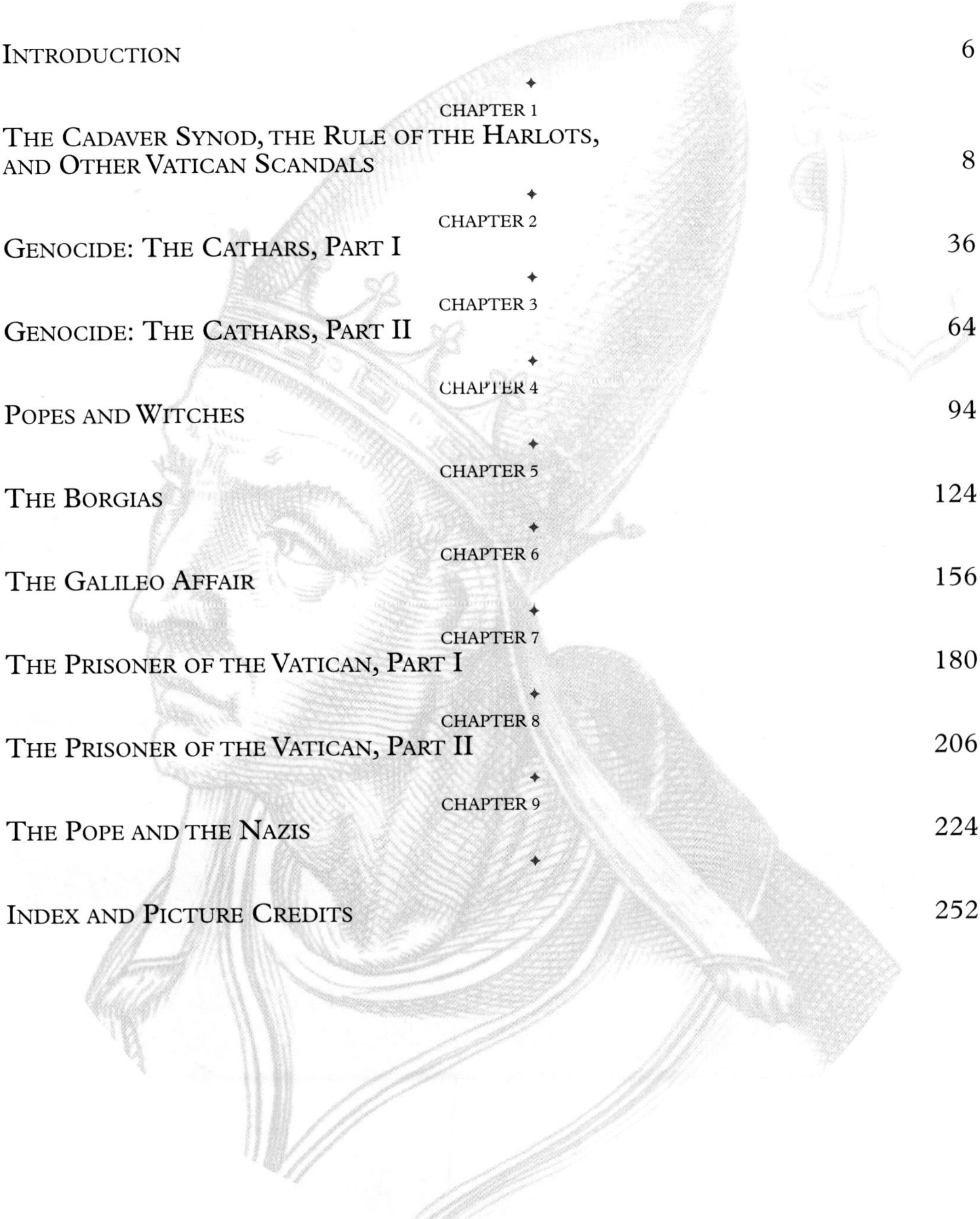

IN HONOREM PRINCIPIS APOST PAVLVS V BVR
SIVS ROMANVS PONT MAX AN MDCXII PONT VII

INTRODUCTION

The Pope in Rome holds the oldest elected office in the world. In the nearly 2,000 years it has existed, the papacy has helped forge the history of Europe, and has also reflected both the best and the worst of that history. Several popes schemed, murdered, bribed, thieved and fornicated, while others committed atrocities so appalling that even their own contemporaries were shocked.

This was especially true of the darkest days of the papacy's dark history when Christendom was gripped by a hysterical fear of witchcraft or any dissent from the path of 'true' religion as ordained by the popes and the Catholic church. Some of the most heinous crimes ever committed in the name of religion – all of them with papal sanction – occurred during the five centuries or so during which a ferocious struggle raged over Europe to eliminate 'error': any belief, practice or opinion that deviated from the official papal line.

Virtual genocide, for example, eliminated the Cathars, an ascetic sect centred around the southwest of France, who believed that God and the Devil shared the world. In 1231, the first Inquisition was introduced to deal with them. Inquisitors used horrific tortures such as the rack and the thumbscrew to extract confessions. The end was often death in the all-consuming flames of the stake. As well as heretics, thousands of supposed witches, wizards, sorcerers and other 'agents' of the Devil died in the same horrific way.

The Basilica of St. Peter in the Vatican City (left), constructed between 1506 and 1626, is one of the holiest sites in Christendom. To the east of the basilica is the Piazza di San Pietro, or St. Peter's Square, flanked by 284 Doric columns topped by 140 statues of saints (right).

In less savage form, the Inquisition caught up with the 17th-century astronomer Galileo Galilei, who was censured for supporting views about the structure of the Universe that were contrary to Church teachings. Galileo believed in that the Earth orbited the Sun, while the Church taught that the Earth was at the centre of the universe. Galileo ended his life as a prisoner in his own house, and some 350 years passed before the Vatican admitted that he had been right all along.

The Vatican had its own, self-imposed prisoners: the five popes who declined to recognise the Kingdom of Italy and for nearly sixty years refused to leave the precincts of the Vatican. Eventually, in 1929, Pius XI realised that isolation was making the papacy an anachronism and signed the Lateran Treaties that enabled it to rejoin the modern world.

Ten years later, in 1939, the extreme dangers of this modern world were brought home to another Pius – Pope Pius XII – who was confronted with the combatants in World War II, both of whom sought papal sanction for their efforts. Pius XII gave his support to neither, but by following his own path made himself a hero and a saviour to some, but a villain, even a criminal, to others.

THE CADAVER SYNOD, THE RULE OF THE HARLOTS, AND OTHER VATICAN SCANDALS

One thousand years ago and more, political instability was rife in Rome. At that time, the image of the papacy was everything from outlandish to weird to downright appalling. All kinds of dark deeds stuck to its name. Corruption, simony, nepotism and lavish lifestyles were only part of it, and not necessarily the worst.

During the so-called 'Papal Pornocracy' of the early tenth century, popes were being manipulated, exploited and manoeuvred for nefarious ends by mistresses who used them as pawns in their own power games. With some justification, this era was also called the Rule of the Harlots.

Benedict IX (above), one of the most scandalous popes of the 11th century, was described as vile, foul, execrable and a 'demon from Hell in the disguise of a priest'. St Peter's Basilica in Vatican City (left) was by tradition the burial site of St Peter, the first Bishop of Rome and first in the line of papal succession. Here its dome rises above the facade begun in 1605 by the architect Carlo Maderna.

HOW TO FIND A MISSING POPE

So many popes were assassinated, mutilated, poisoned or otherwise done away with that when one of them disappeared, never to be seen again, it was only natural to scan a list of violent explanations to find out what had happened to him. Death by strangulation in prison was a frequent cause. Had the vanished pope been hideously mutilated and therefore made unfit to appear in public? Had he made off with the papal cash box? Or should the brothels and other houses of ill repute be searched to find out if he was there? Often, there was no clear answer and explanations were left to gossip and rumour.

A VARIETY OF VIOLENT ENDS

The variety of violent ends suffered by popes during the Papal Pornocracy was astonishing. For example, in 882 CE one pope, John VIII, failed to die sufficiently quickly from the poison administered to him. His assassins, losing patience, smashed his skull with hammers to move things along. A tenth-century pope, Stephen IX, suffered horrific injuries when his eyes, lips, tongue and hands were removed. Amazingly, the unfortunate man survived, but was never able to show his mutilated face in public again. Pope Benedict V decamped to Constantinople in 964 CE after seducing a young girl, taking the papal treasury with him. Benedict was obviously a free-spending pontiff, for the money ran out before the end of the year and he returned to Rome. He soon resumed his bad old habits but was finally killed by a jealous husband who left more than one hundred stab wounds on his body before throwing him into a cesspit.

Another pope, Boniface VI, was elected to the Throne of St Peter even though he had twice been downgraded for immorality. As so often happens with events that took place sufficiently long ago to gather legends, Boniface either died of gout, or was poisoned or deposed and sent away to allow another pope, Stephen VII, to take his place. Either way, Boniface disappeared from history but he did so with suspicious rapidity: his reign lasted only 15 days. Afterwards, Stephen was let loose on the many powers and privileges of the papacy that he was expected to use for the benefit of his sponsors, the mighty House of Spoleto in central Italy and its domineering chatelaine, the Duchess Agiltrude, the instigator of the scandalous Cadaver Synod of 897 CE.

Pope John VIII was murdered in 882 CE, but only after he had failed to die by poison. Instead, he was battered to death by his killers.

One thing was certain, though: by the ninth century, the papacy and the popes were the playthings of noble families like the Spoletans, who controlled cities such as Venice, Milan, Genoa, Pisa, Florence and Siena, among others. Through their wealth and influence, and their connections with armed militias, these families formed what amounted to a feudal aristocracy. They were generally a brutish lot, willing to bring the utmost violence and cruelty to the task of seizing and controlling the most prestigious office in the Christian world. Once achieved, though, their newfound power could be ephemeral, for the reigns of some of their protégés were very short indeed. There were, for example, 24 popes between 872 CE and 904 CE. The longest reign lasted a decade and another four came and went within a year. There were nine popes in the nine years between 896 CE and 904 CE, as many

> By the ninth century, the papacy and the popes were the playthings of noble families.

pontiffs as were elected during the entire twentieth century. This meant, of course, that the papal See of Rome was in a constant state of uproar, as the struggle for the Vatican had to be fought over and over again.

THE DEADLY DUCHESS

Stephen VII was one of the short-lived popes, promising the House of Spoleto, in central Italy, a taste of papal power that turned out to be a brief 15 months in 896 CE and 897 CE. Stephen was almost certainly insane and his affliction appears to have been common knowledge in Rome. This, though, did not deter the Duchess Agiltrude from foisting him onto the Throne of St Peter in July 896 CE. Agiltrude, it appears, had a special task for Pope Stephen, which involved wreaking revenge on her one-time enemy, the late Pope Formosus.

Like most, if not all, legendary glamour heroines of history, Agiltrude was reputed to be very beautiful, with a sexy figure and long blonde hair. However that may be, she was certainly a formidable woman with a fearsome taste for retribution. In 894 CE, Agiltrude took her young son, Lambert, to Rome to be confirmed by Pope Formosus as Holy Roman Emperor, or so she expected. She found, though, that the venerable Formosus had ideas of his own. He preferred another claimant, Arnulf of Carinthia, a descendant of Charlemagne, the first of the Holy Roman Emperors. The pope realized that Agiltrude was not going to stand by quietly and watch as her son was displaced, and knowing well the turbulent temper of the Spoletans, he saw trouble coming. So, Formosus appealed to Arnulf for help.

Arnulf, for his part, had no intention of being forced to give way to an underage upstart like Lambert or his implacable mother. He soon arrived with his army, sent Agiltrude packing back to Spoleto and was crowned Holy Roman Emperor by Formosus on 22 February 896 CE. The new emperor at once set out to

Stephen was almost certainly insane and his affliction appears to have been common knowledge in Rome.

Pope Formosus was rumoured to have been poisoned before his death in 896 CE, but he suffered horrific injuries afterwards. Several of his fingers were cut off and he was beheaded before being thrown into the River Tiber.

BENEDICT IX, THE THREE-TIMES POPE

Benedict IX was born in around 1012 into a family with plenty of political, military and papal muscle. Two of his uncles preceded him as Pope Benedict VIII and Pope John XIX, and his father, Alberic III, Count of Tusculum, was influential enough to secure the Throne of St Peter for him when he was around 20 years of age. Needless to say, Benedict was one of the youngest popes ever, and he was highly placed in the dissolute stakes as well. Benedict was described as 'feasting on immorality' and 'a demon from Hell in the disguise of a priest'. He was also accused of 'many vile adulteries and murders'. A later pope, Victor III, charged him with 'rapes, murders and other unspeakable acts'. Benedict's life, Pope Victor continued, was 'so vile, so foul, so execrable that I shudder to think of it'. For good measure, Benedict was also indicted for homosexuality and bestiality.

Benedict's hold over his throne was tenuous. His enemies forced him out of Rome in 1036 and again in 1045, when he sold his office for 680 kilograms of gold to his godfather, John Gratian, the Archpriest of St John Lateran who afterwards became Pope Gregory VI. The payment drained the Vatican treasury so greatly that, for a time, there was not enough money to pay the papal bills.

Having secured his booty, Benedict set off for a life of leisure and pleasure at one of his castles in the country. He had plans to marry, but the lady in question, a second cousin, turned him down. Within a few months, Benedict was back in Rome, attempting to retrieve his throne. He failed and was driven out by infuriated nobles in 1046. Another attempt met the same resistance, and Benedict was finally thrown out in 1048.

In 1049, Benedict was accused of simony, but failed to appear in court to answer the charges. As punishment, he was excommunicated. After that, Benedict more or less disappeared from the records. The exact date of his death remains unknown. It may have taken place in 1056 while he was preparing to launch a renewed attempt at retrieving the papal throne. Another date for Benedict's demise was 1065, when he had seemingly repented of his numerous sins, and died as a penitent at the Abbey of Grottaferrata in the Alban Hills, 20 kilometres (12 miles) southeast of Rome.

Benedict IX is said to have ended his outrageous life as a humble penitent at the church of Santa Maria di Grottaferrata, a small town in the Alban hills southeast of Rome.

pursue Agiltrude, but before he could reach Spoleto, he suffered a paralyzing illness, possibly a stroke. Pope Formosus died six weeks later, on 4 April 896 CE, reputedly poisoned by Agiltrude. By all accounts, he had been an admirable pope, well known for his care for the poor, his austere way of life, his chastity and devotion to prayer, all of them admirable Christian virtues – and remarkable – in an age of decadence, self-seeking and barbarism.

Pope John VIII (seated) gives a papal blessing to Charles the Bald, King of West Francia in northwestern France after his coronation as Holy Roman Emperor in 875 CE.

But whatever his virtues, Formosus could not entirely escape the poisonous atmosphere of violence and intrigue that permeated the Church in his time. It was all too easy to make enemies and so become exposed to their vengeance and bile. It was also possible that Formosus was too honest and outspoken for his own good. It was, for instance, an unwise move to oppose the election of Pope John VIII in 872 CE, particularly when Formosus himself had been among the candidates. It was bad policy, too, to have friends among Pope John's enemies who were perennially plotting against him. They were so intent on destroying him that they sought help for their nefarious plans from the Muslim Saracens, who were the sworn enemies of Christianity.

This was an age when the enemies of popes had a habit of disappearing or ending up dead. The writing on the wall was easy to read, and when his plotter friends fled from the papal court, Formosus fled with them. This, of course, implied that he was one of the conspirators. As a result, he was charged with some lurid crimes, such as despoiling the cloisters in Rome, and conspiring to destroy the papal see. Formosus was punished accordingly. In 878 CE, he

Such accusations and penalties, made against an elderly man of proven probity and morality were clearly ludicrous and had all the appearance of a put-up job.

was excommunicated. This sentence was withdrawn, though, when Formosus agreed to sign a declaration stating that he would never return to Rome or perform priestly duties. In addition, the Diocese of Porto, in Portugal, where Formosus had been made Cardinal Bishop in 864 CE, was taken from him.

ALL WAS FORGIVEN – FOR A WHILE

Such accusations and penalties, made against an elderly man of proven probity and morality were clearly ludicrous and had all the appearance of a put-up job. Fortunately, all was later forgiven. After the death of John VIII in 882 CE, his successor as pope, Marinus I, recalled Formosus to Rome from his refuge in western France, and restored him to his Diocese of Porto. Nine years later, Formosus was himself elected pope and it was during his five-year tenure that he made a very serious mistake: he crossed Duchess Agiltrude and the House of Spoleto. He also made other enemies over his policies as pope, which included trying to eradicate the influence of lay (non-ordained) people in Church affairs.

Quite possibly, this was why the death of one of her enemies and the incapacity of the other were not enough for Agiltrude. She had in mind something much more dramatic and gruesome. Once Formosus' successor as pope, Boniface VI, had gone, the way was

clear for Stephen VII, the candidate favoured by Agiltrude and her equally malicious son Lambert, to step up to the plate and do their bidding.

THE DARK WORKINGS OF HATRED

In January 897 CE, Stephen announced that a trial was to take place at the church of St John Lateran, the official church of the pope as Bishop of Rome. The defendant was Pope Formosus, now deceased for nine months, for whom Stephen had developed a fanatical hatred. Stephen was a thoroughly nasty piece of work but the source of his hatred is not precisely known: it is possible that just being a member of the House of Spoleto relentlessly prodded along by the fearsome Agiltrude was enough. Even so, hatred, however obsessive, could not easily explain the horrors that featured in the posthumous trial of Pope Formosus some time in January 897 then nine-months dead.

The dead pope was not tried in his absence. At Agiltrude's prompting, Formosus – or rather his

Pope Stephen VII put on a very dramatic show at the 'trial' of the dead Pope Formosus, whose mouldering corpse was dug up from its grave to play its grisly part in the Cadaver Synod of 897 CE.

rotting corpse, which was barely held together by his penitential hair shirt – was removed from his burial place and dressed in papal vestments. He was then carried into the court, where he was propped up on a throne. Stephen sat nearby, presiding over the 'trial' alongside co-judges chosen from the clergy. To ensure they were unfit for the task, and merely did what they were told, several co-judges had been bullied and terrorized and sat out the proceedings in a lather of fear. At the trial, the charges laid against Formosus by Pope John VIII were revived. For good measure, Stephen added fresh accusations designed to prove that Formosus had been unfit for the pontificate: he had committed perjury, Stephen claimed, coveted the Throne of St Peter and violated Church law.

This illustration of Pope Stephen VII interrogating the dead Pope Formosus portrays the corpse of the one-time pontiff in a rather better condition than it would have been in reality: Formosus had died several months previously.

VATICAN VOCABULARY

SIMONY

Simony, the crime of selling or paying for church offices or positions or offering payment to influence an appointment, was a serious crime within the Church. It took its name from Simon Magus, also known as Simon the Sorcerer, who attempted to bribe the disciples Peter and John. As the New Testament recounts:

> *And when Simon saw that through laying on of the apostles' hands the Holy Ghost was given, he offered them money, saying, 'Give me also this power, that on whomsoever I lay hands, he may receive the Holy Ghost.' But Peter said unto him, 'Thy money perish with thee, because thou hast thought that the gift of God may be purchased with money.'*

NEPOTISM

Nepotism derives from the Latin word *nepos,* meaning nephew or grandchild, and describes the favouritism many popes showed towards their relatives and friends by giving them high positions in the Church they did not merit, either through ability or seniority. It was probably the most common of Church crimes, particularly in medieval times. However, nepotism was almost understandable at a time when popes had personal rivals and enemies and needed people close to them who had already proved their loyalty.

His corpse was stripped of its vestments and dressed instead in the clothes of an ordinary layman. The three fingers of Formosus' right hand, which he had used to make papal blessings, were cut off.

DRAMA AT THE CADAVER SYNOD

Stephen's behaviour in court was extraordinary. The clergy and other spectators in court were treated to frenzied tirades, as Stephen mocked the dead pope and launched gross insults at him. Formosus had been allowed a form of defence in the form of an 18-year-old deacon. The unfortunate young man was supposed to answer for Formosus, but was too frightened of the raving, screaming Stephen to make much of an impression. Weak, mumbling answers were the most the poor lad could manage.

Inevitably, at the end of the proceedings, which came to be called, appropriately, the Cadaver Synod, Formosus was found guilty on all the charges against him. Punishment followed immediately. Stephen declared that all of the dead pope's acts and ordinations were null and void. At Stephen's command, his corpse was stripped of its vestments and dressed instead in the clothes of an ordinary layman. The three fingers of Formosus' right hand, which he had used to make papal blessings, were cut off. The severed fingers – or rather what was left of them after nine months of decay – were handed over the Agiltrude who had watched the proceedings with open satisfaction. Finally, Pope Stephen ordered that Formosus should be reburied in a common grave. This was done, but there was a grisly sequel. Formosus' corpse was soon dug up, dragged through the streets of Rome, tied with weights and thrown into the River Tiber.

Formosus was buried yet again, this time in an ordinary graveyard. Like the rescue itself, the burial had to be kept secret.

Formosus had been revered by many of the clergy and he was popular with the Romans and, before his election in 891 CE, many had rioted at the prospect of another pope being chosen instead. There was, therefore, no shortage of helpers when a monk who had remained faithful to the dead pope's memory asked a group of fishermen to aid him in retrieving Formosus' much misused remains. Afterwards, Formosus was buried yet again, this time in an ordinary graveyard. Like the rescue itself, the burial had to be kept secret. If Formosus' enemies – particularly Pope Stephen and Agiltrude – had learnt of it, it was likely that the body of the dead pope would have been desecrated yet again.

The Cadaver Synod, known more graphically by its Latin name *Synodus Horrenda,* prompted uproar and outrage throughout Rome. This was underlined in the superstitious popular mind when the Basilica of St John suddenly fell down with a thunderous roar just as Pope Stephen and Agiltrude emerged from the church of St John Lateran at the end of the 'trial'. The fact that the Basilica had long ago been condemned as unsafe was less convincing than the idea that the collapse was a sign of God's displeasure. Before long, in much the same vein, rumours arose that the corpse of Pope Formosus had 'performed' miracles, an ability normally ascribed only to saints.

The widespread disgust at the savagery of the proceedings, and its ghastly sequel,

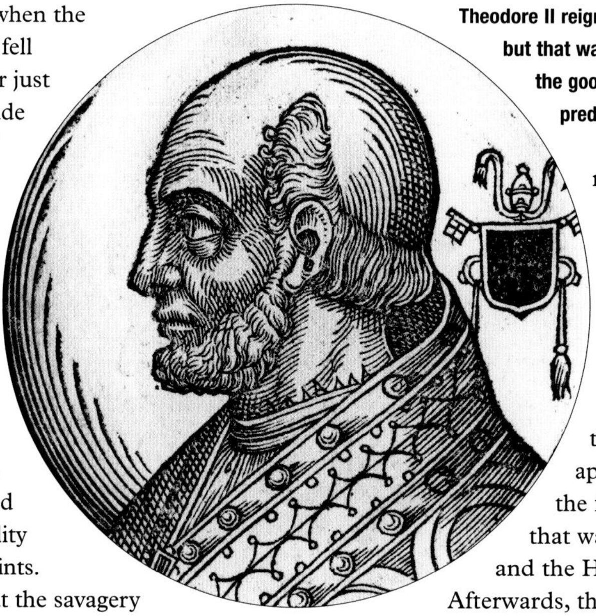

Theodore II reigned as pope for only twenty days, but that was long enough for him to restore the good name of his much abused predecessor, Formosus.

> Stripped of his splendid papal vestments and insignia, he was thrown into prison, where he was strangled.

convinced many clergy that if anyone was unfit to be pope it was Stephen VII. An element of self-interest also featured in the wave of hostility aroused by the Synod. Many clergy who had been ordained by Formosus were deprived of their positions when Stephen nullified the dead pope's ordinations.

POPE STEPHEN MEETS HIS MAKER

Hostility soon translated into action. In August 897 CE, eight months after the Cadaver Synod, a 'palace revolution' took place and Stephen VII was deposed. Stripped of his splendid papal vestments and insignia, he was thrown into prison, where he was strangled. This, though, was by no means the end of the days when the popes and the papacy were mired in disgrace. For one thing, Agiltrude was still around and active and, wherever she was, there was bound to be trouble. Agiltrude was enraged at the murder of her protégé Pope Stephen and moved in fast to restore the influence that had been killed off with him. But she had no luck with the new pope, Romanus, who was placed on the papal throne in 897 CE but remained there for only three months. Romanus, it appears, fell foul of one of the factions at the papal court that was opposed to Agiltrude and the House of Spoleto.

Afterwards, the hapless former pope was 'made a monk' an early medieval European euphemism that meant he had been deposed.

RESTORING FORMOSUS

Romanus's successor, Pope Theodore II, was even less fortunate, but at least he lasted long enough to do right by the much-abused Formosus. Theodore ordered the body of the late pope reburied clad in pontifical vestments and with full honours in St Peter's in Rome. He also annulled the court where the Cadaver Synod had taken place and invalidated its verdicts and decisions. Much to the relief of the clergy dispossessed by Stephen VII, Theodore declared valid once again

> Sergius ... had Formosus' corpse beheaded and cut off three more of his fingers before consigning him to the River Tiber once more.

the offices they had once received from Formosus. It was as if the Cadaver Synod and the lunatic Pope Stephen had never existed. Unfortunately, however, it brought Theodore few, if any, rewards. His reign lasted only 20 days in November 897 CE, after which he mysteriously died. The following year, however, future

POPE SERGIUS III: THE MOST WICKED OF MEN

Sergius III was once described as the source of 'infinite abominations amongst light women' and 'the slave of every vice and the most wicked of men'. His personal as well as his public life as pope was said to be one long procession of scandal and decadence, which included the murder of one, and possibly two popes. It appears that Sergius ordered the murders of both Pope Leo V and the antipope Christopher who were strangled in prison in 904 CE. That done, the way was clear for Sergius to become pope himself. Three years later, Pope Sergius acquired a mistress, Marozia, whose mother, Theodora, 'gave' her to him when she was only 15 years old. Sergius was 30 years Marozia's senior, but it seems he had lusted after Marozia for nine years, ever since they met at the notorious Cadaver Synod of 897 CE. Even from an early age, Marozia had possessed a strong sexual attraction and although she was by no means Sergius' only lover, he never forgot her. Sergius and Marozia had a son, who became John XI, so making Sergius the only pope on record as the father of another pope. As for Marozia, her four-year affair with Pope Sergius, who died in 911 CE, seems to have given her a taste for papal power and the pursuit of pope-making.

The critics of scandalous popes heaped virtually every pejorative they knew on Sergius III and his decadent lifestyle.

trials of dead persons were prohibited by Theodore's successor, Pope John IX.

Ten years later, Sergius III, who was elected pope in 904 CE, dug up Pope Formosus and put him on trial

Not long afterwards, Formosus' headless corpse surfaced again when it became entangled in a fisherman's net.

all over again. Sergius, then a cardinal, had been a co-judge at the Cadaver Synod in 897 CE and became infuriated when the guilty verdict was overturned. This time, Sergius restored the guilty judgement and added some ghoulish touches of his own. He had Formosus' corpse beheaded and cut off three more of his fingers before consigning him to the River Tiber once more. To emphasize his message, Sergius ordered a flattering epitaph for Stephen VII be inscribed on his tomb.

Not long afterwards, Formosus' headless corpse surfaced again when it became entangled in a fisherman's net. Retrieved from the Tiber for a second time, Formosus was returned once more to St Peter's church. Sergius had, of course, contravened the prohibition on posthumous trials declared by John IX so his actions were essentially invalid. Nevertheless, a public statement of Formosus' innocence had to be made and both he and his work were formally reinstated yet again.

The chief instigator of the original Cadaver Synod, Agiltrude, was still alive when Formosus was exonerated for a second time but her position – and her power – had radically altered because, through the extraordinary antics of Stephen VII, she had triumphed over the dead pope in 896 CE. But she had a weakness. Agiltrude's power, while considerable, was essentially second-hand, relying on puppets like Pope Stephen who could be manoeuvred into the positions she wanted them to occupy and from there implement her policies. Also important in Agiltrude's armoury were certain family relationships that gave her the high status she enjoyed from the positions occupied by her husband, Guy of Spoleto, and after him, by their son, Lambert. When Guy died on 12 December 894 CE, Agiltrude instantly lost her standing as Duchess of Spoleto and Camerino, Queen of Italy and Holy Roman Empress. There was still some kudos to be had from Lambert's elevation to all these titles, but he died before his mother in 898 CE and Agiltrude's last family link with power disappeared.

Agiltrude died in 923 CE, but by that time two other women had discovered another way into the corridors of papal power in Rome. They were Theodora and her daughter Marozia, both of them the mistresses of popes. Theodora was described as a 'shameless strumpet' and her two daughters, Marozia and the younger Theodora as possessing reputations not 'much better… than their mother'.

Neither the elder Theodora nor Marozia halted the rapid turnover that had become a regular feature of the papacy. If anything they exacerbated it. In the first years of the tenth century, short pontificates of a year or less persisted, and so did the violent deaths of

Short pontificates of a year or less persisted, and so did the violent deaths of popes that reflected the ongoing struggle for power.

popes that reflected the ongoing struggle for power. Others managed to survive for a year or two but rarely much more. In fact, popes succeeded one another with such rapidity that papal servants made a handsome profit selling off their personal accoutrements and furnishings.

RULE OF THE HARLOTS

But petty theft was very small beer compared to the corruption, licentiousness and venality of this period, which was known as the 'papal pornocracy' or the 'Rule of the Harlots' by those who, with good reason, believed that the papacy was now in the hands of whores. Like the puppets whose strings were so diligently pulled by Agiltrude, the pornocracy popes were eager partners in the

A portrait of Marozia, the 'shameless strumpet' who schemed her way to power in Rome in the 10th century CE and matched her lover, Pope Sergius III, for licentiousness and vice.

FLAMENG DEL.

ISLAND OF DECADENCE

Most of the visitors to Marozia's establishment on the Isola Tiberina in Rome were young aristocrats and various churchmen, including bishops whose way of life was as far as could possibly be from the ascetic Christian ideal. Apart from sex, and lots of it, these men were more interested in chasing boar or in falconry – the standard entertainment of the upper classes in medieval times – and while they attended Mass and other church services, they usually did so with their spurs on, and daggers in their belts. Their horses were at the ready outside, waiting for Mass to end so that their riders could leap into the saddle and dash off for an afternoon's hunting.

These men enjoyed a lavish lifestyle to match. Their houses were the last word in luxury, featuring the finest decor and most expensive hangings in lush velvets. This was the kind of decadent living – and decadent company – Marozia most enjoyed.

John XI, seen here with his mother Marozia on the Isola Tiberina, was only 21 years of age when she engineered his election as pope in 931 CE.

decadence and immorality that characterized this shameless – and shameful – era.

The tenth-century Lombard historian, Bishop Liutprand of Cremona, was virulently anti-Roman and anti-papal. However, rather more than a grain of truth was in the mix when he wrote in his *Antapodosis*, a history of the papacy from 886–950 CE:

> *They hunted on horses with gold trappings, had rich banquets with dancing girls when the hunt was over, and retired with (their) whores to beds with silk sheets and gold embroidered covers. All the Roman bishops were married and their wives made silk dresses out of the sacred vestments.*

Bishop Liutprand branded Theodora and Marozia as 'two voluptuous imperial women (who) ruled the papacy of the tenth century'. Theodora, he maintained, was 'a shameless strumpet...at one time...sole monarch

Marozia kept an establishment on the Isola Tiberina, an island in the middle of the River Tiber where modesty and morality were unknown.

of Rome and – shame though it is to write it – exercised power like a man.' Theodora's second daughter, another Theodora, did not escape censure for she and her sister, Liutprand continued, 'could surpass (their mother) in the exercises that Venus loves'. This was hard on the younger Theodora who, it appears, led a blameless life devoted to good works, but Liutprand's assessment of Marozia was much nearer the mark. For one thing, Marozia kept an establishment on the Isola Tiberina, an island in the middle of the River Tiber where modesty and morality were unknown.

Turning to Theodora, Liutprand described in detail how she seduced a handsome young priest and obtained for him the bishopric of Bologna and the archbishopric of Ravenna. It seems, though, that Theodora later regretted her generosity. She soon missed her youthful lover and in order to have him near her so that she could be his 'nightly companion',

THEODORA'S POPES

Theodora was already a practised pope-maker by the time she engineered John X onto the Throne of St Peter in 914 CE. One of her preferences was for mild-mannered popes she could push around, such as Benedict IV, who reigned uncomplainingly from 900–903 CE. On the other hand, Theodora also had a taste for thoroughgoing cads and debauchees. One of them was Lando I, who was pope for only seven months between 913–914 CE. Little is known about Lando but what was known was pretty dreadful. Lando, it appears, was ruined early on in life by spending too much time in the company of 'lewd women' and, according to a medieval chronicler, was 'at last consumed': this, of course, was chronicler's code for the fate of a sinner felled by punishment from on high.

Pope John X was the lover of Marozia's mother, Theodora. She made him pope in 914 CE, but he was hardly grateful: instead, he deserted her and went off with a younger woman.

she summoned him to Rome. In 914 CE, she made him pope as John X. He was probably the father of Theodora's younger daughter.

BLOTTING THE PAPAL COPYBOOK

Pope John, it appears, fitted well into the pornocratic ethos he found in Rome. He was a skilful military commander who fought and won battles against the Muslim Saracens. But he blotted his copybook, and did it with indelible ink, through his nepotism, the enrichment of his family and his almost complete lack of principle. Far from being grateful to Theodora for his elevation to the most exalted of Church offices, John deserted her once he had set eyes on the delectable young daughter of Hugh of Provence, the future king of Italy.

But Theodora's daughter Marozia was not best pleased at the election – or rather the engineering – of John X onto the Throne of St Peter and she resolved to thwart both him and her mother with a candidate

Like Agiltrude, Marozia was motivated by the same blind hatred, the same remorseless urge for retribution and the same drive to prevail at all or any cost.

of her own: another John, her illegitimate son by Pope Sergius III, who was born in around 910 CE. When John X became pope, Marozia's son was only about four years old, a trifle young for the pontificate, even in early medieval times when teenage popes were not unknown.

Marozia, however, had the time to brew her plans while she waited. She had watched the Duchess Agiltrude in action at the Cadaver Synod and afterwards took her as her role model. Like Agiltrude, Marozia was motivated by the same blind hatred, the same remorseless urge for retribution and the same drive to prevail at all or any cost. And like so many people bent on revenge, Marozia had a long memory that kept past wrongs vividly alive.

In Marozia's eyes, revenge was due at the outset for the death of her first husband, Count Alberic of Lombardy, whom she had married in 909 CE. Alberic was a born troublemaker, reared in a family skilled in the dark arts of intrigue, murder, adultery, simony and almost every other profanity known to decadence. The

The Muslim Saracens, the deadly enemies of Christian Europe, are shown here landing in Sicily, which they conquered in 827 CE. Pope John X led a Christian army to repel the invaders.

Counts of Lombardy were, in addition, adept at making popes, having put seven members of their family on the Throne of St Peter after seizing control of papal elections.

Marozia, no mean exponent of these abuses herself, quickly recognized her husband's potential and the ambition his upbringing had bred in him. She set about encouraging him to challenge Pope John X and march on Rome with a view to seizing the pontiff, and his job with him. For once, though, Marozia made a serious misjudgement. John X was no pushover like so many puppet popes in the 'Rule of the Harlots' but a tried-and-tested military leader with a notable victory to his credit.

In 915 CE, John had taken to the field in person at the head of the army of the Christian League and

smashed the Muslim Saracen forces in a battle close to the River Garigliano, some 200 kilometres north of Rome. Nine years later, Marozia succeeded in persuading Alberic to seize Rome and, probably, unseat Pope John X. But when Alberic marched on the Holy City, his defeat at the battle of Orte in Lazio, central Italy, was just as resounding. Alberic was killed and his body mutilated. For good, ghoulish measure the victorious pope forced Marozia to view what was left of her husband, a horrible experience she never forgot or forgave.

At the same time, she felt obliged to put her revenge on hold, for her mother Theodora was still alive. Perhaps out of a latent respect for Theodora or maybe fearing a backlash from her supporters, Marozia seems to have made no move against John, for the moment at least. Meanwhile, in 924 CE, Pope John stoked Marozia's desire for revenge even further. He allied himself with the former Hugh of Provence, the new King of Italy, so endangering Marozia's power in Rome.

Two years later, in 926 CE, Marozia married a second and highly influential husband, Guido, Count and Duke of Lucca and Margrave, or military governor, of Tuscany. This marriage greatly strengthened Marozia's position, as did the death in 928 CE of Theodora. There were, of course, rumours that Marozia had poisoned her and she was certainly ruthless enough to do away with her own mother. Nevertheless, Theodora's death facilitated Marozia's revenge, for, without his former patroness, Pope John X became more vulnerable. Together, Marozia and her husband Guido saw to it that he soon became even more so.

For good, ghoulish measure the victorious pope forced Marozia to view what was left of her husband, a horrible experience she never forgot or forgave.

MURDER AT THE PAPAL PALACE

The couple arranged the murder of John Petrus, Prefect of Rome, who was Pope John's brother. Petrus had received favours and lucrative offices from John that furious Roman nobles believed were not his due but were owed to

Pope Leo VI was one of the many short-lived popes of the age of pornocracy. He was elected around June 928 CE and reigned for only seven months. Little is known about him, either good or bad, apart from the fact that he is thought to be one of several pontiffs buried in St Peter's Basilica.

them. However, there was more to the killing of Petrus than pure revenge. He got in the way of Marozia's plans by proving a stalwart support for his brother, and a valuable aide in navigating safely the currents of intrigue, violence and betrayal that marked the troubled waters of the tenth-century papacy. But with John Petrus out of the way, the safeguards he provided vanished with him and it was then a simple matter of arresting John and throwing him into prison in the Castel Sant'Angelo. He soon died, either smothered in bed according to Liutprand or a victim of anxiety – for which read stress – in a version of John's death by the French chronicler Flodoard.

On the face of it, Marozia now reigned supreme among the power brokers and pope-makers of Rome, but this impression was deceptive because everything Marozia had worked and schemed for was about to disintegrate. She set up two more puppet popes. The first was Leo VI, who came and went in a single year, 928 CE and, it was rumoured, was poisoned by Marozia after a reign of only seven months. His successor was Stephen VIII, who fared a little better, reigning from 928 CE to the early months of 931 CE. This may have appeared to conform to the typical sequence of events, with short-lived popes succeeding each other and then dying or disappearing. However, behind this familiar routine, Marozia was biding her time until her illegitimate son John reached an age when she could make him pope in his turn. John was 21 years of age, just about old enough to assume the papal crown, when his mother at last achieved her ambition and created him Pope John XI in 931 CE.

> Marozia ... set up two more puppet popes... However, behind this familiar routine, Marozia was biding her time until her illegitimate son John reached an age when she could make him pope in his turn.

Marozia's second husband had died in 929 CE. Three years later, John XI facilitated Marozia's third marriage to her old foe, King Hugh of Italy, who, as the late Guido's half-brother was also her brother-in-law. This relationship contained one of two impediments to the marriage for, under Church law, marriage between in-laws was illegal and tantamount to incest. Another obstacle was the fact that Hugh already had a wife, but that was easily dealt with as Pope John arranged a quickie divorce. The pope also presided at the wedding, lending it an air of legitimacy that, strictly speaking, it did not possess.

John had steered his mother through otherwise impenetrable difficulties, but any satisfaction this gave Marozia was very short-lived. Since her triumph over the late John X, she had reckoned without her second,

> This relationship contained one of two impediments to the marriage for, under Church law, marriage between in-laws was illegal and tantamount to incest.

legitimate, son whose father had been Marozia's first husband Alberic, Count of Tuscany. The young Alberic II, intensely jealous of his elder half-brother and the favour their mother had shown him, soon demonstrated how true he was to the legacy of wickedness his ancestry had given him. Alberic was no friend of his mother's third husband either, and lost no time displaying his dislike. The marriage ceremony was scarcely over and the guests were seated for the wedding breakfast when Alberic grossly insulted King Hugh. Hugh responded in kind, and the exchange of abuses moved on to violence when the King slapped Alberic for being clumsy.

Alberic was incandescent at this public humiliation and swore revenge. What Alberic did next may also have been motivated by rumours that King Hugh intended to have him blinded – a common means in early medieval times for incapacitating rivals while leaving them alive to suffer.

MAROZIA IMPRISONED

Hugh and Marozia had been married only a few months when Alberic roused an armed mob, worked them up into a vengeful fury and advanced on the Castel Sant'Angelo, where the couple were staying. They were

rudely awakened by the commotion outside and Hugh, fearing he would be lynched, leapt out of bed and made his escape. Wearing only his nightshirt, he hid himself in a basket and was carried to safety by servants. He shinned down the city walls by means of a rope and fled, leaving Marozia to face her vengeful son alone. Alberic's vengeance was truly terrible. He imprisoned his mother in the deepest underground level of the Castel Sant'Angelo, and it is doubtful she ever saw daylight again. She was then 42 years old, still beautiful and fascinating, but now she was set to moulder away for the next 54 years into extreme old age.

Alberic ... imprisoned his mother in the deepest underground level of the Castel Sant'Angelo. She was then 42 years old.

Meanwhile, Alberic threw his bastard half-brother, Pope John XI, in jail while he consolidated his power. Once safely installed as ruler of Rome, Alberic released John from prison, but had no intention of setting him free. Instead, he placed his half-brother under house arrest in the church of St John Lateran. Almost all of John's powers as pope were removed from him, leaving him only the right to deliver the sacraments. This, however, was no new experience for Pope John. All that happened was that he passed from the control of Marozia to the control of Alberic, who exercised both secular and ecclesiastical power in Rome.

John lasted four years under the tutelage of his younger brother before dying in 935 CE, leaving Alberic to emulate their mother and grandmother as creator of popes. Over the next 22 years, before his death at the age 43 in 954 CE, Alberic appointed four popes. And on his deathbed nominated his own illegitimate son, Octavian, aged 16, as their successor. Octavian duly became pope in 955 CE, taking the name of John XII, and was a complete and utter catastrophe.

The Castel Sant'Angelo, which stands on the right bank of the River Tiber, was one of the papal residences. The statue of an angel at the top gave the castle its name. It was originally built as a mausoleum by the Roman Emperor Hadrian between 135 and 139 CE.

CELLAM MAXIMAM VETVSTATE FATISCENTEM INGENTI MOLITIONE PRODVCENDAM LAXANDAMQVE
MVSIVVM MVLTIS IAM ANTEA PARTIBVS INSTAVRATVM AD ANTIQVVM EXEMPLAR
NOVAM ABSIDEM OPERE CVLTVQVE MAGNIFICO EXORNATAM TRANSFERRI AVLAM
ET CONTIGNATIONE REFECTIS EXPOLIRI IVSSIT ANNO CHR MDCCCLXXXIV SACRI

The elaborate interior of the Church of St John Lateran, the Cathedral of the Diocese of Rome and the principal basilica of the Vatican. The ceremonial chair of the popes can be seen at the centre.

Pope John XII was so thoroughly dissolute it was rumoured that prayers were offered up in monasteries begging God to grant him a speedy death. There seemed to be no sin that John XII did not – or would not – commit. He ran a brothel at the church of St John Lateran where he put one of his own lovers, Marcia, in charge. He slept with his father's mistress and his own mother. He took golden chalices from St Peter's church to reward his lovers after nights of passion. He blinded one cardinal and castrated another, causing his death. Pilgrims who came to Rome risked losing the offering they made to the Church when the Pope purloined them to use in gambling sessions. At these sessions, John XII used to call on pagan gods and goddesses to grant him luck with throws of the dice. Women were warned to keep away from St John Lateran or anywhere else the pope might be, for he was always on the prowl looking for new conquests. Before long, the people of Rome were

Pope John XII. a thoroughly dissolute pontiff who ran a brothel at the Church of St John Lateran, is shown crowning the Holy Roman Emperor Otto I in 962 CE.

so enraged at John's behaviour he began to fear for his life. His response was to rifle St Peter's church for valuables and flee to Tivoli, some 27 kilometres (16 miles) from Rome.

Pope John, still in exile at Tivoli replied that if the synod deposed him … he would excommunicate everyone involved, making it impossible for them to celebrate Mass or conduct ordinations.

John XII was doing so much damage to the papacy, which was still reeling from the crimes and sins of his predecessors, that a special synod was called to deal with him. All the Italian bishops and 16 cardinals and other clergy (some from Germany), convened to decide what to do with the ghastly young man who was their pontiff. They called witnesses and heard evidence under oath and finally decided on a list that added even more misdeeds to John's already appalling record. Some of these were outlined in a letter written to John by the Holy Roman Emperor Otto I of Saxony.

> *Everyone, clergy as well as laity accuse you, Holiness, of homicide, perjury, sacrilege, incest with your relatives, including two of your sisters and with having, like a pagan, invoked Jupiter, Venus and other demons.*

Pope John, still in exile at Tivoli replied to Otto in terms so malevolent that fear permeated Rome. If the synod deposed him, John threatened, he would excommunicate everyone involved, making it impossible for them to celebrate Mass or conduct ordinations. In Christian terms, this was the worst possible penalty a pope could impose, for excommunication meant being thrown out of the Church, losing its protection and even endangering the immortal soul.

JOHN XII'S REVENGE

In spite of the threatened excommunication, the Emperor Otto deposed John and a new pope, Leo VIII, was put in his place. John, of course, would have

A portrait of Leo VIII, who was backed by the Holy Roman Emperor Otto I but had to fight off a ferocious rival, John XII, before being acknowledged as the true pope. Leo's reign lasted only eight months in 964 and 965 CE.

none of this. When he eventually returned to Rome in 963 CE, his vengeance was infinitely worse than he had threatened. He threw out Pope Leo, but instead of excommunication, he executed or maimed everyone who sat in judgement on him at the synod. John had the skin flayed off one bishop, cut off the nose and two fingers of a cardinal and gouged out his tongue, and decapitated 63 members of the clergy and nobility in Rome.

Then, on the night of 14 May 964 CE, it seemed that all those prayers begging God to intervene and save Rome from its demon-pope had at last reached their divine destination. As a bishop named John

… (Pope John) was surprised in the act of sin by the matron's angry husband who, in just wrath, smashed his skull …

Crescentius of Proteus later described it, 'While having illicit and filthy relations with a Roman matron, (Pope John) was surprised in the act of sin by the matron's angry husband who, in just wrath, smashed his skull with a hammer and thus liberated his evil soul into the grasp of Satan.'

DEATH COMES TO MAROZIA

But the Church was not yet finished with the family of 'harlots' who had spawned nine of the most sinful popes ever to defile the name of the papacy. In 986 CE, 22 years after the dramatic death of John XII, Bishop Crescentius came to the Castel Sant'Angelo to see John's mother, Marozia, who was now 96 years old. Marozia's once ravishing beauty had crumbled into a bag of bones, her shrivelled flesh clothed in rags. The recently elected pope, John XV, had decided to take mercy on her, though his mercy took a form that only the medieval mind would have recognized.

Crescentius laid several charges against Marozia, including her conspiracy against the rights of the

LEO·VIII·PAPA ROMANVS

Marozia was now 96 years old. An executioner slipped into her cell and smothered her with a pillow…

papacy, her illicit involvement with Pope Sergius III, her immoral life and her 'plot' to take over the world. Marozia was also compared to Jezebel, the arch-villainess of the Bible who also 'dared to take a third husband'.

The belief that human wickedness could be caused by demonic possession was common in the early Middle Ages, so just in case Marozia's demons were still present, she was exorcised. Now absolved from her sins and made fit to face her Maker, she died quickly after that. An executioner slipped into her cell and smothered her with a pillow 'for the well-being' it was said, of 'Holy Mother Church and the peace of the Roman people'.

However, the end of the pornocracy and the Rule of the Harlots was not the end of papal debauchery or the influential families who leeched off of it. The papacy had a very long way to go before it finally shed its notorious image as a tool of powerbrokers and parvenus who fronted vested interests whether royal, noble, political or commercial. In fact, it took another thousand years, until the nineteenth century, for the papacy to become the spiritual influence it was always meant to be and the Vicars of Christ no longer ranked high on the list of history's greatest villains.

Pope John XII, once described as 'a true debauchee and incestuous satanist' is shown in a very un-papal pose, dancing with a scantily-clad woman, perhaps intended to portray his mother Marozia.

BONIFACE VIII: A CAPTIVE POPE

One of the first acts of Pope Boniface VIII, the former Benedetto Caetani, was to imprison his predecessor, the gentle and unworldly Celestine V, in the Castle of Fumone in Ferentino, Italy where he died aged 81 in 1296. Boniface soon proved to be an autocrat who decreed in 1302 that 'it is absolutely necessary for salvation that every human creature be subject to the Roman pontiff'.

This approach made Boniface many enemies among the powerful and ambitious kings of Europe, including Philip IV of France who was enraged when the pope claimed in 1302 that all monarchs were subordinate to the Catholic Church. Philip's response was to charge the pope with heresy and demand his resignation. The French king followed this up by invading the pope's palace at his birthplace in Agnani, and imprisoning him.

Boniface spent three days in prison while his captors debated whether or not to drag him in chains to nearby Lyons where he would be put on trial. The charges against Boniface would be the worst that could be devised in a deeply superstitious age. He was accused of wizardry, dealings with the Devil, possessing an idol containing a diabolical spirit and talking to it, revoking his belief in Jesus Christ, declaring the sins of the flesh were not sins and committing other 'crimes', any of which could have seen him burnt at the stake.

ANOTHER POSTHUMOUS TRIAL

Boniface survived the assault by only a month and during that time, he locked himself inside the Lateran Palace in Rome, refusing to let anyone in and planning his revenge. He died there on 11 October 1303, perhaps of natural causes, but possibly by poisoning or strangulation. The vengeful King Philip ordered that Boniface be posthumously put on trial, condemning him as a heretic and therefore not a legal pope. But Boniface's successor Clement V, perhaps having read what had happened to the venerable Formosus four centuries earlier, managed to avert this added shame by spinning out the trial for such a long time that a verdict was never reached.

A statue of Pope Boniface VIII, who got into fearful trouble by trying to impose his autocratic will on the independent-minded kings of 14th-century Europe.

GENOCIDE: THE CATHARS, PART I

Tolerance, today considered a virtuous trait, was a dirty word in medieval Europe. This was particularly true of Christian belief, which developed into a straight and narrow path from which it was dangerous, and frequently fatal, to stray.

One thirteenth-century pope, Innocent III, actually made it a crime to tolerate the presence of heretics in a community. This unbending frame of mind did not arise only from the zealous dogmatism of the medieval Church. It was also a form of self-defence against the challenges that confronted Christianity at this time. The enemies of the Church were strong, determined and dangerous. The Muslims, for example, were dedicated to the spread of Islam throughout the world. Paganism, in its multifarious forms, had monopolized faith in Europe and elsewhere since ancient times and would not relinquish its supremacy lightly.

The heretic Cathars were besieged in the walled town of Carcassonne, France (left), by Catholic forces sent by the pope. The defenders of Carcassonne, both Cathar and Catholic, made heroic efforts against their attackers, whose crusade was instigated by Pope Innocent III (above). Outgunned and outnumbered, their resistance proved futile.

Within the Church, it was felt that the only way to overcome these rivals was to treat their beliefs and practices or, indeed, any dissent that cast the smallest doubt on received wisdom, as heresy or the work of the Devil. The punishments incurred were fearful. Burning dissenters at the stake was meant to purify the world of their presence. Torture was designed to force out the demon possessing an individual and thereby save the victim's immortal soul.

Yet despite the extreme perils involved, Christianity was still confronted from time to time not only by other religions but, perhaps more insidiously, by alternative views of its own basic tenets. One of the most pervasive of these challenges came from the Cathars, a religious sect that first arose in around 1143 in the Languedoc region of modern southwest France. From there, Catharism spread into Spain, Belgium, Italy and western Germany and was well rooted in all these places by the thirteenth century.

Then, Raymond V, Count of Toulouse presented another, much less patient, tougher way to deal with the Cathars. In 1177, the Count asked the General Chapter of the Cistercian Monastic Order for help in dealing with Cathars who, he said, were close to overwhelming his domains in Languedoc. The Cistercians believed they had just the man for the job – Henri de Marcy. Originally a Cistercian abbot, Henri had his own hard-line views about how to go about crushing heresy and heretics: his way was force of arms applied relentlessly and for as long as it took. In 1178, the Cistercians sent him to Languedoc at the head of a high-powered papal legation, including a cardinal, a bishop and two archbishops.

Christianity was still confronted from time to time not only by other religions but, perhaps more insidiously, by alternative views of its own basic tenets.

LOCAL DIFFICULTIES

Henri may have thought he had a simple and straightforward solution, but he rapidly discovered that his task was much more complex than he had imagined. The Cathars were highly regarded in Languedoc and the people, the nobles who ruled them and the resident bishops were not best pleased when outsiders sought to interfere. Targeting the ring of support that gave the Cathars protection therefore became Henri's first task. Top of his list was the renegade Roger II de Trencavel, Viscount of Carcassonne, who had imprisoned William, Bishop of Albi in 1175 over a dispute about which of them could claim the lordship of Albi and with that, supreme power in the area.

A Cistercian abbot, Henri had his own hard-line views about how to go about crushing heresy and heretics: his way was force of arms ... for as long as it took.

In 1209, Pope Innocent III approved the Primitive Rule of the Franciscan Order of Friars. The Rule established the basic disciplines of the monastic life, such as the vows of obedience, chastity and poverty.

CATHARS V CATHOLICS

A painting by Fra Angelico (1395–1485) depicting the Miracle of the Book. Dominican and Cathar books are thrown into the fire. The former miraculously escape the flames while the Cathars' heretical volumes are consumed. St Dominic (with halo) is pictured at left being returned his undamaged book.

From the first, the popes in Rome regarded the Cathars as heretics with dangerously subversive beliefs. It was no wonder that the popes became so alarmed. To begin with, Catharism was a 'dualistic' religion similar to eastern faiths such as Zoroastrianism, which was once based in Persia (present-day Iran). The Cathars believed that the world was evil and had been created by Satan. They identified Satan with the God of the Old Testament, the ultimate blasphemy in the eyes of 'true' Christians. Human beings, the Cathars contended, went through a series of reincarnations before translating into pure spirit, which represented the presence of the God of Love as described in the New Testament by His messenger, Jesus Christ. The Cathars were totally opposed to Catholic doctrine and regarded the Church in Rome as immoral, and both politically and spiritually corrupt.

Naturally enough, within the Church, such ideas that exchanged God for Satan and displaced Jesus from the prime position were considered sacrilegious. They needed to be expunged. In 1147, Pope Eugene III, a former Cistercian monk, 'innocent and simple', as his friend St Bernard of Clairvaux described him, had made wiping out the Cathars an urgent priority after his election two years earlier. But he proved too soft for the task. When he applied gentle persuasion on the Cathars to convert to Catholicism, he soon discovered that they were intensely stubborn and refused even to consider such an idea. Bernard of Clairvaux, acting on Pope Eugene's behalf, managed a few conversions, but not nearly enough to make the major difference required to extinguish the Cathar sect.

Pope Innocent III appears in this medieval manuscript illustration in the act of excommunicating the Albigenses, a name generally given to heretics.

Henri swiftly cut Roger loose by declaring him a heretic and excommunicating him. This was enough to persuade Roger to release the Bishop of Albi, but it was not the end of the matter. In 1179, Roger incurred the wrath of Pons d'Arsac the Archbishop of Narbonne, who had been a member of Henri de Marcy's legation the previous year. The Archbishop accused Roger of lacking sufficient enthusiasm for the fight against heresy and excommunicated him again.

Two years later, in 1181, Henri de Marcy returned to Languedoc. This time, he prepared to attack the castle of Lavaur, but did not need to fight for it. Roger II's wife Adelaide surrendered to him without demur. As a bonus, Henri captured two Cathar Parfaits, or Perfects, the ascetic 'priests' of the Cathar faith who embraced poverty, chastity and celibacy.

VATICAN VOCABULARY

EXCOMMUNICATION

Excommunication means putting a man or woman outside the Christian communion. It was the worst punishment an individual could incur, for it cut them off from the protection of the Church and from contact with Church life. Among other crimes, the punishment could be incurred for committing apostasy, (abandoning Christian beliefs), heresy, schism (division within the Church), attacking the pope personally or procuring an abortion. Anyone who ordained a female priest was also subject to excommunication.

In medieval times, the Catholic Church regarded excommunicants as either *vitandus* (to be avoided or shunned), or *toleratus* (meaning they could have social or business relationships with other Catholics). They were allowed to attend Mass, but could not receive communion, the ceremony celebrating the Last Supper. The ceremony of excommunication was both dramatic and daunting. A bell was tolled as if the excommunicant had died, the book of the gospels was closed and a candle was snuffed out. However, excommunication was not necessarily permanent. If the guilty parties made a statement of repentance, they could be restored to full membership of the Church.

The Archbishop accused Roger of lacking sufficient enthusiasm for the fight against heresy and excommunicated him again.

Yet despite his efforts, Henri's success was limited. The Cathars were proving a very hard nut to crack and appeared to be impervious to any approach the Church might make. In 1204, Innocent III, who had been elected pope in 1198, was so wary of them that he suspected a number of the bishops with sees in the south of France were virtually Cathar collaborators. More faithful, trustworthy advocates of the established Church, including the Spanish priest Dominic de Guzman (the future St Dominic), replaced the maverick bishops. Dominic launched a rigorous campaign of conversion in Languedoc but though unremittingly zealous, he achieved very little. The few converts he managed to make were a poor return for his efforts, which included strongly argued Cathar–Catholic debates in several towns and cities. Even so, the core values of Catharism remained untouched. Eventually Dominic realized why: only Catholics who matched the Cathars for real sanctity, humility and asceticism could hope to change their minds about their faith.

The Cathars were proving a very hard nut to crack and appeared to be impervious to any approach the Church might make.

THE ORDER OF FRIARS PREACHERS

To respond to the formidable undertaking, in 1216 Dominic founded the Order of Friars Preachers, better known as the Dominican Order, dedicated to preaching the Gospels and saving the souls of the Cathars and other heretics. Dominic told the monks who joined the Order:

> *Zeal must be met by zeal, humility by humility, false sanctity by real sanctity, preaching falsehood by preaching truth.*

Like the Cathars, Dominic believed, his monks should eschew all materialistic benefits, live in poverty with only minimal possessions, tramp the roads barefoot and beg for their food. In addition, they must be celibate and keep themselves strictly chaste. Dominic was sure that this way of life, strong on humility and self-sacrifice, was the way to attract the Cathars back to the Church of Rome.

But Dominic was forestalled. Someone much more aggressive and bloodthirsty than himself had already applied a solution that the peaceable Dominic could not consider. After ten years of resolute resistance in which most Cathars maintained their contempt for the Catholic Church and their certainty of its evil nature, Pope Innocent III finally lost patience and turned up the heat. In the spring of 1207, he dispatched a papal legate, Pierre de Castelnau, Archdeacon of Maguelonne, to Provence where he ordered the nobility to actively persecute the Cathars, Jews and any other heretics they might find.

De Castelnau encountered determined opposition from the start. Count Raymond VI of Toulouse, son of Raymond V, and the most powerful lord in Languedoc, was intimately bound up with the Cathars and declined to cooperate. Raymond had friends, relatives, nobles and allies who were devout adherents of Cathar beliefs and did not bother to hide his affection for them. He even made a practice of travelling with a Cathar Perfect in his

Pope Innocent III … dispatched a papal legate, Pierre de Castelnau, Archdeacon of Maguelonne, to Provence where he ordered the nobility to actively persecute the Cathars, Jews and any other heretics they might find.

retinue. When de Castelnau learnt of Raymond's disobedience to an order that effectively came from Pope Innocent III himself, he excommunicated the Count at once and pronounced the traditional anathema upon him. 'He who dispossesses you will be accounted virtuous!' de Castelnau thundered, 'He who strikes you dead will earn a blessing.'

Raymond was not made of particularly stern stuff – he was better at dissembling than defiance – and, apparently frightened, he backed down and promised to carry out the persecutions as required. De Castelnau, it seems, believed him. A few weeks later, he pardoned Raymond and restored him to his rights as a Christian. De Castelnau should have known better: Raymond VI was a natural-born liar who would break his word as soon as he had the chance. This time, though, he opted for a new ploy: he did nothing.

It took some weeks for this non-event to sink in, but when it did, Pierre de Castelnau reacted to Raymond's perfidy with fury. Raymond was accused of condoning heresy in Languedoc, stealing Church property, offending bishops and abbots and supporting the Cathars. At the end of this tirade, de Castelnau excommunicated Raymond once again. Raymond suggested talks to break the impasse, but they got nowhere and the Count resorted to threats and insults in front of several witnesses who later reported what had happened to Pope Innocent in Rome.

THE MURDER OF PIERRE DE CASTELNAU

On 13 January 1208, the dialogue was finally broken off and Pierre de Castelnau and his retinue departed for Rome. The following morning, the travellers reached Arles and rode down to the landing stage to embark on the ferry that would take them across the River Rhône. De Castelnau never made it. Before his

The Miracle of the Books, in which Cathar books burned while St Dominic's Catholic books remained undamaged, is also known as the Miracle of Fanjeaux, after the town in the Languedoc where it occurred. It is pictured here by the Spanish artist Pedro Berruguete (c. 1450–1504).

Raymond VI, Count of Toulouse was forced to do public penance for the assassination of Pierre de Castelnau.

retinue could come to his aid, a strange horseman rode swiftly towards them and killed de Castelnau with a single sword thrust in his back.

Later there were rumours that the murderer was a knight in the employ of the Count of Toulouse. Raymond vigorously denied any involvement and in June 1209, even volunteered to undergo a public scourging as penance for the dark deed. When the punishment was over, the Count, beaten, bloody and sore was obliged to pay his respects at the tomb of de Castelnau, who was already being classed as a blessed martyr. All the same, Raymond was still the principal suspect and remained in disgrace. The assassination of de Castelnau was never solved. But innocent or guilty, Count Raymond protested too late.

A few weeks after the killing, Pope Innocent III lost patience with the diplomatic approach and called for a crusade. This was the so-called Albigensian Crusade named after the town of Albi, a stronghold of the

A strange horseman rode swiftly towards them and killed de Castelnau with a single sword thrust in his back.

Cathars in Languedoc. In this call to arms, Raymond of Toulouse thought he saw a chance to convince the Pope of his Catholic credentials. To this end, Raymond loudly proclaimed his intention to pursue heretics and punish all who aided and abetted the Cathars and their priests. It was all a charade. Raymond was in no way penitent, but it was, of course, politic that he give the appearance of making common cause with the tens of thousands of knights who were gathering at Lyons in eastern France, each of them boasting their own retinue of infantry, archers, grooms and other attendants. Their commander, handpicked by the Pope himself, was the murdered de Castelnau's superior, Bishop Arnaud Amaury, the Cistercian Abbot of Cîteaux. Ruthless and retributive by nature, Amaury was ideal for the task Innocent set him, which was to exterminate the Cathars once and for all. He was both ruthless and retributive and was resolved to wipe out the Cathars by the most brutal means at his disposal.

Together with the *routiers,* the mercenaries who made up a large part of most feudal armies, the Albigensian

Pierre de Castelnau, papal legate to Pope Innocent III, was brutally murdered in January 1208. The deed was done with a sword thrust into his back, rather than a frontal spear attack as shown here.

'ABANDON YOUR LUXURY OR YOUR PREACHING!'

Quite possibly, the extreme measures adopted against the Cathars by Arnaud Amaury, the Bishop of Cîteaux and military commander of the Albigensian Crusade, were in revenge for the humiliating treatment he had received when he went to Languedoc and, like St Dominic and St Bernard of Clairvaux, attempted to persuade the Cathars to relinquish their beliefs. As related in the *Song of the Cathar Wars,* a history of what is now southern France covering the years 1204–18, the Cathars made fun of Amaury, and dismissed him as a fool. 'That bee is buzzing around again,' they said when Amaury preached to them. The Cathars and their Perfects were, of course, devoted to a frugal, ascetic way of life and despised luxury and self-indulgence. But like many clergy of the early thirteenth century, Arnaud Amaury's lifestyle was both ostentatious and hedonistic and the Bishop made the mistake of appearing before the Cathars in all his splendour. As the eighteenth-century French writer Voltaire related in his 1756 *Account of the Crusade against the People of Languedoc:*

'The Abbot of Cîteaux appeared with the entourage of a prince. In vain he spoke as an apostle, the people shouted at him, "Abandon either your luxury or your preaching!"'

Arnaud Amaury, a Cistercian monk, led the crusade that crushed the heretics of southern France.

crusaders were so numerous that as the procession moved southwest into Languedoc, it stretched for more than six kilometres (3.7 miles) along the road. Every man had been promised splendid rewards – full remission of their sins, suspension of their debts and a wealth of Church funds to fill their pockets.

> Amaury was ideal for the task Innocent set him … He was both ruthless and retributive and was resolved to wipe out the Cathars by the most brutal means at his disposal.

'WE WOULD RATHER DROWN'

The crusader army reached its first destination, Béziers, a strongly fortified town on the River Orb in southwestern France, in late July 1209. The inhabitants were in defiant mood. Cathar and Catholic alike, they had no intention of giving in to any demands the crusaders might make. When the Bishop of Béziers arrived and presented the burghers of the town with a list of 222 Cathar Perfects who were to be handed over at once, he threatened that if they did not agree, the town would be besieged next day. The burghers appeared unfazed. They refused to give up any Cathars, Perfects or otherwise, and, according to one chronicler, told the Bishop: 'We would rather drown in the salt sea.'

At that, the Bishop remounted his mule and rode back to the camp the crusaders had set up a day's march away. The following day, 22 July, the inhabitants of Béziers were greeted with a daunting sight. The crusader army had moved up and transferred their camp until it surrounded the walls of the town. They filled the landscape as far as the horizon with their tents, horses, campfires, flags,

The town of Béziers was completely destroyed by the Albigensian crusaders in 1209. This picture shows the town today, with its cathedral in the background.

banners, the elegant pavilions of the crusader lords and their siege machines.

Suddenly, a lone crusader appeared on the bridge that spanned the River Orb near the southern fortifications of Béziers and began to shout insults and threats at the people lining the walls above. A crowd of young men, spoiling for a fight, grabbed spears, sticks and any other makeshift weapon easily to hand, swung open the town gate and surged down the slope to the riverbank. Before he could get away, the lone crusader was seized, thrown to the ground, and soundly beaten. Finally, he was thrown off the bridge into the muddy water of the Orb.

But in their frenzy to get hold of him, the young men of Béziers made the worst possible mistake by leaving open the gate into the town. It was an irresistible invitation to the crusaders who came charging over the bridge and into the narrow streets. Taken by surprise, the defenders scrambled into

VATICAN VOCABULARY

INTERDICT

The excommunication of a town, city or other district, even entire countries, was called being 'placed under interdict'. In practice, this meant that no Christian marriages, funerals or church services could take place as long as the interdict remained in force, although the populations involved *were* allowed to make confession and receive baptism. If a country placed under interdict came under attack, the pope was under no obligation to come to its assistance. In addition, an interdict released the subjects from their oaths of loyalty to the offending ruler, which allowed them to rebel against him with impunity, if they wished.

Kings, emperors or other rulers whose behaviour had offended the Catholic Church usually incurred this blanket form of excommunication. The ruler in question had to repent before the penalty could be lifted and the country could be restored to the Catholic communion. This, for instance, is what happened in 1207 when King John of England refused to accept Cardinal Stephen Langton, the Pope's choice for Archbishop of Canterbury. John was excommunicated and England was placed under interdict until 1212, when the King at last gave in and agreed to Langton's appointment. After that, the interdict was withdrawn.

retreat, intending, perhaps, to put enough distance between themselves and their attackers to regroup and launch an assault of their own. But there was no chance of that.

A crowd of young men, spoiling for a fight, grabbed spears, sticks and other makeshift weapons…

Eventually, there were no survivors, and having disposed of the entire population, Amaury's crusaders prepared to loot and pillage the empty houses. Béziers was an affluent town, offering plenty of prizes and valuables of all kinds. The French knights among Amaury's men believed that they had priority when it came to seizing booty, but to their fury, the servant

BATTLE MADNESS AND SLAUGHTER

Amaury's army was inexorably driven on by what the Vikings of Scandinavia used to call *berserker* (battle madness), and cut down anyone and everyone within range of their broadswords. They burst into a church where a vigil was being held and amid screams of agony, terror and frenzied, but useless, attempts to escape, they slashed, stabbed and slaughtered their way through the congregation until all that was left of them were piles of bloody corpses slumped in the aisles. Next, the crusaders moved on to the church of Mary Magdalene and killed every man, woman and child – Catholic or Cathar – who had been sheltering inside. Around 1000 people died inside the church within a few minutes, leaving only a pall of deathly silence to cover the scene of slaughter. Nearly 700 years later, in 1840, when the church was being renovated, their bones were discovered under the floor of the church. There were hundreds of them, piled roughly together in a huge mass.

There was no escape for the congregation sheltering inside the church at Béziers when the crusaders burst in and started laying about them with their weapons.

> Having disposed of the entire population, Amaury's crusaders prepared to loot and pillage the empty houses.

boys and the mercenaries got there before them. The chronicler William of Tudela described what happened next. He wrote:

> *The servant lads had settled into the houses they had (captured), all of them full of riches and treasure, but when the French (lords) discovered this, they went nearly mad with rage and drove the lads out with clubs, like dogs.*

But before the knights could get their hands on any valuables, William of Tudela continued:

> *These filthy, stinking wretches all shouted out "Burn it! Burn it!" (And) they fetched huge flaming brands as if for a funeral pyre and set the town alight.*

THE RAPE OF BÉZIERS

The buildings in Béziers were mainly constructed of wood. They burnt quickly and easily as the flames ate their way through one quarter after another. Very soon, all that was left was a raging inferno of death and destruction. To their rage and horror, the treasure the French knights hoped to claim burnt to ashes or quite literally melted away before their eyes. The Cathedral of St Nazaire, built some 80 years previously, was said to have 'split in half, like a pomegranate' in the ravening

THE MASSACRE AT BÉZIERS

The massacre that took place at Béziers was not spontaneous. It had been meticulously planned in 1208, even before the Albigensian Crusade began, when Arnaud Amaury, a lawyer called Milo (who was the Lateran Apostolic Notary) and 12 cardinals went to Rome to discuss with Pope Innocent III how the crusade should be conducted. The plan they formulated was consistent with the strategy adopted by Crusader forces in the Holy Land during the First Crusade, which had begun more than a century earlier in 1096. The blueprint for the massacre at Béziers was set out in a manuscript called *Canso d'Antioca,* which a crusader knight, Gregory Bechada, is believed to have written some time between 1106 and 1118. Describing the eleventh-century Crusader army, which the Albigensian Crusaders were to emulate, Bechada wrote:

The inhabitants of Béziers had no chance against the strong, well-armed crusaders who assaulted the town with a variety of weapons, including the deadly crossbow.

> *The lords from France and Paris, laymen and clergy, princes and marquises, all agreed that at every stronghold the crusader army attacked, any garrison that refused to surrender should be slaughtered wholesale, once the stronghold had been taken by force. They would then meet with no resistance anywhere, as men would be so terrified at what had already happened.*

VATICAN VOCABULARY

ANATHEMA

Anathema was the name given to a Church decree excommunicating an individual or denouncing an unacceptable doctrine. As a punishment, however, anathema went beyond excommunication. In the New Testament, there is a reference in Corinthians that says, 'If any man love not the Lord Jesus Christ, let him be anathema.' In Galatians, anathema is named as the punishment for preaching a rival gospel:

> *But even if we, or an angel from Heaven, should preach to you a gospel contrary to what we have preached to you, he is to be anathema.*

The book of John went even further.

> *He that abideth in the doctrine of Christ, he hath both the Father and the Son. If there come any unto you that bring not this doctrine, receive him not into your house, neither bid him God speed: for he that biddeth him God speed is partaker of his evil deeds.*

The Cathedral of St Nazaire ...was said to have *'split in half, like a pomegranate'* in the ravening blaze, before collapsing in ruins. The congregation that had taken shelter there were burnt to death.

---

blaze, before collapsing in ruins. The congregation that had taken shelter there were burnt to death. Béziers was later rebuilt, but the damage had been so extensive that the work took some 200 years to complete.

Before the onslaught, the Catholics had been given the option of leaving the town to escape the punishment that was going to consume the Cathars. Most of them refused, electing to remain and share with their fellow townsfolk whatever fate might bring. This presented the crusaders with a difficulty. How were they to know Catholic from Cathar? It was said that Bishop Amaury ordered, 'Kill them all! God will know His own.' His order was obeyed down to the last drop of blood. Amaury was so elated with the day's work he wrote to Pope Innocent:

> *Our forces spared neither rank nor sex nor age. About 20,000 people lost their lives at the point of the sword.*

Eight centuries ago, the mighty walls of medieval Carcassonne were the scene of savage fighting.

The destruction of the enemy was on an enormous scale. The entire city was plundered and put to the torch. Thus did divine vengeance vent its wondrous rage.

News of the atrocities perpetrated at Béziers soon spread through Languedoc and the rest of southern France. Lords and landowners whose lowland territories might be the next target for Amaury and his avenging army began to rethink their loyalties. One after another, they came to the encampment where the crusaders spent three days after their rampage through Béziers, to pay homage to Amaury and assure him of their support.

But one of the most powerful among the local lords, Raymond Roger III de Trencavel, Viscount of Carcassonne, Béziers, de Razès and Albi, adopted a different approach. Raymond Roger was the son of the

renegade Roger II of Carcassonne and the nephew of the shifty Raymond VI, Count of Toulouse, but he was more astute than either of them. When Raymond VI suggested teaming up to oppose Amaury and his crusaders, Raymond Roger, knowing only too well how perfidious his uncle could be, turned him down. He could not risk the chance that if the going got tough, Raymond VI would resort to his usual Plan B, which was to abandon any agreement they might make and cravenly submit to the enemy.

News of the atrocities perpetrated at Béziers soon spread through Languedoc and the rest of southern France. Lords and landowners began to rethink their loyalties.

If that were to happen, Raymond Roger III had too much to lose. For a start, he could find himself in personal danger and might even be forced to relinquish his lands because of his relaxed, tolerant attitude towards the multicultural society he ruled. Consorting with heretics, as the rabid zealotry of the time would judge this laissez-faire approach, was as bad as actually being a heretic, if not worse.

DIPLOMACY FAILS

Though Raymond Roger was not himself a Cathar, a large number of his subjects belonged to the sect. His territory also included a community of Jews who had for years been responsible for running Béziers, his secondary seat of power after Carcassonne. Carcassonne also had its Jewish community and they, too, could be in grave danger. Amaury's army would undoubtedly have killed them, for the massacre at Béziers had given ghastly proof of how far crusaders were willing to go to express their 'religious' zeal. For this reason, Raymond Roger took the precaution of sending the Jews of Carcassonne out of the city before the crusaders could get there.

However, it was not as easy to shift the much larger Cathar population. For their sake, as well as his own, Raymond Roger first resorted to diplomacy, seeking to make a deal by promising to persecute the Cathars and any other heretics in his territory. Did he mean it? Probably not, but he may well have learnt from his father the value of dissembling to postpone an evil day. His promise was never put to the test for there was no deal. Amaury did not even grant Raymond Roger a meeting to discuss the matter. It was likely, though, that the crusader leader realized that if he were to guarantee the safety of Carcassonne and Raymond Roger's other cities, there would be nowhere else for his loot-hungry followers to pillage.

PREPARING FOR WAR

This cynical response set off alarm bells. Raymond Roger hastened back to Carcassonne and prepared for war. First, he implemented a 'scorched earth' policy so that the crusader army would be denied the chance to live off the land, as was customary in medieval warfare. Raymond Roger ordered the surrounding area to be laid waste: crops and vineyards were to be burnt, windmills and farm implements destroyed and cattle and other herds either slaughtered or driven

Consorting with heretics was as bad as actually being a heretic, if not worse.

into Carcassonne where they could shelter behind the city's huge defensive walls. That done, Raymond Roger's troops made their preparations. With their weapons primed they kept constant watch for the crusaders' approach.

Amaury's army came within sight of Carcassonne on 1 August, ten days after the massacre at Béziers. They quickly calculated that capturing the city, with its mighty fortifications and stout defenders was not going to be a straightforward task. There were no open gates, no weak defences and no easy pickings. In fact, Amaury did not dare let his forces make camp too near the city walls where they might come within range of the fearsome crossbowmen of Carcassonne. The crusader knights parked their tents and pavilions some distance away. So did Amaury's soldiers, who laid their fires and chose their sleeping places well out of the reach of the deadly crossbows and other long-range weapons arrayed against them in Carcassonne.

The bloody hand-to-hand warfare that took place during the battle for Carcassonne in 1209 is vividly depicted on this frieze in the Cathedral of St Nazaire in Béziers.

The defenders of Carcassonne made a brave show, but the truth was that they were totally outnumbered. They were also 'outgunned', for Amaury had at his disposal powerful siege machines and many more archers – the artillery of medieval warfare – than Raymond Roger could mass against him. The day after the crusaders' arrival outside Carcassonne, 2 August, was a Sunday, when making war was banned by papal decree. Amaury's forces had to wait until Monday but as soon as dawn broke, they quickly deployed their battering rams, laid ladders against the walls for heavily armed soldiers to climb, and poured a hail of arrows inside Carcassonne where defenders and citizens alike could be indiscriminately killed.

ATTACK ON CARCASSONNE

The site the crusaders chose for their first attack was Bourg, one of two suburbs of Carcassonne that lay just outside the city. Of the two, Bourg was the less well fortified and defended and after two hard-fought hours, the crusaders were able to force their way through and scatter soldiers and citizens alike. As they fled into Carcassonne proper, seeking the safety they hoped to find behind its walls, archers and crossbowmen standing high on the battlements loosed

MONSTERS OF MEDIEVAL WARFARE

Huge siege machines had been a feature of war as long ago as the eighth century BCE, when the Old Testament recorded that during the reign of King Azariah of Judah, soldiers were using 'engines, invented by cunning men to be on the towers and upon the bulwarks, to shoot arrows and great stones withal'. Much later, the Greeks and Romans also employed siege warfare, subjecting town populations to days and nights of thunderings, shudderings, crashings and the sinister whistle of dozens of arrows raining down from the sky. Streets, squares, houses, churches – anywhere and everywhere townsfolk might be was susceptible to the damage and death dispensed by the siege machines.

By the thirteenth century when the towns of Languedoc came under siege during the Albigensian Crusade, the machines and the fearful destruction they wrought had hardly changed since the days of ancient Rome. A medieval army besieging a castle or town still used catapults, ballistae and battering rams, just as the ancient Greeks and Romans had done. They also employed scaling ladders and siege towers, as well as 'cats' or 'penthouses' to protect themselves against missiles flung down at them by defenders manning the walls.

KICK LIKE A MULE

One engine of war used by the Albigensian Crusaders in Languedoc was developed from the Roman *onager* (wild donkey). The *onager* got its name because it kicked like the rather bad-tempered animal. The trebuchet had a similarly vicious action, using a windlass that twisted ropes or springs. When the ropes or springs were suddenly released, the spoke 'kicked' at a crosspiece on the wooden frame of the trebuchet and the missiles contained in a large cup were propelled forward at speed. This method of firing was known as the 'counterweight' system. Trebuchets were normally used to hurl large stones, but they could also fling incendiary materials like burning pitch or flaming oil. Used this way they truly became weapons of terror and were greatly feared for the way they disfigured anyone standing in their path.

The ballista, which was invented by the Romans, was much like the hand-held crossbow but on a much

A siege tower (top) enabled an attacking army to draw level with the defenders of a besieged town and fire their arrows directly at them. The battering ram (bottom) was a crude but effective weapon for breaking down walls, while the sharpened stake (in background) could destroy a wall by picking its stones apart.

larger scale. Built exclusively of wood, it included a very powerful spring frame that enabled the engine to throw a stone or other object weighing more than 22 kilograms over a distance of around 366 metres. The ballista could also be loaded with a mass of arrows that fell inside a castle or city in massively destructive and often inescapable showers.

FIRE AND FEAR

The end of conventional siege warfare, as practised since Biblical times, arrived in the early fourteenth century, with the introduction of gunpowder and with that, firearms and field guns, such as the primitive but effective vasi, terror weapons of another more novel kind. The *vasi*, also known as *pots de fer* (iron pots) were first illustrated in an English manuscript of around 1327 as a vase-like weapon lying on its side with an arrow sticking out of its muzzle. At the rear end, a gunner stood with a red-hot rod poised over a firing hole. Vasi and their successors let off thunderous explosions, setting woodwork defences on fire and

In medieval warfare, mining was used to make the walls of a castle collapse by destroying their base. A fire was lit to destroy the wooden posts holding up the tunnel.

pounding walls, town gates and towers into a mass of rubble. Even the mightiest monsters of medieval warfare up to that date had been unable to achieve this destruction.

But 'mining', a silent, insidious method of warfare, proved even more terrifying than the siege engines. This involved digging under the foundations of a castle or walled city and temporarily shoring up the walls with small wooden stays. The resulting tunnel was stuffed with straw soaked in oil and anything else that would burn and then set alight. As the stays burned through, the walls collapsed. This tactic had a devastating effect at Carcassonne. The defenders of Castellar sited at the top found their foothold suddenly gone as they fell, along with a mass of loose stone that smashed to rubble as it hit the ground. Most did not survive.

The inhabitants of Carcassonne were allowed to leave the town after its capture by the Albigensian crusaders, led by Simon de Montfort IV. However, they were only allowed to take the clothes they stood up in.

down blast after blast of fire upon the attackers, all to no avail. A mass of crusaders poured inside Bourg, but this time, they were not intent on slaughter. Their targets were the water wells by the River Aude. Soon they had these had under control together with the northern approaches to Carcassonne.

The loss of the wells was a severe blow to the defence of the city, but the people of Carcassonne fought on. On 7 August, when the crusaders tried to storm Castellar, the other, southern, suburb of the city, they were plastered with rocks, arrows and other missiles, which sent them running for shelter among the nearby trees. It was obvious to the crusader knights that the time had come to deploy the trebuchets, ballistas, mangonels and catapults – all formidable siege machines. Between them, these deadly pieces of equipment poured clouds of rocks, pebbles, flaming firebrands and anything else they could launch over the walls of Castellar and into the streets. Anyone caught out in the open was likely to be injured, maimed or killed.

AVENGING BÉZIERS

Now that the walls were breached, the crusaders swarmed into Castellar and in the ferocious fight that followed, most of the defenders were killed. The crusader lords left a small garrison in Castellar and retired back to their camp. But revenge was not long in coming. Lords, whose lands lay in the highlands around the valley of the River Aude close by the Pyrenees Mountains, and supported by Raymond Roger, arrived. These men, unlike their more cautious lowland counterparts, were the type who preferred death to surrender and with Raymond Roger at their head, they charged out of Carcassonne and fell on the garrison, slaughtering them to the last man. Béziers, they might have thought, was avenged.

But the short, sharp action seems to have been observed from the crusader camp and suddenly, a large troop of armed knights, much more numerous than Raymond Roger's men, came riding towards them. Roger's men hastily retreated into Carcassonne and swung the gate closed. The city itself was once more secure, but within its walls a fearful drama was being acted out. The shortage of water caused by the loss of the wells was fouling the city's cisterns and poisoning what little water they still contained. In the boiling August weather people, young and old, began to die. Sickness and fevers spread and a cloud of flies settled on the bodies of the dead as they lay rotting in the streets.

Amaury had at his disposal powerful siege machines and many more archers than Raymond Roger could mass against him.

THE END AT CARCASSONNE

The situation could not go on. Around the middle of August, two weeks after Amaury's army arrived outside Carcassonne, an emissary from the crusaders arrived. He had a simple but chilling message: surrender now or share the fate of Béziers. Raymond Roger recognized the end when he saw it. He agreed to parley and under a guarantee of safe conduct, rode to the crusader camp to meet with the Count of Nevers, Hervé de Donzy. Neither

his family, nor his followers saw Raymond Roger, Viscount de Trencavel, alive again.

What happened in the privacy of Hervé de Donzy's tent never became known and even contemporary chroniclers, usually eager for any shred of gossip and rumour, failed to reveal any clue. The only facts to emerge at this juncture were that, to their great relief and puzzlement, the Carcassonnois – Cathar, Catholic and Jew alike – were told they could go, but had to leave everything behind except for the clothes they stood up in.

Knights on horseback are shown fighting at close quarters during the siege of Carcassonne in this Languedoc manuscript.

They departed, passing one at a time through a narrow postern gate under the sharp eyes of crusader guards who watched out for any sign they were trying to smuggle out any of their possessions.

'Not even the value of a button were they allowed to take with them,' one chronicler recorded. Or, as another chronicler expressed it, the Carcassonnois took away 'nothing but their sins'. Precisely how Raymond Roger managed to obtain freedom for his people in Carcassonne was, and remained, a mystery, although it has since been suggested that the real purpose of the crusader attack was not the destruction of the Cathars, but the elimination of its dangerously tolerant viscount who preferred to consort with heretics rather than follow the 'true' faith of Christ. However that may be, once the city was empty and

> It has since been suggested that the real purpose of the crusader attack on Carcassonne was not the destruction of the Cathars, but the elimination of its dangerously tolerant viscount who preferred to consort with heretics rather than follow the 'true' faith of Christ.

the now destitute Carcassonnois had gone, Raymond Roger was brought back in chains, forced down into the depths of his castle, the Chateau Comtal, and manacled to the wall of its dungeon. On 10 November 1209, 13 weeks later, he was found dead. He was 24 years of age.

Raymond Roger left behind a five-year-old son, Raymond Roger IV, but despite efforts over many years, the heir to Trencavel never received his patrimony. Instead, the Trencavel lands were given to Simon de Montfort IV, father of the more famous baron of the same name who became Sixth Earl of Leicester and pioneered parliamentary power in England later in the thirteenth century. On 15 August 1209, the elder de Montfort was made Viscount of Béziers, Carcassonne and all the other possessions once owned by the Trencavel family.

SIMON DE MONTFORT IV

Subsequently, de Montfort, who succeeded Arnaud Amaury as military leader of the crusade, blamed the death of Raymond Roger on dysentery and added a vague mention of 'divine punishment' for sheltering and supporting the heretic Cathars. The idea of direct punishment from God for sins was very seductive to the medieval mindset, for it demonstrated God's active involvement in human affairs. Even so, many Languedocoise were unconvinced and strongly suspected foul play. They were not alone, although six years passed before anyone voiced these suspicions in public, at the Fourth Lateran Council of 1215. The occasion was significant for Pope Innocent III himself summoned the Council. Innocent was present when Raymond de Roquefeuil, one of the lords who also attended the Council directly accused Simon de Montfort of murder. De Roquefeuil went further, and implicated the Pope. He told Innocent II:

> *As the (crusaders) have killed the father and disinherited the son will you, My Lord, give him his fief and keep your own dignity? And if you refuse to give it to him, may God do you the grace to add the weight of his sins to your own soul!*

These were fighting words few would have dared address to a pope, but Innocent, it seems, merely answered: 'This shall be seen to.' The murder charge was no news to Pope Innocent who had already told Arnold Amaury in 1213 that Raymond Roger had been 'wretchedly slain'. All the same, nothing was done to restore the rights of Raymond Roger IV and the Trencavel family.

The Chateau Comtal, built in the late 12th century, was the inner fortress of Carcassonne and was selected as a UNESCO World Heritage Site in 1997.

Above: The seal of Simon de Montfort IV, showing a horseman taking part in a hunt, with hunting horn raised and hunting hounds alongside.

After the fall of Carcassonne on 15 August 1209, the city, silent and deserted, was thoroughly looted and despoiled. Once that sordid task was done, Amaury and his crusaders went home, carrying fortunes in gold, silver, jewels and other prizes so rich that even the most impoverished among them were set up for life. The few weeks they had spent in Languedoc, punctuated by atrocity and pillage and tainted with innocent blood has long been accounted one of the most sordid episodes in Christian and papal history. But though they severely damaged the Cathars, killed them by the thousand and created a tide of refugees that swelled the population of other cities in Languedoc, the crusaders failed to destroy them or disturb their beliefs. Nor did they convert Cathars to the Catholic faith in sufficient numbers to claim a decisive triumph over heresy.

LOOT, LAND AND POWER

Evidently, the work of 'purifying' the Church of heresy was not yet finished, which was why the Pope issued the call to crusade every year. But, the purpose behind it began to change after news of the Albigensian 'success' at Béziers and Carcassonne alerted new recruits from all over Europe. Before long, thousands came to join the party. For large numbers of them, their first thought was not to perform the work of God and the Church, but to satisfy the prime motives of feudal warfare: the acquisition of loot, land and power.

The chief beneficiary of this new, materialistic ethos was Simon de Montfort IV who ranked quite modestly

Amaury and his crusaders went home, carrying fortunes in gold, silver, jewels and other prizes so rich that even the most impoverished among them were set up for life.

among the great feudal lords and landowners of the time until he was given the Trencavel holdings in Languedoc. Before that, de Montfort's estates in France were few. A more substantial inheritance was his half share, with his mother, in the Earldom of Leicester in England. This, though, became purely theoretical in 1207 when John, King of England confiscated the earldom and appropriated its revenues. In this context, de Montfort, a courageous, but cruel commander known for his 'treachery, harshness and bad faith', was bound to seek recompense by some

It took Pope Innocent III some time to discover that de Montfort and his new 'crusaders' were serving themselves rather than God, and before he did, more cities were attacked and plundered, more populations were terrorized, and more atrocities were committed.

other means. Languedoc gave him his chance, and once in command of the crusader army, he made the most of it.

It took Pope Innocent III some time to discover that de Montfort and his new 'crusaders' were serving themselves rather than God, and before he did, more cities were attacked and plundered, more populations were terrorized, more atrocities were committed even though the appearance of crusade was provided by the killing of hundreds more Cathars. Eventually, in 1213, Innocent ordered an end to the crusade against the heretics of Languedoc. The soldiers of Christ, he believed, had better things to do, such as ending the power of the Muslim Moors in Spain or reconquering Jerusalem, lost to the Saracens in 1187.

The Pope's decision came too late. By 1213, after four years of war and persecution, the Albigensian Crusade took on a life of its own in which the elimination of the Cathars was entwined with the territorial ambitions of feudal lords and kings and one vital, inescapable fact: despite all the damage the Crusade had done so far, the destruction of castles and cities, the slaughter of thousands of people and the

Simon de Montfort IV suffered a bizarre death. He was hit on the head by a stray stone from a nearby catapult during the siege of Toulouse in 1218.

A l'aube du 25 juin
de l'an 1218.
Montfort eut d'abord
son cheval blessé et

ruin of as many lives, the Cathars, though weakened, had survived with their heretic faith intact. This, Pope Innocent was told by the strong-minded Arnaud Amaury, was no time to leave the field. The fight, in which Amaury had already invested so much time and effort, had to go on. Innocent had no option but yield

The Cathar War, as the Albigensian Crusade was also called, dragged on for another 16 years and outlived some of its chief protagonists.

The seal of Count Raymond VII of Toulouse shows him on horseback with the cross of Toulouse on his shield and on his horse's caparison, or cloth cover.

to the logic of the situation, and he rescinded his call for an end to the Albigensian Crusade only five months after issuing it.

THE END OF THE CRUSADE

But the ultimate downfall of the Cathars was not brought about solely by military action, as Arnaud Amaury probably envisaged, or by wholesale conversion, as Pope Innocent may have hoped. The Cathar War, as the Albigensian Crusade was also called, dragged on for another 16 years and outlived some of its chief protagonists. Pope Innocent died in 1216. Simon de Montfort was killed in 1218 when a stray stone from a catapult struck him on the head during his seige of Toulouse. And Arnaud Amaury died in 1225.

Four years later, the Albigensian Crusade came to its close after the French defeated Raymond VII of Toulouse, son of Raymond VI. It was reckoned that in the 20 years it lasted, around one million people were killed as the horrors of Béziers and Carcassonne were repeated over and over again. At the Treaty of Paris, signed on 12 April 1229, Raymond VII ceded his castles and his lands, which by that time included Languedoc, to the French King, Louis IX. This was a belated triumph for Louis' grandfather, the wily and treacherous Philip II Augustus, who entered the Wars late (in 1215), but 14 years later, posthumously scooped the pool. With this, Raymond's landholdings shrank to a limited area, with the city of Toulouse as his only notable possession.

This, though, was not all. On the day the Treaty was signed, Raymond was made to suffer the utmost humiliation. The start of the Crusade 20 years earlier had been signalled by the public penance of Raymond's father, Raymond VI. Now, his son marked the end of the Crusade with the same punishment. Forced to endure public penance, Raymond VII was whipped with a bundle of birch twigs in the square outside the Cathedral of Notre Dame in Paris. Afterwards, he was thrown into prison. Most significant, though, was the promise extracted from him to use his army to aid in the persecution of the Cathars.

THE INQUISITION RETURNS

At this time, the hunt for Cathars and other heretics was entering a new and much more deadly phase. Gregory IX who was elected pope in 1227 was not content, as previous popes had been, to call for a crusade and then leave it to the military to do the dirty work. He had a better, though much more chilling idea. He reinvented the Episcopal (bishops') Inquisition, as a method of dealing with heretics that was first introduced in 1184 but had never quite fulfilled its purpose.

The bishops who had been supposed to conduct the Inquisition seemed to have little taste for hunting heretics and even less for the terrifying punishments they had to impose. Some bishops were unable to recognize heresy when they saw it. Others were too closely tied to the families in their diocese to contemplate the possibility that they might find themselves persecuting their own kin. These problems effectively stymied the bishops' Inquisition for as Pope Innocent III put it in 1215:

> *It often happens that bishops, by reason of their manifold preoccupations, fleshly pleasures and bellicose leanings, and from other causes, not least the poverty of their spiritual training and lack of pastoral zeal, are unfit to proclaim the word of God and govern the people.*

In some places, the people were, in any case, barely governable, for the mob frequently took charge when an alleged heretic was uncovered and immediately administered their own summary justice.

The new, papal or Roman Inquisition introduced by Pope Gregory was not only meant to discourage such abuses, but to bring better organization, more efficiency and greater dedication to the business of saving souls from heresy, and punishing – severely – anyone who refused to recant. In this more retributive form, the Inquisition became, and remained for centuries, a byword for torture, terror and unimaginable suffering.

The bishops who had been supposed to conduct the Inquisition seemed to have little taste for hunting heretics and even less for the terrifying punishments they had to impose.

In 1231, Pope Gregory IX, who was elected in 1227 near the end of the Albigensian Crusade, introduced the Inquisition which even today, remains a byword for terror and suffering.

GENOCIDE: THE CATHARS, PART II

The Inquisition introduced by Pope Gregory IX in 1231 was designed to fight all heresy wherever it occurred in Catholic Europe, but its first target was the unorthodox brand practised and preached by the Cathars.

The danger the Cathars presented to the established Church lay in their vast numbers, the support of high-ranking nobles, like Raymond VI of Toulouse and his son, Raymond VII, the spread of Cathar territory in southwest France and northeast Spain and the resilience that enabled them to survive, with beliefs stubbornly intact, the 20 gruelling years of the Albigensian Crusade. However, the sequel to the Treaty of Paris, which brought the Crusade to an official close in 1229, was even more punitive and lasted even longer. Ultimately, the fight against heresy was to outdo most other conflicts of medieval times in the cruelty and terror that was used to achieve its ends.

The mass burning (left) of Cathars at their stronghold of Montségur in 1244 finally broke the back of the Cathar faith. Pope Gregory IX (above) appointed the Dominican friars as chief investigators of heresy.

EXTREME MEASURES

As far as the medieval Church was concerned, extreme measures were justified when heresy placed Christianity in mortal danger. The foundations of society itself were at stake, for the freethinking heretic, who rejected the 'one true Church' and chose

The freethinking heretic, who rejected the 'one true Church' and chose his own beliefs and practices, was a fundamental threat to the faithful.

Gregory IX established the Papal Inquisition in 1231, although unlike the Dominicans he appointed, he did not personally approve the use of torture as a tool of investigation.

his own beliefs and practices, was a fundamental threat to the faithful. The Church, after all, was the bedrock on which their peace of mind rested, and its teachings were central to their certainties. Rob them of that, and mayhem would follow.

Over the next quarter of a century, the sieges of towns and castles and the massacres of their inhabitants continued, but it was not the mixture as before. It was infinitely worse. Pope Gregory's Inquisition gave an extra edge to atrocity as inquisitors exploited the wide-ranging powers he allowed them. Even their job description, *inquisitor hereticae pravitatis* (inquisitor of heretical depravity), was a terrifying term with its overtones of madness and the link that superstition made with demons, devils and their evil.

NO QUARTER GIVEN

The Cathars were fully aware that no quarter would be given once the Dominicans got down to work, and when the Inquisition was set up in Languedoc in the Spring of 1233 thousands of them fled to safer places

Pope Gregory's Inquisition gave an extra edge to atrocity as inquisitors exploited the wide-ranging powers he allowed them.

such as Caudiès de Fenouillèdes or Montségur, both of them on the French side of the Pyrenees. Montségur was remarkable for its fortress, sited high among the snow-capped mountain peaks. It was easy to feel safe in such remote refuges, but not everyone was able to elude the Inquisition or seek safety elsewhere.

Inevitably, a climate of dread and suspicion began to pervade Toulouse and other cities of Languedoc where anyone, Cathar or not, could be betrayed to the Inquisition and so incur its terrible penalties. Loyalty to the Church and its teachings was supposed to be the prime motive for leading inquisitors to heretics. But there were

DOMINICAN INQUISITORS

The Dominicans, members of the Order of Friars Preachers, who were to be the pope's chief inquisitors were a special type of monk, purposely trained by their Spanish founder Dominic de Guzman to mirror the asceticism, poverty and piety of the Cathar Perfects. De Guzman, who was canonized as St Dominic only 13 years after his death in 1221, perceived that the Perfects' humble, self-denying way of life was the key to the devotion they earned among the Cathars. The Dominicans, he decided, must match the Perfects for piety and self-sacrifice if they were going to succeed in saving Cathar souls for Rome. They had to live in the world, not within the confines of the monastery, and like the Cathar Perfects, communicate directly with the people and eschew all luxury, and the self-indulgence too eagerly embraced by too many churchmen.

Unfortunately, Dominic did not take sufficient account of the self-righteousness inherent in the strictly puritan way of life, nor of the way it produced a sense of moral superiority that ran counter to the self-effacement he tried to instil in his followers. In addition, extremes have always bred extremists, and fanatics who would today be classed as psychopaths were drawn to the Order of Friars Preachers by the chance the Inquisition offered to use barbarity disguised as righteous zeal. The pope may or may not have recognized them for what they were. But just the same, he welcomed them to the ranks of his inquisitors and dispatched them to France and elsewhere in Europe where many Dominicans became notorious for conduct that was horrific even by the brutal standards of the time. It was no wonder that, ultimately, the Dominicans became widely known as 'The Black Friars'.

St Dominic, founder of the Dominican Order, is shown here performing self-flagellation. The practice, also called 'mortification of the flesh', was eventually outlawed by the Catholic Church in the 14th century.

THE APPALLING FATE OF MADAME BOURSIER

Madame Boursier, an elderly Cathar lady and native of Toulouse was on her deathbed when Dominican inquisitors arrived at her home a few doors down from the city's cathedral on 5 August 1234. She was about to endure a shocking fate.

The Cathars of Toulouse had kept quiet about their beliefs, hoping to avoid persecution, and till now, the dying and delirious old lady had been one of these secret *credentes* (believers). Until, that is, she was betrayed to the Dominicans by one of her own servants. One of the Dominican monks, Guillaume Pelhisson, was an official inquisitor, another, Raymond du Fauga, Bishop of Toulouse was a man with an overdeveloped taste for cruelty and guile. When the two Dominicans entered Madame Boursier's house and climbed the stairs to her room, her family became terrified: they had long been under suspicion of heresy and believed that now, they had reached the end of the line. This was certainly so for Madame Boursier.

One member of the family, hoping to warn the old lady of her dangerous visitors, whispered to her that the 'Lord Bishop' had arrived. But Madame Boursier was too far advanced in her delirium. She imagined that the Cathar Perfect, Guilhabert de Castres was at her bedside. Raymond du Fauga let her go on believing it and pretended to be the Perfect as he encouraged her to be true to her Cathar beliefs for, as he told her: 'The fear of death should not make you confess anything other than that which you hold firmly and with your whole heart.' To the horror of her relatives, the poor old lady condemned herself out of her own mouth and the Bishop, having made certain of his victim, declared his true identity and pronounced the death sentence, effective immediately.

In a scene rarely matched for sheer malevolence, even in the annals of the Inquisition, the helpless old woman was tied to her bed, carried downstairs and along the street outside to a field that lay beyond the city limits. There, a bonfire had already been lit, and in front of a large and curious crowd, Madame Boursier and her bed were flung into the flames. Barely conscious, the old lady may have been too far gone to be aware of what was happening to her, nor to ever have known how her own servant had been tempted to accept the payment offered by the Inquisition to anyone who denounced a heretic.

Strewn on the floor in front of this Dominican monk are some of the instruments of torture used by members of his Order to root out heretics.

Pope Gregory IX is shown in this 14th century manuscript receiving lists of accused heretics from the inquisitor kneeling before him.

other agendas at work. Piety was all too often outmatched by a range of personal reasons, such as the chance to pay off old scores, get rid of an inconvenient rival or otherwise satisfy the warped imaginations of mischief-makers and misanthropes.

THE INQUISITOR ARRIVES IN TOWN

The papal inquisition did not care about motives. Its inquisitors were trained to net all the victims who were betrayed to them and at the same time close any loopholes that might enable them to escape the 'justice' they were supposed to dispense. First in was an inquisitor who arrived in a town, consulted the local clergy and then called on all males over the age of 14 and all females over the age of 12 to declare their loyalty to the orthodox Catholic faith. Needless to say, those who refused were instantly classed as sinners and, most likely, heretics. The inquisitor gave them one week to think over their position, confess their wrongdoings and denounce themselves.

After that, those who still refused to cooperate were summoned to appear before the Inquisition and its frightening, insistent interrogators. They presented themselves, knowing full well that no one was safe, not the dying, like Madame Boursier, nor the sick, nor the lunatics whose ravings were accepted as solid evidence.

Where the late Pope Innocent III had used the gentle, diplomatic approach, sending Cistercian monks among the Cathars to debate their beliefs and hopefully convert them, Gregory IX was much more proactive. He preferred to manipulate the situation and exploit baser human instincts in order to gain the results he wanted. Inevitably, where Innocent failed, Gregory succeeded. To achieve his ends, he gave preference to Dominicans who were adept at terrorizing witnesses and so confusing them that they soon reached a state where they could barely think straight.

Piety was all too often outmatched by a range of personal reasons, such as the chance to pay off old scores.

INSISTENT INTERROGATION

Did they know of any heretics? Had they seen them, how often, where and when? Who was with them? Who visited them? Had they seen anyone treat a Cathar with reverence or revered him themselves? Did they know of any bequest made to heretics and, if so, how much was it worth and who drew up the deed? Faced with this persistent pressure, designed to trip them up

BURNING THE REMAINS OF THE DEAD

Even the dead were not immune from this orgy of telling tales. The 'accused' soon learnt – or thought they learnt – how to elude the inquisitor's need for more and more fodder for their endless probing and quizzing. When required to give a list of names, the longer, the better, they identified dead men and women who, they imagined, could escape any punishment the inquisitors could impose. How wrong they were. The next thing they knew, the interrogators had appeared in the local cemetery to dig up corpses. No matter what their state of decomposition, the bodies were piled on a cart and taken to a specially designated place of 'execution'.

As the cart rolled through the streets, the priests accompanying them intoned: 'Whoso does the like, will suffer a like fate!'

Once they reached their destination, the rotting cadavers were bound to stakes. The fires were lit and they were ceremonially burnt. It was a macabre, utterly grotesque sight but the rest of the punishment was carried out as if the dead 'heretics' were still alive. Their houses were razed to the ground. Their families lost everything they owned. Some were imprisoned, or were forced to wear yellow crosses to show that they were indelibly stained by the sins of a 'heretic' relation.

Cathar heretics are abused and beaten as they march to a fiery death in this 19th-century colour lithograph.

The 'accused' as they were called in the manuals of the Inquisition, were not allowed to know whether or not they were themselves suspected of heresy.

or make them contradict themselves, most people would say anything, not matter what, to escape the barrage of quick-fire questioning. Loyalty, love, friendship, decency and honesty were all abandoned as victims, sensing danger, made desperate bids at self-defence. The 'accused' as they were called in the manuals of the Inquisition, were not allowed to know whether or not they were themselves suspected of heresy. Fear-filled imagination drove them to divulge scores of names and so provide the Inquisition with yet more suspects.

INQUISITORS UNDER ATTACK

The burning of dead 'heretics' and other excesses committed by inquisitors provoked widespread disgust, and this soon led to serious revolts and even murder. In 1235, two years after the Inquisition first arrived in Languedoc, three inquisitors died after they were hurled down a well some 30 metres (100ft) deep. Another, Arnold Catalan, whose sphere of operations was at Albi, was set upon by an infuriated mob after he

The victims of the sadistic Konrad von Marburg, the Pope's inquisitor in Germany, soon learned that it was a waste of their final breaths to ask him for mercy.

condemned and burnt two heretics and did the same to several corpses he had exhumed.

In his history of the Inquisition in Toulouse between 1230 and 1238, Graham Pelhisson, a Dominican who was himself an inquisitor, described what happened next:

> *The people of Albi sought to throw him into the River Tarn but at the insistence of some among them, released him, beaten, his clothing torn to shreds, his face bloody…*

The burning of dead 'heretics' and other excesses committed by inquisitors provoked widespread disgust, and this soon led to serious revolts and even murder.

This, though, was not an isolated incident for as Pelhisson continued:

> *The chief men of the region, together with the greater nobles and the burghers and others, protected and hid the heretics. They beat, wounded and killed those who pursued them…many wicked things were done in the land to the Church and to faithful persons.*

Another victim of this violent backlash was Konrad von Marburg. In 1227, the year he was elected pope, Gregory IX engaged von Marburg to wipe out heresy in his native Germany. Konrad was already an infamous sadist at the time, but as a reign of terror, his work in Germany outdid everything he had previously 'achieved' and inevitably led to his murder in 1233.

THE TERRIFYING KONRAD VON MARBURG

Before he was appointed a papal inquisitor, Konrad von Marburg had acted as advisor and confessor to Elisabeth, the widow of Prince Ludwig IV of Thuringia, who died of plague in 1227. Before long, Konrad held the unfortunate Elisabeth in thrall. He replaced her favourite ladies-in-waiting with two termagants and punished her for lapses by slapping her on the face or hitting her with a rod. It was an exceptionally harsh regime which, combined with the ascetic lifestyle she led after her husband's death, damaged her sufficiently to kill her at the age of 24. She was afterwards canonized as St Elisabeth and became for many an icon of misused womanhood.

There was more than a hint of what Elisabeth had gone through at the hands of the brutal Konrad in his later conduct as the pope's inquisitor in the German districts of Hesse and Thuringia. A rumour that he was in the area could create panic. According to some reports, panic changed to hysteria if he appeared in person, riding through a town or village accompanied by his grim-faced assistant, a man called Dorso, and a character named John, who had only one eye and one hand.

There was good reason for this terror. Konrad saw heretics everywhere and those he did not see, he fancied were hiding from him in castles, churches and even in monasteries and nunneries. Actual guilt or proof of guilt became superfluous because Konrad would accept almost any accusation as fact and judged suspects guilty of heresy unless they could prove they were innocent. This was easier said than done, for Konrad employed mobs whose task it was to find heretics, terrify confessions out of them and burn them at the stake if they refused to recant. Victims had one chance to avoid this fate: they could denounce more 'heretics', not from any real knowledge, but by deliberately falsifying evidence. Hundreds, maybe thousands, Cathars and Catholics alike, were accused of heresy, and, in their turn, offered the chance to live if they would agree to incriminate others. If they refused, Konrad was not one to hang around waiting for them to make up their minds. Many of his 'heretics' were burnt at the stake on the same day they were charged.

Konrad did not confine himself to snaring minnows for the Inquisition. He aimed for the top, implicating priests, aristocrats and other high-ranking notables in sins and shortcomings that qualified them for punishment. One of his victims was the Provost of Goslar, Heinrich Minnike, another was Heinrich II, Count of Sayn, who was found guilty of participating in'satanic orgies'. Minnike burnt at the stake, but the Count fought back and was exonerated by the bishops of Mainz. They refused to reverse their verdict as Konrad demanded.

Needless to say, Konrad made enemies wherever he went and after he left Mainz to return to Marburg, the inevitable happened. On 30 July 1233 while on the road, Konrad was waylaid by knights who murdered both him and his assistant Dorso. It was suspected, but never proved, that the assassins were in the pay of Heinrich II.

The widowed Queen Elisabeth of Thuringia, who was canonized as St. Elisabeth in 1235, visits a hostel for the poor which she founded.

In 1230 Pope Gregory IX ordered his chaplain and confessor, St Raymond of Peñaforte, to compile a collection of ecclesiastical laws and rulings. He is seen here being handed the collection, known as the Decretals of Pope Gregory IX.

POPE GREGORY'S GUILE

The killing of the pope's man, whatever the circumstances, was usually treated as a great scandal, virtually an insult to the pontiff himself. The death of Konrad of Marburg, however, drew a guileful response from Pope Gregory IX. He could not have been unaware of Konrad's barbarous doings and yet he wrote to the archbishops of Cologne and Trier in terms that subtly shifted the blame onto them.

'We marvel' the pope told the two archbishops 'that you allowed legal proceedings of this unprecedented nature to continue for so long among you without acquainting us of what was happening. It is our wish,' Gregory continued disingenuously 'that such things should no longer be tolerated and we declare these proceedings null and void. We cannot permit such misery as you have described.'

THE MURDEROUS ROBERT LE BOUGRE

Gregory had to be much more direct when it came to handling Robert le Bougre, another of his extremist inquisitors who was, it seems, a former Cathar turned Dominican monk. The zeal of the convert can be a terrible thing and Robert certainly proved that dictum through the way he conducted the fight against heresy in his designated area, which was Burgundy in east central France. There, Robert was responsible for a wave of executions, notably at Charité-sur-Loire where he ordered the burning of 50 heretics. This brought him into conflict with the Archbishops of Rheims and of Sens who saw the executions as an infringement of their rights. They had to concur, they maintained, before heretics were convicted. Some bishops claimed the right to amend sentences passed on the guilty and others demanded inquisitorial courts of their own.

Pope Gregory, a master of dissimulation, professed surprise at this reaction. By appointing Robert le Bougre and other inquisitors he had, he claimed, sought to lighten the bishops' workload. What he had actually done, of course, was to erode their legitimate powers. Nevertheless, Gregory met the aggrieved bishops halfway. In 1234, he suspended Robert le Bougre, barely a year after appointing him. But Robert was not dismissed. After an interval to allow tempers to cool, he reappeared with a new title, Inquisitor General of the Kingdom of France, and he made his previous depredations look like small beer.

For three years, between 1236 and 1239, Robert headed the Inquisition in Châlons-en-Champagne, Cambrai, Péronne, Douai and Lille, and burnt another 50 victims. He returned to the province of Champagne in 1239, where the Cistercian chronicler Alberic de Trois-Fontaines was eyewitness to a mass execution at Mont-Aimé in which no fewer than 183 'heretics' were burnt to death. Subsequently, nothing more was heard of Robert le Bougre, apart from a rumour that he died in jail after long years of imprisonment.

Reigns of terror, as conducted by the likes of Konrad of Marburg or Robert le Bougre, were inevitable when the weapons provided by the pope for his inquisitors to use included those that most terrified the medieval mind. Excommunication and interdict, for example, meant exclusion from the Church and its sacraments. More worldly punishments, such as imprisonment, dispossession, exile and even torture were also used to bring people to heel and make them cooperate with the Inquisition. Refusal was, of course, considered tantamount to heresy and incurred the same punishments.

> The killing of the pope's man, whatever the circumstances, was usually treated as a great scandal, virtually an insult to the pontiff himself.

Two Dominican brothers, Peter Seila and William Arnald, who were commissioned as inquisitors by the pope in 1233, deployed virtually the full range of papal penalties in Languedoc, the chief target of the Inquisition. One of their methods involved speed, with arrest, trial, conviction and penalty following each other in quick succession. This was how the most eminent Cathar Perfect in Toulouse, Vigoros de Bacone, came to be burnt at the stake before his friends and supporters were able to organize a defence for him. Seila and Arnald went on to exhume the bodies of alleged Cathars and burn them. They imprisoned scores of people, Cathars or Catholics, they seemed not to care, and bullied the authorities in Toulouse into providing them with armed soldiers to help in the work of arresting, detaining, trying and executing 'heretics'.

Eventually, after more than two years, Count Raymond VII of Toulouse had had enough. Raymond had been forced to accept the Inquisition, and this far,

An inquisitor makes an accusation in this painting by the French artist Jean Paul Laurens (1838–1921).

he had cooperated, if reluctantly, with Seila and Arnald. His reasons were simple: he could not afford another war like the one that had all but ruined him in 1229. But once Seila and Arnald went too far, Raymond felt impelled to report them to the pope.

He complained that the two Inquisitors were 'noxious' and appeared 'to be toiling to lead men into error rather than towards the truth'. Raymond had the backing of Queen Blanche, the mother of the French king, Louis IX, who told Pope Gregory that his inquisitors had breached the bounds of decency.

A FORMIDABLE FOE

The Count and the Queen were fortunate to catch the pope at a difficult moment. Gregory was embroiled with Frederick II, King of Germany and Sicily and Holy Roman Emperor, a secular-minded ruler whose aim in life was to spread his own power throughout Italy at the expense of papal influence. According to the pope, Frederick was 'the beast that surges up from the sea laden with blasphemous names...his gaping mouth offending the Holy Name...hurling his lance at the tabernacle of God and His Saints in heaven'. With such a formidable foe confronting him, Gregory had to win allies wherever he could. He was even willing to enlist heretic Languedoc on his side. It was known that Frederick had designs on Provence, in southeastern France and Raymond, seizing his chance, offered to aid the pope

This 15th-century manuscript depicts the Great Schism of 1378 to 1415, when there were rival popes based in Rome and at Avignon in France, prompted by the death of Gregory IX.

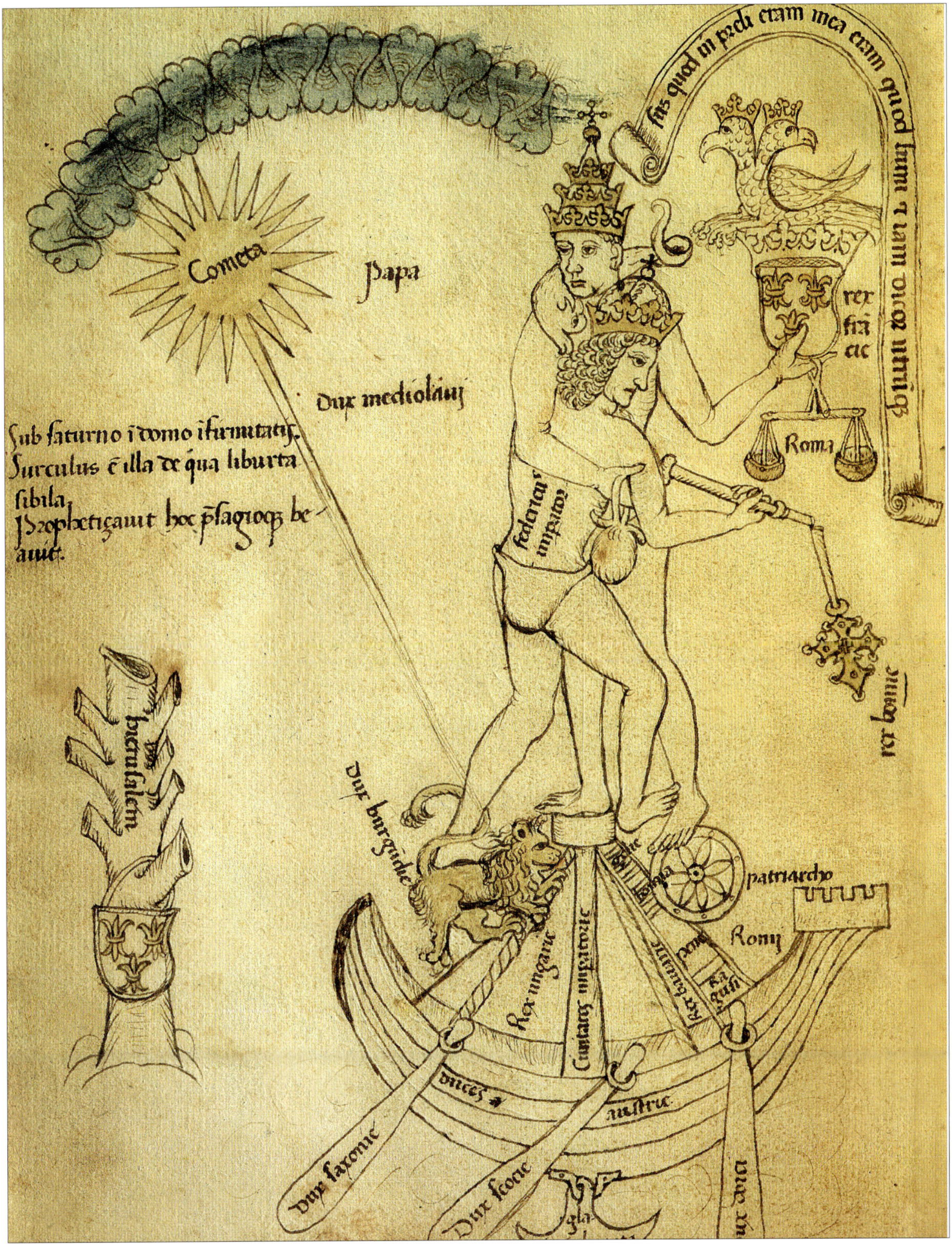
Cometa
Papa
Roma
patriarcho

Queen Blanche of Castile (top left) who protested against the excesses of the Inquisition, was the wife of King Louis VIII of France and the mother and regent of King Louis IX. Famous for her clemency, she is shown in the lower part of the picture releasing unjustly imprisoned serfs.

in thwarting him. Raymond's price, however, was the withdrawal of Seila, Arnald and the apparatus of the Inquisition from Toulouse and Languedoc.

FIGHTING BACK

Pope Gregory declined to go that far, but he did attempt to rein in his inquisitors and pressure them to be more lenient. Gregory even travelled to Languedoc, in an effort to soothe the outrage caused by his overzealous inquisitors. Encouraged by these concessions, Raymond prepared to adopt a harder line with Seila and Arnald. He was almost pre-empted when the inquisitors ordered the arrest of several courtiers in his personal entourage who had Cathar sympathies. But Raymond succeeded in getting them away, beyond the reach of the Inquisition. At his behest, the soldiers detailed to arrest the courtiers escorted them out of Toulouse to the safety of the surrounding countryside. Seila and Arnald were infuriated and tried to get their revenge by turning on several consuls serving in the government of Toulouse. They failed to get far, though, for they soon found themselves unceremoniously dumped out of the city. Other Dominicans, together with the Archbishop of Toulouse, were assaulted by a furious mob who threw stones at them as they fled all the way back to Carcassonne. Once there, the Dominicans excommunicated their attackers and put Toulouse under interdict.

Pope Gregory even travelled to Languedoc, in an effort to soothe the outrage caused by his overzealous inquisitors.

They soon returned under Gregory's orders. However, the pope had to be careful not to punish Raymond too harshly because he needed the Count as an ally in the struggle with Emperor Frederick. For this reason, the pope lifted the interdict on Toulouse and appointed a watchdog to rein in the Dominicans and their taste for brutality.

WORSE THAN THE DOMINICANS

Stephen of St Thibéry was a Franciscan friar from an order known for its gentleness and diplomacy, but he was a disastrous choice. Far from holding back the Dominicans, as Pope Gregory expected, Stephen outdid them in his zeal to expunge the Cathars and their heresy by the most retributive means at his disposal. The ruthless questioning began again, and the dead were exhumed once more and burnt along with the living. Suspected 'heretics' were bullied into confessions and, to save themselves, betrayed others.

The pressure they exerted was so great that it cracked two of the most prominent Cathar Perfects in Toulouse, Raymond Gros and Guillaume de Soler, who informed on scores of other Cathars and betrayed details about their families, their friends and their activities. Needless to say, Gros and de Soler became marked men and the Inquisition had to organize protection to save them from the fury of Cathars and others who had once trusted them implicitly.

DECEIVING THE INQUISITORS

The two traitors were safe enough, for any move against them would have identified their attackers as Cathars and heretics. Instead, the Cathars became cunning and hid behind a screen of deception. Some Perfects shed their simple robes for the less easily identifiable clothes worn by ordinary people. Perfects had been vegetarians, but now they ate meat and made sure they were seen doing it in public.

Perfects had been vegetarians, but now they ate meat and made sure they were seen doing it in public.

Probably the most drastic change in their habits involved the separation between male and female Perfects who, traditionally, were supposed to keep strictly apart. Now they went out in pairs so that

ASSASSINATION AT AVIGNONET

During the morning of 28 May 1242, the Franciscan Stephen of St Thibéry together with the Dominican William Arnald and eight scribes were journeying through the countryside between Toulouse and Carcassonne. On the way, they halted at various villages to hear confessions from accused heretics and see their names inscribed in the Inquisition registers.

There was nothing unusual about this, for the Inquisition seemed to be everywhere in Languedoc, and was likely to turn up in any town or village at any time to ferret out incriminating information. It was all part of the terror they spread throughout the province. The likes of Stephen and William Arnald often relied on the power of intimidation which they exercised over the Languedocois who went in mortal dread of being 'sent to the wall', the dungeon in Carcassonne where prisoners were kept in small, damp cells and left there to subsist, if they could, on a diet of bread and water.

However, what was unusual this time was a lack of bodyguards and other armed protection to see Stephen, William and their scribes safely from one destination to the next. That evening, they reached the fortified town of Avignonet where Raymond d'Alfaro, (Raymond VII's bailiff and brother-in-law) was waiting in the castle to receive them. Lodgings for the two friars had been arranged in the castle keep where they were eating their evening meal when William-Raymond Golairan, one of d'Alfaro's men checked up on them.

Satisfied that Stephen and William Arnald suspected nothing, Golairan left the castle and rode out to Antioch Wood, a small group of trees where he met up with Pierre-Roger de Mirepoix, Joint Lord of Montségur with the aged Raymond de Pereille, and his group of heavily armed knights. All of them were Cathar *credentes* who normally acted as guards at Montségur. This meeting was, of course, pre-arranged. Peter Roger chose a dozen or more knights and at dusk, sent them off to Avignonet, their battleaxes slung from their belts and a troop of horsemen following behind. By the time they reached Avignonet, it was pitch dark.

While the Cathar knights hid in an abattoir beyond the town walls, Golairan returned to the castle keep and saw that Stephen, William and their scribes had retired to bed. Then, he went outside, to the castle ramparts and opened the gate to admit Peter Roger's knights. Silently, they made their way over cobbled streets to the castle entrance where some 30 Avignonetois awaited them, armed with meat cleavers and clubs. Together, they slipped into the castle courtyard and made their way towards the keep. They proceeded in silence up the stairs and along the stone corridors until they reached the heavy oak door that led to the inquisitors' quarters. There were no guards protecting it. One of the Cathar knights swung a two-headed battleaxe at the door, which split with a tremendous crash.

BLOODY ASSAULT

Before anyone inside knew what was happening, dozens of men were in the room, slashing with knives, slicing with axes and cleavers and bringing cudgels and clubs hammering down on their heads. The assault went on and on until the attackers were sure that everyone was dead, by which time a deathly silence hung over the room and the stone floor was slick with blood. The assassins lit torches and grabbed everything they could see – candlesticks, money and the one thing they were really looking for: the inquisitors' register of names. All the pages were torn up and set alight. Before long the Inquisition's 'evidence' was nothing but a pile of smoking ashes.

The assassins left Avignonet without being detected and returned to Antioch Wood where Peter Roger was waiting for them. He was expecting a special gift, the skull of William Arnald, which he planned to make into a drinking cup. Roger was disappointed to be told that the skull had been left behind, shattered into pieces by the fury of the Cathars' onslaught, but its state at least told him how successful the raid had been.

Peter of Verona, a Dominican monk, was killed by Cathar assassins on 6 April 1252 while travelling on the road to Milan, Italy. He is pictured here miraculously writing *Credo in Unum Deum* (I believe in one God) on the ground in his own blood in the seconds before death.

anyone who saw them, including the Dominicans, would assume that they were married couples. The best defence was of course, to leave the towns altogether and there were numerous Cathar Perfects sheltering in the safety of Montségur, but they did not neglect their followers. Perfects would slip back into town in disguise, their pastoral visits known only to a very few local Cathars. Their business done, they left the same way, in strict secrecy.

The Inquisition was well aware that something clandestine was going on in Languedoc, but was generally unable to catch the perpetrators. Inquisitors were, needless to say, thoroughly detested. To protect themselves and their entourage of clerks and scribes at Albi and Carcassonne, they had to borrow armed guards from the French in order to function. Sometimes, the inquisitors were locked out and were unable to enter some towns, like Toulouse, but there was always the surrounding countryside to be raked over, potential heretics to interrogate and punishments and penances to be handed out.

ANOTHER REBELLION

As time went on, the level of hatred increased until, in 1240, it provided an opportunity for Raymond Roger IV de Trencavel, the son of the tragic Raymond Roger III who had died mysteriously at Carcassonne in 1209, to intervene. Now aged 35, Raymond Roger IV had been living in exile for 30 years but had not given up hope of winning back his lost inheritance. He assembled an army of exiles in Aragon, northeast Spain, and marched them across the Pyrenees Mountains into Languedoc. He enjoyed some small initial success, liberating Limoux, Alet and Montréal from the French. But serious business began when Raymond Roger laid siege to Carcassonne where he was welcomed into the suburbs of Bourg and Castellar. From there, in fewer than five weeks, he launched eight assaults on Carcassonne proper. This, though, was where his run of success came to an abrupt end.

The French reacted swiftly, sending an army into Languedoc and chasing Raymond Roger IV out of Carcassonne and all the way to nearby Montréal. Now

Known to Catholics as the 'stronghold of Satan', the Cathar town of Lavaur near Toulouse was assaulted and pillaged by the Albigensian crusaders on 3 May 1211. The population was massacred.

Montségur, the last major stronghold of the Cathars, was built at a height of 914 metres (3,000ft) near the Pyrenees mountains in the south-west of what is now France.

the besieger was besieged as the French surrounded the town. The fighting, however, was so fierce and so costly that both sides opted for a truce. Afterwards, Roger Raymond was forced back into exile in Aragon.

If Roger Raymond had hoped to receive help from Count Raymond VII of Toulouse, he was disappointed.

Perfects would slip back into town in disguise, their pastoral visits known only to a very few local Cathars.

At that time, Count Raymond had to cover his own back, because he could not afford to offend Pope Gregory IX. But by 1242, times had changed. Pope Gregory died in 1241 and was succeeded by Celestine IV, who expired, probably of old age, after only 17 days. Celestine's successor, Innocent IV, was involved in a power struggle with Gregory's old foe, the Holy Roman Emperor Frederick II. Innocent IV felt so insecure in Rome that he eventually fled to Genoa and remained there until Frederick's death in 1250.

The confusion this caused in Rome gave Raymond VII the opportunity he had awaited for 13 years. His nobles too were itching for a chance to get at the detested French and reclaim their own lost lands and estates. In addition, Raymond had gained support from the kings of England and Navarre and Castile and Aragon in Spain. At last, Raymond was able to make a bid to free his former territories from the grasp of the French and drive away the Dominicans, the Inquisition and their ghastly apparatus of cruelty and death.

Raymond Roger IV had been living in exile for 30 years but had not given up hope of winning back his lost inheritance.

The inquisitors, rather than military objectives, were Raymond's first targets in the rebellion that began on 28 May 1242. Although he was not actually present to see the deed done, there was little doubt that Raymond was behind the murder of the inquisitors that took place a few days later and the

destruction of their supposed 'evidence' against heretics in Languedoc.

CELEBRATIONS IN LANGUEDOC

News of the killings at Avignonet flashed across Languedoc, where the hard-pressed Cathars and Catholics celebrated this strike against the dreaded Inquisition. One clergyman even rang the bell of his church to mark the occasion, and the assassins were received back at Montségur as heroes. The raid at Avignonet had, however, been only a prelude to a series of military attacks on castles, the Dominicans' houses and the palaces of bishops, all of them legitimate targets for the vengeance the Languedocois wrought against the hated French and the Inquisition they promoted. Meanwhile, towns and villages across the province seemed to be energized by Avignonet and rose up to seek revenge for the atrocities, indignities and cruelties the Inquisition had brought to once peaceful and affluent Languedoc.

But sadly, inevitably, both revolution and rejoicing were short-lived. Despite the illustrious names who had signed up to back Raymond VII – King Henry III of England, Hugh de Lusignan, whose family were prominent crusaders, Roger Bernard, Count of Foix – all of them crumbled before the forces of France. The King and de Lusignan were thrashed in battle, and the Count, though a son and nephew of Cathar

The inquisitors ... were Raymond's first targets in the rebellion ... there was little doubt that Raymond was behind the murder of the inquisitors that took place a few days later and the destruction of their 'evidence' against heretics in Languedoc.

Perfects, defected to the enemy and used his army to hammer Raymond VII to a defeat that would prove permanent. Raymond's other allies in Aragon, Castile and Navarre read the runes and quietly backed out. Once again, in January 1243, Raymond and King Louis IX signed a treaty that turned back the clock to 1229, when Languedoc had come under French rule at the Treaty of Paris.

INACCESSIBLE MONTSÉGUR

The assassins of Avignonet were never caught, but Montségur, the fortress where the plot had been conceived, remained as the last major outpost of Cathar resistance in Languedoc. Catholic clergy and

The mighty castle of Montségur, which was built after 1204 in preparation for the day when, inevitably, the Cathars would have to make a stand against their persecutors.

An illumination from a Languedoc manuscript shows Montségur finally captured by troops commanded by Hugh de Arcis, seneschal (steward) to Louis IX of France.

inquisitors had long called Montségur the 'Synagogue of Satan' and as far as they were concerned, recent events had shown how fully it lived up to that name. Montségur had to be destroyed because it was not just another fortress, but a safe haven where hundreds of Cathars, Perfects and *credentes* alike, had sought the asylum that only the high mountains and inaccessible crags of the Pyrenees could give them.

In 1242, some 500 refugees, both Cathars and Catholics, were living inside Montségur. Of these, 200 or so were Perfects who made their homes in huts and caves around the castle. Knights, men-at-arms and their wives, mistresses and children, many of them related to the Perfects, had also moved in to take advantage of the protection offered by the fortress. There was also a continuous flow of *credente* pilgrims who secretly visited this symbol of the Cathar faith for spiritual guidance and then returned home as secretly as they had come.

Montségur served these purposes for nearly 40 years, ever since 1204, when its ruling lord, Raymond de Pereille, realized that one day, the Cathars would have to make a stand against the Church that had labelled them heretics. To prepare for that day, de Pereille rebuilt the castle that overlooked the village of Montségur from its dizzying height of 914 metres (3000ft), high enough to provide a panoramic view of the woods and valleys that covered the landscape for miles around. Over the years, Montségur had sheltered dozens of Cathar Perfects on the run from persecution. Later, they returned for refuge again and again, whenever the witch-hunt was renewed. But the crisis conditions caused by the Inquisition and its excesses were a hint of something much more serious in the future – the 'final solution' to the Cathar question.

Just how close that solution had come was made plain in the spring of 1243 when the view from the castle revealed troop movements in the terrain far below. On the orders of Hugh de Arcis, seneschal to King Louis IX, knights, soldiers and their equipment began arriving from Aquitaine, Gascony, and other

There was also a continuous flow of *credente* pilgrims who secretly visited this symbol of the Cathar faith for spiritual guidance and then returned home as secretly as they had come.

regions of France and an encampment was set up on the eastern side of Montségur.

One Church dignitary, Pierre Amiel, Bishop of Narbonne, pitched his elaborately ornamented tent directly beneath Montségur. The scene was soon festooned with flags carrying the *fleur de lys*, the symbol of France, or the Cross to emphasize the holy purpose of the enterprise.

The thousands of men camped below provided a daunting sight, but this did not, as yet, denote that a siege was imminent: much more manpower was required before Hugh de Arcis had enough forces to surround the fortress. Even then, he could not achieve total encirclement. The perimeter of Montségur measured more than three kilometres (2 miles) and was not continuous – defiles and ravines that could provide escape routes from the castle interrupted it here and there. It was also impossible to

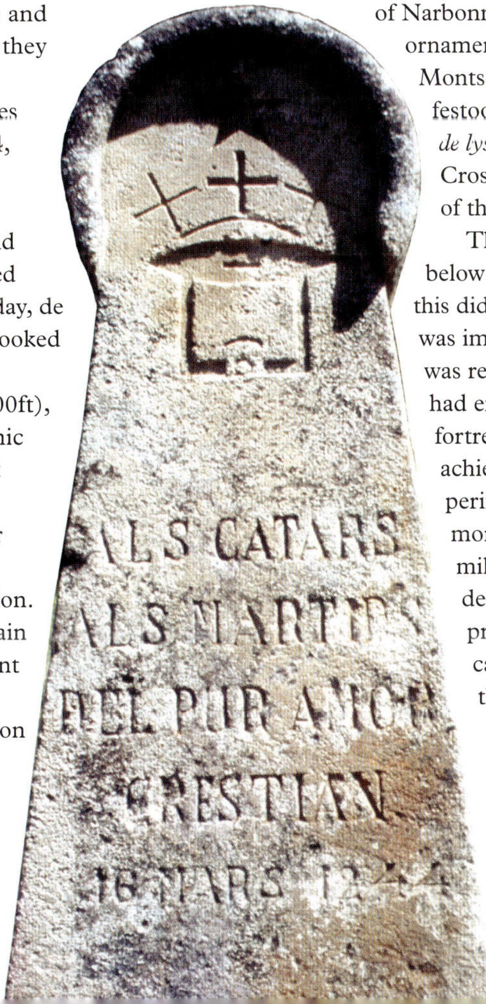

The monument to the 221 Cathars and others who died at the stake in the 'Field of the Burned' at Montségur on 16 March 1244.

use siege machines on the slopes of the Pyrenees that backed Montségur.

DEFENDING MONTSÉGUR

Inside the fortress, Pierre-Roger de Mirefoix's problems were just as acute, but different. The Cathar Perfects were pacifists and totally opposed to war. Even in this dire situation, they would not fight. This left Pierre Roger with only 98 men to defend the castle. To some extent, this disadvantage was cancelled out by the principle that attackers ascending from

> The thousands of men camped below provided a daunting sight, but this did not, as yet, denote that a siege was imminent.

below were always at the mercy of defenders sited above and so it proved at Montségur. The French forces made several attempts to climb the precipitous goat paths, covered in spiny gorse, that led to the

At the Council of Lyons in 1245, Innocent IV deposed the twice excommunicated Frederick II, the Holy Roman Emperor, after Frederick threatened him.

summit of Montségur, but they were soon driven back down again when de Mirefoix's men loosed on them showers of stones, crossbow quarrels and other missiles. There was, though, one way the French could get at the defenders without even leaving the ground. They fired arrows almost vertically over the walls of the castle to land among the Cathars at the top. Around a dozen defenders were felled by this means and the loss of each was a serious blow.

Nevertheless, Pierre-Roger de Mirefoix's meagre force managed to keep the attackers at bay for eight months, well into winter, when icy weather and dwindling food supplies began to exact their depredations on both sides of the siege. A few days before Christmas, when snow began to blanket the French encampment, Hugh de Arcis accepted that

The last of the Cathar fortresses, at Quéribus, 728 metres (2388ft) up in the Pyrenees mountains, was assaulted and captured in August 1255.

lesperance de tous ceulx qui le
gardoient cuidans quil feust
es angoisses de la mort. Il
ouurit la bouche et les pre
mieres paroles quil dist fu
rent quil demanda la croix
et la print devotement pour
aler oultremer. Et depuis
lors en avant il devint de plus
en plus grant aulmosnier
et desirant dacomplir le saint
voiaige et secourir la sainte
terre de promission. La cite
fut celle propre annee que le
Roy saint loys se croisa pres
que toute gastee et destruitte.
par une maniere de gens
Sarrazins appellez turffains.
Lesquelz entre aultres villes
prindrent par force la sainte

THE LAST OF THE CATHARS: THE AUTIER BROTHERS

The brothers Pierre and Guilllaume Autier were in their fifties, both well educated and well-to-do but not especially devout. Pierre, who had a sardonic wit, was fond of saying that making the sign of the Cross was useful only for swatting flies. Then, in 1296, to the amazement of all who knew them, the Autier brothers suddenly 'got religion' and took up a new, ascetic life as small-time peddlers.

They spent some time in Italy, but resurfaced in their native Languedoc in 1300, where Pierre began to preach the Cathar faith. He was very successful. Before the Inquisition caught up with him, he had converted around 1000 families. But in 1305, he was betrayed to the Inquisition, while his brother Guillaume was quickly apprehended and burnt at the stake with all but one of the new Perfects Pierre had created.

The one who escaped was called Sans Mercadier and he committed suicide rather than experience the agony of burning to death. Pierre Autier remained at large for another four years until he was finally caught and in April of 1310, burned in public in front of the cathedral of St Stephen in Toulouse.

after the long stalemate, his troops might soon become demoralized and could start to drift home. A drastic, even dramatic, move was required, but the risks would be considerable.

ASSAULT ON ROC DE LA TOUR

De Arcis called for volunteers. The men who came forward were Gascons, experienced at living in mountain country close to the Pyrenees. Their orders were almost tantamount to a suicide bid. They were to capture a part of the fortifications known as the Roc de la Tour (Tower Rock), which was built on top of a stone column sited on the summit ridge of Montségur.

This involved, first of all, climbing the cliff that gave access to the fortification, and doing it at night while carrying heavy weapons. When darkness fell, the Gascons began to climb the Roc, feeling their way up hand over hand, foot by foot and trying not to dislodge any stones or pebbles that might betray their presence to the guards at the top. The Gascons completed the perilous climb without mishap. Surprise was total. The Cathar guards, unable to fight back swiftly enough, were killed in an instant or thrown over the cliff edge to their deaths.

The fall of the Roc de la Tour was a disaster, all the more so because its capture made it possible for the French to winch their mangonels and other siege machines to the top and start crashing heavy stone missiles directly into the fortress. A snowstorm closed in on the castle, but the attackers moved inexorably forwards, dragging their siege machines with them. As the onslaught of stones kept drumming down into the fortress, dozens were killed and injured. The French advance was unstoppable. Rumours began to circulate: Count Raymond VII was coming to the rescue and the Emperor Frederick II was sending troops to break the siege. Any hopes that were aroused came to nothing and by 2 March 1244, Pierre Roger de Mirefoix realized that the only thing he could do was surrender.

RECANT OR BURN

Considering the savage handling of crime and punishment that typified medieval times, the terms laid down by Hugh de Arcis were not overly draconian. The murders at Avignonet and any other crimes committed in the past were forgiven and the inhabitants of Montségur were given two weeks to think over their options: either submit to interrogation by the Inquisition and recant, or refuse to do so and burn at the stake.

In the event, the Cathar Perfects in Montségur declined to cast aside their beliefs and seek forgiveness from Archbishop Amiel. Instead, they prepared for death. Whatever meagre belongings they possessed, they distributed them among their families and friends. They comforted their distraught relatives and gave themselves over to prayer.

Some Cathar *credentes,* who were not liable to the death penalty, were inspired to join the Perfects and burn with them. On Sunday 13 March 1244, 21

The isolated Cathar fortress of Quéribus still stands today, a testament to its value as a border stronghold. Its thick stone walls were most recently restored in the period 1998 to 2002.

credentes, including the wife and daughter of Raymond de Pereille, requested the *consolamentum,* the Cathar version of the Last Rites given to Catholics, in which they were enjoined to lead a chaste, ascetic life. Those lives had only three more days to run.

In the meadows below Montségur, a patch of ground surrounded by a palisade was being prepared for a bonfire of burnings, using wood chopped down from the nearby forests. Rows of stakes were set in the ground, ropes to tie the Cathars were piled up, torches to light the fires were stacked, and ladders were propped up against the palisades.

THE BURNING GROUNDS AT MONTSÉGUR

Early on the morning of 16 March, a procession of 221 men and women began to wind down the path that led from the summit of Montségur to the bottom of the slope. The Cathar leaders went barefoot, wearing nothing

When they reached the burning ground, they climbed the ladders and were bound together onto the stakes in pairs, back to back.

but their coarsely woven robes. When they reached the burning ground, they climbed the ladders and were bound together onto the stakes in pairs, back to back. The rest followed until row upon row of men and women filled the enclosure.

When all was ready, Archbishop Amiel gave the signal for flaming brands to be thrown in among them. The soft murmur of praying was audible, only to be drowned out by the crackle of the fire as it climbed up the stakes and set everyone and everything alight. As the blaze grew and the human forms at its centre disappeared, the crackle turned to a roar and smoke, thick, black and choking, began to fill the valleys, dirty the meadow grass that grew between them and finally curl up into the sky.

THE LAST CATHAR FORTRESS

The fall of Montségur did not see the end of the military crusade against the Cathars. There was another fortress, their last, at Quéribus, which was besieged and captured in August of 1255. But the Cathars did not need Quéribus to teach them that the back of their faith had already been broken in the burning ground at Montségur. The heart had gone out of it. Even Raymond VII who had championed the Cathars for so long and sacrificed so much for their cause deserted them and in 1249 helped the Inquisition to organize more burnings at Agen, northwest of Toulouse. Raymond died three months later, in September of the same year.

Thousands of *credentes,* exhausted by years of secrecy, living in the suspense and fear of discovery, had become mortally afraid of the Inquisition and its power to ruin lives, condemn and kill. They recanted to save themselves and to confirm their new devotion to the Church. In so doing they betrayed neighbours, friends and even family to the remorseless Inquisition.

A small number of captured Perfects were persuaded to renounce their beliefs, turn Catholic and provide long lists of Cathar sympathizers. They, in turn, fell into the hands of the Inquisition whose powers were increased in 1252 when Innocent IV, who had been elected pope in 1243, gave his permission for the Inquisition to use torture to get at the truth. But he made conditions. Euphemistically termed 'putting the question', torture, Pope Innocent instructed, must not include cutting off limbs, spilling too much blood or causing death.

CATHARISM IS CONSIGNED TO HISTORY

Even so, the end of Catharism and the Cathars did not come quickly. Rather, its beliefs and believers were gradually ground down by well trained, zealous inquisitors backed by a bureaucracy of informers, torturers, instruction manuals, registers of suspects and, of course, the all-pervasive terror the Inquisition inspired. Thousands of Cathars disappeared into dungeons, never to be seen again or if they were, they emerged as compliant shadows of their former selves, too terrified of the stake to speak their minds. By the end of the thirteenth century, few people, if any, were willing to dispute the view of the medieval world as sanctioned by the pope and the Church. It was, in fact, left to a pair of eccentric brothers from Languedoc and a one-time murderer to sound the last trumpet for the Cathars. By the time it was all over and the Cathars were history, it had taken 112 years, the reigns of 19 popes and thousands of violent deaths before the Church of Rome, its crusaders and its inquisitors and torturers finally prevailed.

THE LAST OF THE CATHARS: GUILLAUME BÉLIBASTE

The murderer turned Cathar who finally closed the book on the Cathar heresy was Guillaume Bélibaste. He began life as a shepherd tending his flocks high up in the Corbière hills near the River Aude in Languedoc. In 1306, Bélibaste killed another shepherd in a brawl and went on the run to escape the law. During his wanderings, he encountered Philippe d'Alayrac, one of Pierre Autier's Cathar Perfects who was hiding from the Inquisition. Together, the shepherd and the Perfect fled over the Pyrenees into Catalonia, in northeast Spain. Before he was hunted down by the inquisitors and burnt at the stake, d'Alayrac initiated Bélibaste into the Cathar faith. By this means, Bélibaste came to believe that not only was the world a wicked, evil place but that it was ruled by four demons: King Philip IV of France, Jacques Fournier, Bishop of Palmiers, Pope Boniface VIII and Bernard Gui, a merciless inquisitor based at Carcassonne.

Guillaume Bélibaste believed that Pope Boniface VIII, pictured, was one of the four demons who ruled the earth. Bélibaste was burned at the stake in 1321.

It was not long before Bélibaste had gathered in a flock of *credentes* who, like himself, had fled for safety to Spain. For nearly five years, this Cathar community was undisturbed, or so it seemed. What they did not know was that in 1317 they had admitted to their ranks a certain Arnold Sicre who was a secret agent employed by Bishop Jacques Fournier. Sicre bided his time until he could betray Guillaume Bélibaste to the Inquisition. His chance came in the spring of 1321, when, with others, he accompanied Bélibaste on a journey into France to see Bélibaste's aged aunt, Alazais, who had generously financed her nephew's small Cathar community. Two days into their journey, armed men, tipped off by Sicre, broke down the door of the house in Tirvia, on the Spanish side of the Pyrenees, where Bélibaste and his companions were staying. All of them were arrested. Guillaume Bélibaste completed his journey over the mountains and into France in chains. He was put on trial for heresy, but the verdict was never in doubt. In the autumn of 1321, he was led into the courtyard of the castle at Villerouge-Termenès in Corbières where a stake awaited him. A blazing torch was applied, the flames surged upwards and in a matter of minutes, the last of the Cathar Perfects met his end.

POPES AND WITCHES

Belief in witches and wizards, spells, sorcery and curses stretch back at least to Biblical times. Such beliefs were an attempt to explain the mysteries and dangers of life on Earth. Before people understood the real reasons behind an earthquake, flood, thunderstorm, failed harvest, outbreak of disease or other disaster, they blamed the forces of evil or mischievous spirits and influences.

Spells were already enough of a problem in ancient Babylon, in 1760 BCE, when falsely casting them incurred the death penalty in the Code of Hammurabi. The Biblical book of Deuteronomy refers to sorcery as an 'abomination', Exodus states, 'Thou shalt not suffer a witch to live.' The Book of Samuel recounts how, during the late eleventh century BCE, King Saul 'hath cut off those that have familiar spirits and the wizards, out of the land'. Women, particularly old women, were associated with witchcraft early on, and a thousand years after Saul, in the first century BCE, 80 of them were sentenced to death at Ashkelon, in Palestine, which was then a province of the Roman Empire.

King Philip IV of France (above), who initiated the persecution of the Knights Templar in 1307, is also pictured in the medieval manuscript illustration at left. Four Templars are prepared for execution in the presence of their king and persecutor.

At that stage, witchcraft and the other 'dark' arts were classified as sins or crimes that disturbed law and order, spread fear and unrest and angered God. But in the early Middle Ages, when the fledgling Christian Church and its popes became involved, their concept of the subject was different. Now, Christianity considered witchcraft as heresy, along with all other beliefs that ran contrary to those preached by the Church.

St Augustine of Hippo (left) is shown arguing with the Manichean Bishop Faustus of Mileve in around 383 CE. Manicheans believed that God and the Devil were perennially fighting for possession of the human soul.

DELUDED VICTIMS OF EVIL

Early Church practice treated those who fell for the enticements of the Devil as deluded victims of evil rather than criminals. Far from indicting them, Church authorities recommended that they be instructed in the foolish and fallacious nature of witchcraft. However, to underline its strong stand against the Devil, Church authorities followed the pronouncement of St Augustine, Bishop of Hippo in Algeria. In around 400 CE, Hippo had declared that anyone who believed in witchcraft was de facto a heretic. In 785 CE, this belief was specifically outlawed at the Council of Paderborn in western Germany. Here, it was declared that sorcerers must be reduced to the status of serfs or slaves and handed over to the service of the Church. Sorcery and magic were in themselves wicked pursuits and even studying them placed souls in danger.

Fighting magic, sorcery and witchcraft were not simply spiritual matters, designed to bring all who called themselves Christians into a universal belief system. Behind the battle lay Church politics, which sought to rid Europe of paganism. Pagan witchcraft and the superstition it fostered stood firmly in the way of the Christian ambition to establish a monopoly of faith across the continent. To this end, the Church waged a long and costly war against the pagans, which was not won until 1386, when King Wladyslaw III of Lithuania, the last of the pagan states, became a Christian as a wedding present to his child bride Queen Jagwiga of Poland.

The statue of King Wladyslaw II Jagiello of Poland, formerly the pagan King Wladyslaw III of Lithuania, which stands in Central Park, New York.

Two suitably ugly witches cast a spell to ensure bad weather, with a rainstorm breaking above them.

locusts or the failure of crops meant that they were in the inescapable grip of dark, evil forces.

The evidence, they believed, was all around them. Most medieval villages had their strange looking or ugly old women, or people disfigured by disease or born with what we would now call genetic defects, and they were always first in line to take the blame when anything went wrong. This seems to have become common in thirteenth-century Switzerland and Croatia, where reports of witches and witchcraft rose to near-epidemic proportions after Pope Gregory IX set up the first, Papal, Inquisition in 1231.

POPE GREGORY AND THE FIRST INQUISITION

Gregory was what would now be called hard-liner, and was so utterly determined to stamp out heresy in all its forms that he went beyond even the broad bounds of his times. He sent zealous, often fanatical, inquisitors to gather evidence of witchcraft, sorcery and similar activities. As far as is known, the pope never questioned their findings, even though some were clearly sadists. One of them, Gregory's protégé, was the notorious Konrad of Marburg, tormentor of the Cathars, whose excesses eventually prompted his assassination in 1233. Six

it was declared that sorcerers must be reduced to the status of serfs or slaves and handed over to the service of the Church.

Pagan beliefs possessed a remarkable tenacity, nurturing the idea that witches could change shape or lay terrible curses on anyone

years earlier, Konrad had been commissioned by Gregory to wipe out heresy in Germany, and was under orders to pursue the Luciferians, or Satanists who were, it was said, openly worshipping the Devil and subverting Christians to their odious beliefs. Konrad soon fulfilled his commission with his customary diligence. He uncovered, he claimed,

But it was one thing to spread Christianity to those who were intellectually attracted to it or who had a use for it (in Wladyslaw's case, an advantageous marriage). It was quite another to convince less educated, less calculating minds driven under the influence of popular fears and pagan practices.

PAGAN BELIEFS

Pagan beliefs possessed a remarkable tenacity, nurturing the idea that witches could change shape or lay terrible curses on anyone who refused to give them alms. It was natural for illiterate, uneducated people to conclude that everyday experiences like the death of a child, a plague of numerous nests of 'devil worshippers' and achieved an appalling death toll. High birth or position protected no one. Some 80 men, women and children were burnt as heretics at Strasbourg and bishops went to the stake along with the rest. Nobles, commoners, priests – anyone and everyone who fell under suspicion – were considered guilty unless and until they could prove they were innocent.

THE HORRORS OF TORTURE

In the atmosphere of terror and suffering, amid the screams of agony and assailed by the stench of fire and roasted flesh at the burning grounds, the urge to confess – if only the torture would stop – made proving innocence well nigh impossible. Many victims appeared to go mad under the instruments of torture, which included some of the most excruciating ever devised, such as head and limb crushers, slow stranglers, or 'cats' paws', which shredded flesh. All caused unimaginable pain.

Nobles, commoners, priests – anyone and everyone who fell under suspicion – were considered guilty unless and until they could prove they were innocent.

One of the most devilish of torture devices and the most widely used was the *strappado*, described by Philip Limboch in his *History of the Inquisition* published in 1692:

> *The prisoner has his hands bound behind his back, and weights tied to his feet and then he is drawn up on high, until his head reaches the pulley. He is kept hanging in this manner for some time, so that all his joints and limbs may be dreadfully stretched… Then suddenly, he is let down with a jerk, by slacking the rope, but kept from coming quite to the ground, by which terrible shake his arms and legs are all disjointed.*

The *strappado* and other instruments of torture were sometimes blessed by priests to acknowledge the 'holy' work they were doing in revealing heresy. The ravings of their victims were taken as true confessions of wrongdoings, which they had never committed or even imagined. But confession did not always save them, for

The *strappado* and other instruments of torture were sometimes blessed by priests to acknowledge the 'holy' work they were doing in revealing heresy.

scores of innocents, having 'cleared' their consciences and possibly named other 'heretics' still died later in the all-consuming flames of the stake.

A CREDULOUS POPE

Pope Gregory was fully complicit in all of this. He had extraordinary confidence in Konrad von Marburg and his other inquisitors and accepted without question virtually everything they told him. This included the news that Satan regularly appeared at witches' sabbaths, and there transformed himself into a toad or a pale shadow or a black cat. Black tomcats became a particular target for Gregory. In his papal bull *Vox Rama* issued in 1233, he condemned black cats as animal incarnations of Satan for their sinister ability to 'vanish' in the dark and the supposed role they played as 'familiars' to witches. Cats were often placed in baskets and burnt at the stake along with their equally hapless owners. Simply owning a black cat could be

VATICAN VOCABULARY

PAPAL BULL

A papal bull is a pronouncement, charter or decree issued by a pope, usually for public consumption. The contents of papal bulls may be news of a bishop's appointment, the canonization of a new saint, the announcement of excommunications or forthcoming Vatican Council. The bull takes its name from the *bulla* (seal) attached to the document, which is most often made of metal, but might also be made of lead or, for very solemn occasions, of gold.

A victim (centre) undergoing the agonizing torture known as *strappado* which stretched and dislocated the limbs.

taken as 'proof' of a link with Satan and thousands of the animals were thrown into fires and burnt alive in an attempt to extinguish the Devil's presence on Earth.

TORTURE BECOMES OFFICIAL

Pope Gregory IX died in 1241, and Innocent IV, who was elected pope two years later, took up his work against heresy. In the meantime, Konrad of Marburg had been using torture on his victims on a freelance basis. Innocent IV made torture official papal policy in 1252 and unleashed some outlandish confessions. Old women, whose ugliness and often crooked physique created an image of witches still standard today, owned up to having sex with the Devil and producing invisible children. They were burnt at the stake just the same, but left behind a fearful legacy. In the fevered climate of the witch-hunt, the fact that no one had ever seen their 'children' did not cast doubt on their existence; it just made them all the more sinister.

But witchcraft was no longer confined to crazy, terrified old women. Husbands began to suspect their wives of being secret witches, which meant that their children were the spawn of Satan. Friends, relatives, neighbours, even passers-by in the street were scrutinized for eccentricity or other 'unusual' behaviour. Witches were believed to be everywhere and no one could know their identity or what they were going to do. In this atmosphere of hysteria, it seemed that the Evil Eye of ancient folk belief was watching, ready to wreak havoc, and that the Antichrist was about to triumph and consign all humanity to hellfire.

> Old women, whose ugliness and often crooked physique created an image of witches ... owned up to having sex with the Devil and producing invisible children.

Innocent IV, whose tomb is shown here, was elected pope in 1243. He continued the witch-hunting work of his predecessor, Gregory IX, and made torture to extract confessions official in 1252.

THE KNIGHTS TEMPLAR ON TRIAL

The series of show trials that epitomized this dreadful perception of witchcraft and heresy took place after 1307, when Clement V, who had been elected pope two years earlier, agreed to investigate heresies and abominable sexual and religious practices allegedly committed by the Knights Templar. The Templars were a military order originally founded in 1118 after the First Crusade against the Saracens, and since then had built up a distinguished record of service to Christendom and the Crusader kingdoms in the Holy Land.

This medieval illustration shows two Knights Templar being burned at the stake while spectators watch impassively. Gruesome death and unimaginable suffering were spectator sports in the grisly Middle Ages.

This, though, did not save them from scrutiny once King Philip IV of France made accusations against them. Quite possibly, Pope Clement did not know, or

THE ORDER OF THE KNIGHTS TEMPLAR

The Templars had been the first, and were the wealthiest and most influential, of the religious and military orders formed to manage the new situation in the Holy Land that followed the success of Christian armies in the First Crusade of 1095–99. The Muslim forces were decisively defeated and Crusader realms were set up in Tripoli, Antioch, Edessa and most prestigious of all, in Jerusalem. These new acquisitions needed an administration and some form of defence. For this purpose, military and religious orders of chivalry were created soon after the conclusion of the Crusade. In addition to the Knights Templar, these included the Knights Hospitaller, who provided medical services, and the Knights of the Holy Sepulchre, whose task it was to defend this most important centre of Christian worship in Jerusalem.

Like the Hospitallers, the Templar Order was mainly composed of Frankish knights. Their task was to provide armed escort and protection for the pilgrims who made the long and arduous journey to the Holy Land, because travelling involved many dangers. Unarmed pilgrims were ambushed, robbed, killed, kidnapped and even sold into slavery by bandits who specialized in swift, hit-and-run tactics and then melted away into the desert landscape.

The first Knights Templar who volunteered to guard and protect the pilgrims against such merciless enemies were only nine in number, but they were well suited to the task. All of them were of noble birth, all well connected to powerful families and all well trained in military tactics. They were all extremely devout Christians, and had adopted the highest ideals of the Christian lifestyle, devoting themselves to the poverty and chastity, obedience and humility of monks. They were willing to beg for their food and lead pure, exemplary lives. Their original name, the Poor Knights of Christ and the Temple of Solomon said a great deal about them.

And yet, ironically, and in the end tragically, the Poor Knights became the richest crusader Order. This

was not of their own doing, but arose from the rich revenues that were lavished on them by admiring aristocrats and churchmen. Young men from rich families who joined the Order and brought their personal wealth with them also filled Templar coffers.

Popes awarded the Templars special privileges, including exemption from the ban on usury (money lending), which allowed them to set up banks and other financial institutions. These enabled them to offer safe deposits loans, credit, trustee services and strongholds for keeping jewellery, gold or other treasure secure. Several European princes and even some wealthy Saracens entrusted the Templars with their substantial treasuries.

In time, the Templars became property owners with a total of 870 castles, schools and houses. They also built extensively, constructing churches, mills, bridges and city walls. In the Holy Land, the Templars constructed several major castles, on strategic sites in Jaffa, Acre and Sidon. These belonged to a new generation of fortress architecture. They were of unprecedented size and sophistication and included the first concentric castles. One of them, at Safed in the Jordan valley was part of a string of Templar fortresses designed to guard against incursions from the Muslim Emirate of Damascus. It took two years to build at a cost in today's terms of around £40 million. Its walls were over 18 metres thick and 52 metres high, and the castle's seven towers rose to an overall height of nearly 38 metres above the walls. The whole edifice, which required a garrison of 2000 men and £2 million a year to maintain, was cut from solid rock.

But the power, wealth and influence of the Templars proved to be their undoing once the envious King Philip IV of France set to work to bring them down. It took the King seven years to destroy the Templars by means of lies and false accusation, and virtually every other dirty trick he could come up with.

This imposing scene shows the inauguration of Jacques de Molai as Grand Master of the Order of the Knights Templar in around 1298.

maybe did not care to know, that the charges had been manufactured by Philip, who feared Templar power and coveted Templar wealth, nor that the incriminating evidence later presented was falsified. The craven Clement was essentially a creature of King Philip, who dominated him and had already hounded to death one of his predecessors, Pope Boniface VIII, in 1303. After that, no pope dared challenge the increasingly mighty kings of Europe. Clement V did as he was told. The upshot was the torture, imprisonment and death at the stake of scores of Templars and, in 1312, the dissolution of the Templar Order.

The downfall of the Templars shocked European Christendom. If such a rich, powerful, favoured, propertied organization, could be so completely ruined in just a few years, what chance was there for ordinary people who lacked the Templars' privileges and influence? The answer was, of course, none.

Clement V did as he was told. The upshot was the torture, imprisonment and death at the stake of scores of Templars.

WHITE MAGIC

Even good deeds apparently achieved by means of sorcery were regarded as works of the Devil. This lesson was learnt the hard way in France, in 1390, when a man named Jehan de Ruilly accused Jehenne de Brigue of witchcraft after she had used sorcery to cure him of a spell laid on him by Gilette, the mother of his two illegitimate children. De Ruilly, it appears, was at death's door, with barely a week to live, when de Brigue showed him how to make a wax doll of Gilette and suckle a pair of toads. He made a miraculous recovery.

At first, de Brigue professed to know nothing about sorcery or witchcraft, but at her trial, it emerged that she had learnt how to cast spells and summon up a demon named Haussibut to help her in working her cures. It was Haussibut who aided de Ruilly's treatment by revealing to de Brigue that Gilette had hexed him. Despite the beneficial nature of her activities, Jehenne de Brigue was sentenced to burn. She was saved from

This 16th-century woodcut shows a crowd of men and women accused of witchcraft being burned together in a pit.

the stake at the last moment when a re-trial was ordered early in 1391. However, the case against de Brigue grew more and more serious from then on.

She was stretched out naked on a trestle, ready to be tortured, when she started to make lurid confessions. She admitted helping Macette de Ruilly (de Ruilly's wife), prepare a poison to use on her husband so that she could be free to carry on an affair with a curate. Macette denied the story, but when stretched on the rack, she changed her mind and also started to confess. De Brigue and Macette de Ruilly were both found guilty of sorcery and of making a pact with the Devil. They were taken to Châtelet-Les Halles, in the centre of Paris, where they were forced to wear a conical mitre decorated by devils, the sign of the heretic. Next, they were placed in the pillory to be misused and insulted at will by the Parisians. Finally, they were burnt alive at the Pig Market where de Brigue and Macette died at the stake on 17 August 1391.

Even good deeds apparently achieved by means of sorcery were regarded as works of the Devil.

Witch trials continued on into the fifteenth century and assumed an even more brutal and sinister character in Switzerland. Here, in 1428, alleged witches, who were said to fly across the country and use their demonic powers to make men and women infertile, were forced to make confession under torture. Such witches were said to destroy crops, remove milk from cows and kill and eat children at sabbath feasts.

> Stretched out naked on a trestle, ready to be tortured, she started to make lurid confessions.

They were accused of indulging in obscene dances at their sabbaths, kissing the Devil's rump and participating in wild sex orgies, during which the Devil could change his sex and so enjoy men as well as women in a single night.

During the proceedings, it was believed, the Devil would leave a special mark on the witches' bodies. The discovery of this mark was as good as a death sentence, for once the inquisitors found it, they tested it by 'pricking' with a needle or other sharp instrument: if no blood were drawn or pain were felt, all hope of escape was gone. In Switzerland, some 200 men and women were burned. By 1450, at Briançon, on the French side of the Alps, 110 women and 57 men accused of witchcraft died at the stake.

Men were also targeted in this way in Normandy, in northern France, where the Inquisition at Evreux sentenced Guillaume Edeline, prior of Saint-

A woman accused of witchcraft is shown being undressed by her accusers in a 16th-century torture chamber. One end of the rack, a torture device to stretch victims and dislocate their limbs, can be seen at the bottom right of the picture.

Germain-en-Laye to life imprisonment in 1453 for having sex with a succubus (a female demon who was believed to seduce men while they slept). His sentence included punishment for flying on a broomstick and kissing a goat underneath its tail.

Witches were said to destroy crops, remove milk from cows and kill and eat children at sabbath feasts.

Robert Olive of Falaise fared worse. In 1456, he was burnt for flying to witches' sabbaths.

This, though, was only a prelude to a full-scale witch-hunt that began in Arras, in the Pas-de-Calais region of northeast France in 1459. One of the first victims was Deniselle Grensières; a mentally retarded woman who was repeatedly tortured by Pierre le Broussart, a Dominican and the chief inquisitor of Arras. Eventually, Deniselle confessed and named four women and the artist Jehan la Vitte as her associates. One of the four women, terrified of being tortured, killed herself before she could be handed over to le Broussart. La Vitte also took drastic action. When he was threatened with torture, he feared that he might weaken and name names in his turn. To avoid this, la Vitte tried to cut out his tongue, but all he did was cause deep lacerations around his mouth. This made talking difficult, but la Vitte still had his hands and was obliged to write his account of how men and women

This 16th-century woodcut shows a popular image of dealings with the Devil in which a man and a woman dance in a circle with demons. The musical accompaniment is provided by a violinist perched in the nearby tree.

suddenly found themselves transported to the Devil's meeting place. La Vitte next recounted how the Devil, who assumed human form though his face remained hidden, obliged everyone to kiss his backside, then sit down to a banquet. Afterwards, the lights were extinguished – the signal for an orgy to begin. 'Each (man and woman) took a partner,' la Vitte told the Inquisition, 'and knew each other carnally.' In the spring of 1460, la Vitte, Deniselle Grensières and the three surviving women she had named were declared heretics and were forced to wear the Devil's mitre. All five of them were burnt.

MORE VICTIMS FOR LE BROUSSART

They left behind a long list of people they had betrayed to le Broussart and once they were ashes, he lost little time in arresting yet another round of victims. This time, though, his list included several distinguished names – men and women of noble birth or high social standing, bishops and other prelates, judges and high-ranking administrators. Some of them managed to bribe their way out of danger, while others were

> La Vitte was threatened with torture. He tried to cut out his tongue, but all he did was cause deep lacerations around his mouth.

assured that in exchange for a confession they could keep their property and other wealth – and their lives. These assurances came to nothing. Once they had confessed, they were burnt to death, like the ordinary folk on le Broussart's list, and feudal overlords or the local bishops seized their goods and estates.

A BACKLASH FINALLY ARISES

By this time, the excesses of the witch-hunt had reached such heights that they provoked a backlash. Churchmen in Arras urged le Broussart to declare an amnesty for those he had imprisoned. When he refused, the bishops of Arras and Amiens, together with the Archbishop of Rheims took matters into their own hands. They started to quash the charges of witchcraft that came before them for judgement and pronounced witches' sabbaths as nothing but hysteria and imagination. At this point, the Parlement of Paris, formerly the council of the kings of France, stepped in and freed some of le Broussart's prisoners. Jean Jouffrey, Bishop of Arras released the rest.

> Assurances came to nothing. Once they had confessed, they were burnt to death.

The Parlement went further, though. Its members condemned le Broussart for acting 'in error and against the order and dignity of justice'. The inquisition at Arras did not escape censure, either. The inquisitors, it was stated, had 'conducted a false trial and one without due process of law'. The inquisition, the Parlement continued, had perpetrated 'inhuman and cruel interrogation and tortures... such as squeezing the limbs, putting the soles of the feet in the fire and making

VATICAN VOCABULARY

THE INDEX OF PROHIBITED BOOKS

The Index of Prohibited Books or *Index Librorum Prohibitorum* was a list containing works banned for Catholic readers by the Church. Prohibited books could contain a variety of 'errors', including heresy, immorality, explicit sex or other subjects that were deemed contrary to the teachings of the Catholic Church. The first Index was published, not in Rome, but in the Netherlands in 1529. Subsequent printings appeared in Venice in 1543 and Paris in 1551. In 1571, a special body was set up to investigate books that might need to be censored. Named the Sacred Congregation of the Index, its task also included updating the books already on the index and labelling others as possibilities for publication if alterations were made. These were described as *donec corrigatur* (forbidden if not corrected) or *donec expurgetur* (forbidden if not purged.) Lists of corrections – some of them very long – were made for the authors as means of making their work more acceptable.

The Congregation was disbanded in 1917 and the Index itself was no longer published after 1966.

In his papal Bull *Summis desiderantes* of 5 December 1484, Pope Innocent VIII ordered harsh measures to be taken against witches and magicians in Germany.

They started to quash the charges of witchcraft that came before them for judgement and pronounced witches' sabbaths as nothing but hysteria and imagination.

the accused swallow oil and vinegar'. Prayers, it was suggested, should be said for those who had died.

The mood was very different when Pope Innocent VIII was contemplating the problem of witchcraft and heresy in Germany in 1484. There was no chance of clemency here, for in a bull issued in that year, Innocent outlined a very disturbing situation. He announced:

> *It has recently come to our ears that in some parts of upper Germany... many persons of both sexes... give themselves over to devils male and female, and by their incantations, charms, and conjurings, and by other abominable superstitions... offences, crimes, and misdeeds, ruin and cause to perish the offspring of women, the foal of animals, the products of the earth, the grapes of vines, and the fruits of trees, as well as men and women, cattle and flocks and herds and animals of every kind, vineyards also and orchards, meadows, pastures, harvests, grains and other fruits of the earth; that they afflict and torture with dire pains and anguish, both internal and external, these men, women, cattle, flocks, herds, and animals, and hinder men from begetting and women from conceiving... it shall be permitted to the inquisitors to exercise their office of inquisition and to proceed to the correction, imprisonment, and punishment of the aforesaid persons for their said offences and crimes...*

Simply to deny charges of heresy or witchcraft was to prove the charges true.

CLOSING LOOPHOLES

He did not say so in so many words, but Innocent's new offensive against witches and heresy closed important loopholes in previous practice and represented guilt by accusation with no hope of reprieve. Simply to deny charges of heresy or witchcraft was to prove the charges true and this applied as much to bishops, theologians or other Church worthies as it did to the lowliest serf or peasant. In addition, speaking up in defence of the accused or attempting to prove charges of witchcraft false were also considered signs of a heretic at work.

What followed was nothing short of a massacre masterminded by two Dominicans specially chosen for the task by the pope himself. They were Heinrich Kramer and James Sprenger, also known as the Apostle of the Rosary. These two became the joint authors of *Malleus Maleficarum*, usually known as *The Witches' Hammer*. It was published in around 1486 and reprinted in 28 new editions by 1600. *The Witches' Hammer* was a

The burning of witches at Derneburg Castle near Hanover, Germany, is illustrated here in a book published in 1555.

Ein erschröckliche geschicht/so zu Derneburg in der Graffschafft Reinsteyn/am Hartz gelegen/von dreyen Zauberin/vnnd zwayen Mañen/Jn etlichen tagen des Monats Octobris Jm 1 5 5 5. Jare ergangen ist.

Die alte Schlang der Teüffel/dieweyl er Got/vnd zůvoran den Sun Gottes/vnsern Herrn Jesum Christum/vnd das gantze menschliche geschlecht/fürnemlich vmb vnsers Haylands Christi willen hasset/hat er sich bald im anfang/vnd kürtzlich nach der erschaffung vmb dz weibßbild/als vmb die/welcher same seinen kopff zertretten solt/angenomen/dieselbigen durch sein hinderlist vnd lugen/zů dem jämerlichen fal/deß vnglaubens vñ vngehorsams wider Got gebracht/Darauß das gantz menschlich geschlecht/in ewige verdamnuß vñ verderben komen were/so Christus vnser Hayland/den zorn des Vatters nicht weckgenomen/vnd das gericht wider vns auffgehaben het. Nu behelt der alte Feind gleichwol alten haß wider Christum/vnd vns/für vñ für/vnd helt auch sein alte weyse/er setzet sonderlich dem weiblichen gschlecht hart zů/als dem schwecheren werckzeug/damit er sie von Christo wegreysse/vñ in ewige verdamnuß füre/vñ wie er zů Eua sprach/sie wurden werdẽ wie die Götter/Also bläßt er noch das gifft in der weyber hertzen/lernet sie zaubern/auff das er sie klůg mache/das sie mehr wissen dann andere leüt/vnd also den Göttern geleich werden/damit macht er sie jm anhengig/vnd zů Teüffels dienerin/ja auch zů Teuffels breüten/wie dise jämerliche geschicht/welche warhafftigklich also wie vnden angezaiget/am Hartz ergangen ist/Die derhalben also gemalet vñ geschriben/im druck auß gangen. Auff das doch die rohelose welt/zů Gottes forcht erwecket/vnd von dem Gottlosen wesen abgeschreckt werden/ Dann Gott der allmächtige derhalben solche Exempel vns sehen laßt/das er damit vnsere harten hertzen durch dise erschröckliche exempel / zur forcht Göttliches gerichts/vnd straffe erwecke/man mag es malen/predigen/singen vnd sagen/vñ wie man jmer kan den leüten einbilden/damit der laydige hauffe ein wenig zů Gottes forcht/gehorsam/vnd zucht gezogen werde/besonder zů disen letsten zeyten/in welchẽ der listige Sathan/dieweyl er mercket/das der tag des gerichts sich nahet/gar rassend toll vnd vnsinnig ist/vnd bede durch sich vnd seine gelider/ grewlicher weyse/wider Christum vnd sein armes heüfflein wüttet/Die ellende welt aber dargegẽ so frey sicher in allem můtwillen dahin lebet/als ob der Teuffel vor langst gestorben sey/vnd kain Got/kain gericht oder straff/verhanden were/Der Almächtig Got vnd vatter/vnsers Herrn Jesu Christi/wölle dem grimmigen feinde wehren/sein armes heüfflein vor jm vnd seinen glidern schützen vnd handthaben/seinem vnd der seinen wütten vnd toben/einmal ein ende machen/durch Jesum Christum Amen.

Folget die geschichte / so zů Derneburg in der Graffschafft Reynstein am Hartz gelegen/ergangen ist/ Jm October des 1 5 5 5. Jars.

Auff den Dinstag nach Michaelis/den ersten Octobris/seind zwů Zauberin gebrandt/die eine Gröbische/die ander Gißlersche genañt/ vñ hat die Gröbische bekandt/das sie Aylff jar mit dem Teüffel gebület habe/vñ wie man dieselben Gröbischen zů der Fewrstat gebracht/vnd an die saul mit Ketten geschlagen/vnd das Fewr angezündt/ist der büle/der Sathan komen/vnd sie in lüfften sichtigklich vor yederman weckgefürt. Am Donerstag/nach dem die Gröbische vñ die Gißlerschin am Dinstag zůvor seind gerichtet worden/das ist den 3. Octobris/seind dise bede Frawen auff den abend in der Gißlersche hauß komen/vnd der Gißlerschen man zur thür hinauß gestossen/das er nider gefallen vnnd gestorben ist/welches ain Nachbaur gegen vber gehöret/vnd zů gelauffen ist/durch die thür gesehen/das zway weyber bede eytel fewrige/vmbs fewr gedantzet/der Gißlerschin man aber/lag vor der thür vnd war todt. Am Sonnabendt nach Dionisij/das ist der 12. Octobris/ist der Gröbischen mañ gerichtet worden/vmb der vrsach willẽ/das er bey seines weybs schwester geschlaffen hat/welche er zůvorn zum weybe gehabt/vñ darnach die Gröbischen genomen/Des Montags darnach/das ist der 14. Octobris ist ain weyb die Serckschen genandt/auch verbrandt worden/der vrsach/das sie des Herrn Achamanual for identifying and punishing witches, and contained most, if not all, the folk beliefs current at the time. It was primarily designed to instruct judges and magistrates in techniques for interrogating witches and establishing their guilt. The book, which benefited from the wide distribution afforded by the new printing press, was just as popular among Protestants as it was among Catholics and copies could be found in courtrooms where they were regularly consulted by both judges and magistrates until well into the eighteenth century.

But the truthfulness of the book was always in doubt. After all, the subject of witchcraft depended heavily on fear, gossip and superstition, and this was particularly true at the height of the campaign of hunting and burning witches. In 1487, when Kramer sent a copy of the book to the Faculty of Theology at the University of Cologne, hoping to gain an endorsement for the work, he was severely put out when, instead, it was pronounced both unethical and illegal. Undeterred, Kramer forged an endorsement from the University and included it in future editions.

The frontispiece of *Malleus Maleficarum*, the manual of witchcraft usually known as *The Witches' Hammer* and first published in 1486. It was used to identify and punish witches until well into the 18th century.

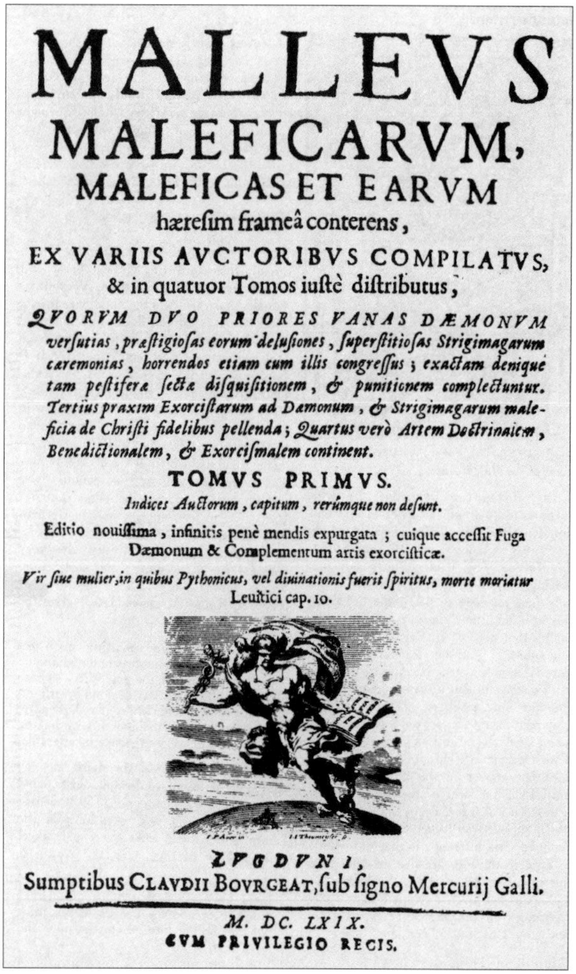
MALLEVS
MALEFICARVM,
MALEFICAS ET EARVM
hæresim frameâ conterens,
EX VARIIS AVCTORIBVS COMPILATVS,
& in quatuor Tomos iustè distributus,
QVORVM DVO PRIORES VANAS DÆMONVM versutias, præstigiosas eorum delusiones, superstitiosas Strigimagarum cæremonias, horrendos etiam cum illis congressus; exactam denique tam pestiferæ sectæ disquisitionem, & punitionem complectuntur. Tertius praxim Exorcistarum ad Dæmonum, & Strigimagarum maleficia de Christi fidelibus pellenda; Quartus verò Artem Doctrinalem, Benedictionalem, & Exorcismalem continent.
TOMVS PRIMVS.
Indices Auctorum, capitum, rerúmque non desunt.
Editio nouissima, infinitis penè mendis expurgata; cuique accessit Fuga Dæmonum & Complementum artis exorcisticæ.
Vir siue mulier, in quibus Pythonicus, vel diuinationis fuerit spiritus, morte moriatur Leuitici cap. 10.
LVGDVNI,
Sumptibus CLAVDII BOVRGEAT, sub signo Mercurij Galli.
M. DC. LXIX.
CVM PRIVILEGIO REGIS.

The Witches' Hammer was primarily designed to instruct judges and magistrates in techniques for interrogating witches and establishing their guilt.

He also managed to get round the condemnation of Pope Innocent VIII, who was apparently unnerved over the savagery he had unleashed. In 1490 Innocent ordered *The Witches' Hammer* to be added to the Index of Prohibited Books. However, Kramer had a copy of the papal bull of 1484, together with more endorsements, printed at the beginning of the book, so giving the impression that Innocent had approved it.

DISAPPEARING ORGAN

But intellectual scepticism about witches was no match for popular belief, which clung on grimly to myths and fantasies, however outlandish, even when scholars, theologians – and popes – rejected them. One typical anecdote in *The Witches' Hammer* told of the Devil's ability to rob a man of his male organ, which, it appears, simply disappeared from its natural place. Fortunately, the organ magically reappeared after the man in question managed to retrieve it from a woman who had bewitched him. Another story recounted how a rival bewitched a young wife on her wedding day. As her husband recounted:

> *In the time of my youth I loved a girl who importuned me to marry her; but I refused her and married another*

This rather fanciful engraving shows what might have been one of the medieval tortures designed to root out witches and heresy.

A 16th-century woodcut showing the meal eaten at the Witches' Sabbath, at which men and women socialized with devils and demons. The meal was followed by a wild sex orgy.

girl... But wishing for friendship's sake to please her, I invited her to the wedding. She came, and... raised her hand and, in the hearing of the other women who were standing round, said, 'You will have few days of health after today.'... It happened just as she had said. For after a few days my wife was so bewitched that she lost the use of all her limbs, and even now, after ten years, the effects of witchcraft can (still) be seen on her body.

THE UNUSUAL AND THE UNEXPLAINED

Stories like these rang bells with ordinary folk, for dread of the odd, the unusual, the unexplained or the mystifying had deep roots in their pagan past and was still prevalent in medieval times. So was a fear of sex and sexuality among churchmen and not just for its connection with original sin. The sex drive was a terrible enemy, for it deprived men and women of control and stole away both virtue and virginity. Kramer and Sprenger demonstrated this fear to the full in T*he Witches' Hammer* and Sprenger at least was a thoroughgoing misogynist, writing:

I would rather have a lion or a dragon loose in my house than a woman... Feeble in mind and body, it is not surprising women so often become witches... A woman is carnal lust personified... if a woman cannot get a man, she will consort with the Devil himself.

Armed with ideas like this and with a brief from Pope Innocent giving them the power to do virtually as

Torturing a victim on the wheel virtually shredded the body to pieces. A monk stands by with pen and paper, presumably waiting to write down a confession.

they pleased, Kramer and Sprenger set off across Germany to root out witchcraft and heresy wherever they could find it. This was a no-holds-barred expedition and the inquisitors used lies, maltreatment and psychological pressure along with physical torture to get the convictions they wanted. They flogged their victims until the blood ran. They used the rack, thumbscrews and crushers of various kinds. But these were just the preliminaries.

A TARIFF OF TORTURES

The real refinements, which came later, were listed on a tariff of tortures drawn up by Hermann IV of Hesse, Archbishop of Cologne. One option involved cutting out a victim's tongue and then pouring hot metal into their mouth. Another entailed cutting off a hand and nailing it to the gallows, presumably before the condemned witch was hanged. None of this came free, though. The victim's family was charged a fee for the privilege and they also had to pay for the expense of a celebratory feast if the victim died under torture.

A German chronicler left a graphic account of the ghastly suffering caused by an instrument of torture known as The Wheel, which, he wrote, turned its victims into

> *a sort of huge screaming puppet writhing in rivulets of blood, a puppet with four tentacles, like a sea monster, of raw, slimy and shapeless flesh mixed up with splinters of smashed bones.*

This was a no-holds-barred expedition and the inquisitors used lies, maltreatment and psychological pressure along with physical torture to get the convictions they wanted.

One woman, whose name remains unrecorded by history, showed remarkable endurance, which must have proved extremely frustrating for Kramer and Sprenger. She was tortured no fewer than 56 times, but failed to confess. This was very unusual because most people would say anything, do anything, admit anything or betray anyone in order to make the torture stop. They owned up to midnight pacts with the Devil where they sold him their souls for gold, to poisoning wells with a glance of their Evil Eye, to laying spells on others. They admitted to having sex with the Devil, bearing monsters as a result and feeding this offspring with newborn babies. They told how in the dead of night, they had attended witches' sabbaths where they worshipped the Devil, performed the Black Mass and afterwards indulged in wild sex orgies until dawn. Some said they had collected male organs, 20 or 30 of them at a time, and placed them in birds' nests where they moved around on their own and were fed on oats and corn.

A 17th-century woodcut showing witches being hanged while others, behind the tower grille, await their turn.

Sometimes, Kramer and Sprenger were able to achieve mass confessions in which an entire convent of nuns revealed that they had been regularly visited by the Devil and all of them had fornicated with him. But the inquisitors soon found that despite torture and the burnings, the numbers of witches they encountered did not decrease. On the contrary, the numbers kept rising and the crimes to which the heretics and witches confessed became more and more bizarre and obscene as time went on. A change of strategy was required and the inquisitors knew where to find it.

FALSE OFFERS OF CLEMENCY

Their own book, *The Witches' Hammer,* which outlawed nothing as long as it could produce a confession, suggested that better inroads might be made into the ranks of evil through offers of milder punishment. But in many cases, the new strategy prompted even more 'witches' to confess in exchange for minor punishments. They could even earn themselves a pardon – or so they were told – if they gave away other witches. Many of them eagerly grasped the opportunity to name names. But where this strategy fell down was

The inquisitors soon found that despite torture and the burnings, the numbers of witches they encountered did not decrease.

on the principle, also enshrined in *The Witches' Hammer,* that inquisitors could lie to witches, deceive them, mistreat them, do anything they liked to and with them and do so with impunity. Many women who admitted to being witches went to the stake complaining loudly that they had been promised their freedom and were ensured they would avoid the fearful fate that now awaited them.

There was also a mystery here. Witches were deeply feared, and were considered formidable foes capable of terrible retaliation. People believed that witches could cast spells, vanish into thin air and perform other supernatural acts to confound their enemies. Why, then, were they so easy to discover? Why were they unable to resist torture? Why did they make such copious confessions and, above all, never hit back at their tormentors? It was firmly believed that witches could curse their inquisitors, strike their torturers blind and emerge from the flames of the stake unscathed. Yet not once had any of these things happened.

Neither Heinrich Kramer nor James Sprenger, nor even the pope himself had an answer to this puzzle. All

One woman showed remarkable endurance ... She was tortured no fewer than 56 times, but failed to confess.

Jean Bodin, the Inquisitor-General of Besançon, France, hounded a woman called Desle la Mansenée on flimsy evidence and had her burned as a heretic and sorceress in 1529.

Guillemette Babin, with wrists bound, stands before Jean Bodin and another inquisitor being questioned about her relationship with the Devil, whose marks have been found on her body.

they could do was accuse, torture, condemn and burn in ever-greater numbers in the hope that the evil they were fighting would somehow be overcome. Tragically, many hundreds, including scores of small children, died in mass burnings, yet the evil remained. One bishop in Geneva, Switzerland, apparently burnt 500 victims within three months. In Bamburg in northern Bavaria another bishop disposed of 600 people, and in Würzburg, also in Bavaria, 900 perished at the stake. And so it went on. In 1586, a century after *The Witches' Hammer* was first published, 118 women and two men were burned to death for casting a magic spell that made the winter last longer.

THE INQUISITOR GENERAL

Although the hunting and burning of witches was most zealously pursued in the fifteenth and sixteenth centuries in Bavaria in southern Germany, other regions came close to matching these activities. One of them centred around Besançon in the province of Franche-Comté. At the time, Franche-Comté was a fief of the Holy Roman Empire where, in 1532, the Carolina Penal Code was enacted decreeing that sorcery was a criminal offence punishable by death at the stake. Whereas the Parlement of Paris was able to put brakes on hunting and burning witches in the more truncated France of the time, it had no jurisdiction over Franche-Comté. Here, in 1529, Jean Boin, the Inquisitor-General of Besançon, began eavesdropping on local gossip at the village of Anjeux. What he heard convinced him that Anjeux was a hotbed of witches, at the centre of which was a married woman named Desle la Mansenée.

One bishop in Geneva, Switzerland, apparently burnt 500 victims within three months.

There was no evidence against her at this early stage, but Bodin made the most of what he could get. The sheer number of her accusers convinced him that la Mansenée had a case to answer. The deposition of one accuser, Antoine Godin, was typical of the hearsay 'evidence' considered conclusive for the purpose of witch trials. Godin, who was aged around 40, reached back some 30 years to his boyhood to recall talk that labelled la Mansenée a witch and a sorceress. Her son, Mazelin, had told how his mother attended the witch's sabbath, flying there backwards on a twisted willow stick. Godin also testified that he had heard villagers say that Desle la Mansenée had stolen threads from a spinning staff, which she intended to use for the purposes of witchcraft. When around two-dozen other villagers of Anjeux backed up Godin's 'proof' Boin made ready to act.

CONDEMNED BY GOSSIP AND RUMOUR

Desle la Mansenée protested her innocence, but even so, she was imprisoned and tortured and before long began to confess. It was much the same story as before – copulation and making a pact with the Devil, flying to the sabbath, participating in orgies, renouncing her Catholic faith and for good measure, making destructive hailstorms and poisoning cattle with a mysterious black powder. The inquisition made a surprise decision, though. Desle la Mansenée was sentenced to death for murder, heresy and apostasy, but not for witchcraft. This dubious mercy meant that she was hanged rather than burned, although her body was consigned to the flames after her execution on 18 December 1529, just to make sure her evil had been eliminated.

By this time, the more scientific ideas of the Renaissance were beginning to seep into concepts of how the law should operate. Judgements were no longer to be based on gossip, hearsay, mass hysteria and the excesses of zeal, but in a cooler intellectual climate founded on a logical, legalistic approach. The new thinking promised a fundamental transformation in the workings of justice and introduced the idea that reason was a far better guide than fear or fantasy. It was a lack of reasoned argument and intelligent proof

Desle la Mansenée was sentenced to death for murder, heresy and apostasy, but not for witchcraft. This dubious mercy meant that she was hanged rather than burned, although her body was consigned to the flames after her execution.

that had raised concerns in the Parlement of Paris nearly 70 years before. But this rational approach, with its intimations of mercy and fair play, counted for nothing with the likes of Jean Bodin, a French jurist, economist and philosopher whose book, *La Démonomanie des Sorciers (On Witchcraft)* was published in Paris in 1580.

THE STRANGE CASE OF THE MADONNA ORIENTE

The Madonna Oriente, also known as *La Signora del Gioco* (The Lady of the Game) was a strange religious personality described by two Italian women, Sibilla Zanni and Pierina de Bugatis, who stood trial for witchcraft before the Roman Inquisition in 1384. The inquisitors heard tales about occult rituals practised by the Madonna at the houses of wealthy Milanese families, which included using magic to bring dead animals back to life and other similar 'miracles'. Zanni and de Bugatis confessed that they had performed white magic for healing wounds or disease or ensuring fertility. Nevertheless, the Roman Inquisition came to the conclusion that the two women were deluded and their stories were nothing but fantasy. They were punished with only a minor penance and released. But the word 'magic' whether black or white was lethal in the context of the Inquisition, even if it was used in a religious context. Six years later the two women were re-arrested. They were put on trial again on the much more serious charge of consorting with the Devil. Both, inevitably, were found guilty and were executed in 1390.

Bodin was one of the most outstanding political theorists of the sixteenth century and ranked high among its greatest scholars. Yet he shared with illiterate and uneducated peasants the common fears and prejudices of his time. For a start, he believed that the ordinary rules of prosecution could not apply to witchcraft. He wrote:

Proof of such evil is so obscure and difficult that not one out of a million witches would be accused or punished if regular legal procedures were followed.

Instead, Bodin advocated the use of torture, even on children and the disabled, as the way to agonize confessions out of suspects. In this way, Bodin believed, it was impossible for any witch to escape punishment. From his point of view, suspicion of witchcraft was as good as proof and rumours were also valid because, as far as he was concerned, gossip about witches was invariably true.

Bodin advocated the use of torture, even on children and the disabled, as the way to agonize confessions out of suspects. In this way, Bodin believed, it was impossible for any witch to escape punishment.

In Bodin's world, anything – absolutely anything – was justified as long as it uncovered witches and witchcraft. Children could be forced to betray their parents, and once a charge of witchcraft had been laid, the accused must always be found guilty. Bodin suspected anyone who did not believe in sorcery of being a sorcerer, and he believed that judges who failed to execute convicted witches must themselves be executed.

As a judge, Jean Bodin recommended that witches be branded with hot irons, but he was not too happy about burning them alive. In his view, burning was too quick, for it was all over within a mere 30 minutes. Bodin, however, had a dark secret that could have made him a victim of his own advice. Since 1567, when he was 37 years of age, he had been possessed by a demon. Fortunately, it was a friendly demon and it touched him on the right ear if he was doing wrong and on the left if he contemplated doing what was right. Luckily for Bodin, the Inquisition never caught up with him.

The efforts of inquisitors in Toulouse and Narbonne were encouraged by such popes as John XXII, who issued a series of papal bulls exhorting them to increase their witch hunts and treat witchcraft as heresy

A SUPERSTITIOUS POPE

France, of course, had been the original stamping ground of the Inquisition when the hunt was on for the Templar and Cathar heretics in the fourteenth century. The persecutions did not stop there. The efforts of inquisitors in Toulouse and Narbonne were encouraged by such popes as John XXII, who issued a series of papal bulls exhorting them to increase their witch hunts, treat witchcraft as heresy and condemn suspects accordingly. Pope John was one of the most superstitious of pontiffs. He believed his enemies were using sorcery to kill him, and in 1317, he ordered them to be tortured into confessing. Three years later, John told the inquisitor at Carcassonne, which lay in Cathar country, to pursue sorcerers and magicians and anyone who tried to raise demons or made wax images for the purpose of inducing sickness or death. As a result of John XXII's encouragement, 1000 suspects were arrested in Toulouse and Carcassonne by1350 and 600 of them were burnt at the stake.

Activities like these, and the fervour that drove them, were still going strong in Jean Bodin's time more than two centuries later. Bodin died in 1596, but even after that, there was plenty of mileage left in the pursuit of suspects in both the Catholic and the Protestant countries of Europe.

This was the case even though, in 1623, Pope Gregory had spoken the last word on the subject from the Vatican in an ordinance entitled *Omnipotentis Dei* (The Omnipotence of God).

Gregory, a reformer by nature, ordered that sadistic punishments should be reduced, if not abandoned altogether, and that the death penalty be limited to those who were 'proved to have entered into a compact with the Devil and to have committed murder with his assistance'.

It took a very long time for the witch hunters to get the message. It was as if witch hunting and burning had taken on a ghastly life all its own that even papal injunctions could not halt. If anything, the parameters of guilt had been extended beyond witches and sorcerers to a new class of heretics, including fortune tellers, necromancers, enchanters and most lurid of all, werewolves.

MORE WITCH-HUNTING IN GERMANY

Nevertheless, witches still accounted for the majority of victims burnt at the stake or imprisoned. In Germany, where King Maximilian I became an enthusiastic witch hunter after succeeding to the throne of Bavaria in 1597, up to 2000 witches were burnt in the small town of Riezler, and as many again in Augsburg and Freising. In the German state of Bamburg, 600 witches perished in the flames in the ten years up to 1633, and more than 900 in the nearby town of Würzburg. Among this last number, a total of 157 people died in 29 mass executions in Würzburg, including boys aged 10 and 12.

Reports of the sadistic excesses committed by inquisitors in Spain (this was before Tomas de Torquemada became Inquisitor General) caused Pope Sixtus to undergo a change of heart about allowing inquisitions. In 1482, he issued a papal bull putting a stop to the inquisition in Spain. The attempt was short-lived, though. King Ferdinand re-applied the pressure, Sixtus resisted briefly and made conditions, but ultimately, in 1483, he caved in and withdrew both his conditions and the bull.

Sixtus died in the following year, but Ferdinand made sure that the next pope, Innocent VIII, received and understood the same message. As Innocent had already proved, he was sufficiently hard-line in dealing with heresy and witchcraft in Germany, but Ferdinand

Pope John XXII, shown here at prayer, was a controversial pope in the early 14th century. His papal seat was at Avignon in modern France, rather than in the Vatican.

THE SPANISH INQUISITION

This painting by Francisco Rizi (1608–1685) shows the burning of heretics at an *auto da fé* in the Plaza Mayor in Madrid in the presence of King Charles II of Spain in the late 17th century.

During the Spanish Inquisition, a latecomer to the scene in 1478, the mass burning of heretics at the *auto da fé* (act of faith), became a public entertainment complete with the Mass, processions, the full pageantry of the religious and civic authorities and hundreds, sometimes thousands of spectators. The authorities of the Spanish Inquisition were always pleased to see a large crowd. In their estimation, there was nothing like an *auto da fé* to instil the fear of God and dread of the Devil into the faithful. Unlike its papal predecessor, though, the Spanish Inquisition did not operate under the aegis of the pope, but on the authority of King Ferdinand and Queen Isabella of Spain. This came about after King Ferdinand blackmailed Pope Sixtus IV into allowing him to create an inquisition by threatening to withdraw Spanish military support at a time when the Muslim Turks were endangering Rome.

This arrangement challenged the spiritual power of the papacy and Sixtus was never happy about it, especially after it became clear that the methods of the inquisition in Spain were even more barbaric than almost anywhere else.

Gregory XV, who was elected pope in 1621, but reigned for only two years, made the last, though much more merciful, papal decree against witches and magicians, the *Omnipotentis Dei*, on 20 March 1623.

TOMAS DE TORQUEMADA, A NAME TO FEAR

The Inquisitor General of the Spanish Inquisition, Tomas de Torquemada, is pictured here with King Ferdinand and Queen Isabella of Spain.

The Spanish use of torture and terror took inhumanity to previously unimagined heights. At the centre of the horror was Tomas de Torquemada, Inquisitor General of the Spanish Inquisition. Torquemada, born in 1420, was a sadist whose name is still a byword for excessive harshness and fanaticism more than five centuries after his death. Torquemada was willing to use any means, however bestial or dishonest, if it meant rooting out heresy and exposing the false *conversos,* the Jews and Muslims whose pretended conversion to Christianity had been designed to deflect persecution.

Torquemada was instrumental in the burning of Jewish and Muslim books and was one of the chief supporters of the Alhambra Decree, which pronounced the mass expulsion of the Jews from Spain in 1492. Yet, ironically, Torquemada himself had Jewish ancestry: his grandmother was said to be a *converso* and there was another convert from Judaism further back in his family. However that may be, the young Torquemada displayed nothing but vile hatred for Jews and Judaism and did everything he could to separate himself from his inconvenient ancestry.

As a youth, Torquemada became a Dominican monk and was known to be devout, ascetic and zealous. Little else is known about his life until, at the age of 54 in 1474, he became prior of the convent of Santa Cruz in Segovia in northern Spain. Soon afterwards, he was appointed confessor to the young Queen Isabella of

Castile and eventually became advisor to both the Queen and her husband, King Ferdinand of Aragon. The royal couple were so impressed with Torquemada that in 1483, they appointed him Inquisitor General of the Spanish Inquisition.

Torquemada was nothing if not thorough. He introduced the policy that every Christian in Spain, including girls over the age of 12 and boys over age 14, had to be accountable to the Inquisition for the purity of their faith. Under cover of anonymity, people were encouraged to tell tales on their neighbours, colleagues and even members of their own families if they were suspected of committing acts of heresy.

Sinners could be fined, imprisoned, tortured, burnt at the stake or subjected to all four of these punishments. When it came to the ultimate penalty, the stake and the fire, Torquemada offered his victims a choice of how they were to be burned. By kissing a crucifix they could be strangled, and therefore die, before being set alight. An apology for wrongs purportedly committed allowed for a speedy death by fast-burning logs. But those who maintained their innocence or retracted their forced confessions were made to suffer a prolonged death by slow burning green wood.

Tomas de Torquemada remained Inquisitor General for nine years, until 1492, when the last of the Jews and Muslim Moors were expelled from Spain. This, he considered, completed his work and he retired to the monastery of St Thomas at Avila. By that time, though, Torquemada had built up a fearful reputation for excessive cruelty and fanaticism, a reputation that made him both feared and detested in Spain. The feeling against him was so intense that he refused to travel anywhere without the protection of his 50 mounted guards and 250 armed soldiers. Convinced that his numerous enemies were out to poison him, Torquemada kept an antidote, the powdered horn of a unicorn, close by on the dining table whenever he ate a meal. These precautions were unnecessary, for when Torquemada died in 1498, aged 78, it was from natural causes.

Nevertheless, the hatred he inspired lived on and as late as 1832, more than 330 years after his death, and two years before the Spanish Inquisition was finally abolished, desecrators broke into Torquemada's tomb, removed his bones and burnt them.

wanted to put his own mark on his inquisition, not take his orders from Rome. Once Pope Innocent had backed off, the Spanish Inquisition moved on, later expanding its field of operations to ensure that the false *conversos*, and other heretics who escaped to Mexico, Peru and other Spanish colonies in America were eliminated in their turn.

In the event, another 350 years went by before a Royal Decree finally abolished the Spanish Inquisition in 1834. By that time, more than 15 generations of inquisitors had handled some 150,000 cases of heresy. Up to 5000 cases incurred the death penalty in trials held between 1560 and 1700 alone. But the records were fragmentary and incomplete, covering some periods but not others, so that final figure for victims murdered may never be known.

LOOKING BACK AT THE PAST

It has been reckoned by scholars that overall, between 40,000–100,000 men, women and children, to say nothing of thousands of black cats and several dogs, were tortured and killed in the five centuries and more when the fear of the Devil and all his works held Europe in thrall and popes and inquisitions struggled to prise Christendom from his wicked grasp. Of all the witch trials in Europe, some 12,000 are known to have ended in executions.

By 1834, more than 15 generations of inquisitors had handled some 150,000 cases of heresy. Up to 5000 cases incurred the death penalty between 1560 and 1700 alone.

Long after Europe had finally emerged from this appalling phase, historians, scholars and psychiatrists looked back at this terrible period in the continent's history and saw it as a gigantic delusion. More than that, the hunting of witches, with its tortures and forced confessions, was an ongoing nightmare brought on by fear, ignorance, fanaticism, suppressed sexuality and rampant hysteria. The shame and disgrace of this chapter of history clung to Europe for a long time.

THE BORGIAS

Power in the city-states of Renaissance Italy was frequently a family affair. And the families in question were truly formidable. The Visconti and Sforza of Milan, the Medici of Florence, the d'Este of Ferrara, the Boccanegra of Genoa or the Barberini, Orsini and della Rovere families shared some or, more often, all of the symptoms characteristic of their breed.

They were intensely greedy for wealth and status, and could not resist enriching their relatives with high-ranking titles and the lavish lifestyles that went with them. Their power could frequently be secured by violence, murder and bribery and ruthlessness comparable only to the methods of the Italian families involved in organized crime centuries later.

This portrait (left) of Pope Alexander VI, formerly Rodrigo Borgia, was painted by Juan de Juanes (1500–1579), often called the 'Spanish Raphael'. Alexander was probably the most controversial pope ever to have reigned, and remains infamous today.

The greatest power of all resided, of course, in the papacy and the immense influence the popes exerted over both the religious and the secular life of Catholic Europe. Several rich and famous families, including the Medici, the Barberini, the Orsini and the della Rovere, provided the Church with popes from their own ranks, but the most notorious of them all were the Borgias. The first of the two Borgia popes was the aged Calixtus III, formerly Alonso de Borja, who was elected in 1455.

From the start, Calixtus III excelled at nepotism. He set out to pack the Vatican bureaucracy with his relatives and place them in lucrative Church posts. Two

THE RISE OF THE FIRST BORGIA POPE

The de Borja family (as the surname was originally spelt) came from Torre de Canals, which lay in the foothills of the mountains to the south of Valencia in the kingdom of Aragon. The de Borjas became landed gentry when they were granted estates as a reward for their services fighting Muslim Moors who had ruled in Spain since the eighth century ce. Essentially, though, the Borjas were adventurers and opportunists, with ambitions to rise above their minor status. The member of the family who made these ambitions come true was Alonso de Borja.

Born in 1378, Alonso was a brilliant student, entering Lérida University to study law when he was only 14 years old. While still in his teens, he became a university lecturer and afterwards entered the service of King Alfonso V of Aragon as a diplomat and advisor. De Borja's greatest success came when he helped bring an end to the so-called Great Western Schism in which rival popes, mainly based in Avignon (now in France), disputed their claims to the papacy with the popes in Rome. Alonso de Borgia used a mixture of promises, charm and threats to make the rival antipope, Clement VIII, give in and recognize Martin V, the pope in Rome, as the true pontiff. In reward, a grateful Pope Martin appointed Alonso de Borja to the prestigious post of Bishop of Valencia.

In 1444, de Borja was made a cardinal. Now 66 years of age, he had led an exemplary life of strict piety and virtue. This was in sharp contrast to many of his fellow cardinals who preferred to enjoy worldly pleasures and luxuries with their mistresses and illegitimate children. In 1455, when Pope Nicholas V died and the time came to choose a successor, Cardinal de Borja was a frail 77-year-old. He was crippled by gout and spent most of his time propped up in bed. Consequently, when the cardinals met in conclave to elect a new pope, de Borja was not even considered as a candidate. But the two would-be pontiffs who fought the election were compromised, for they were, respectively, the representatives of the rival Colonna and Orsini families. A stalemate ensued and the conclave was forced to look for a third candidate.

The only possible alternative was Cardinal de Borja, for he was the only one with an unblemished reputation and was not bound to powerful family interests. He was also extremely old, not likely to survive for long, and his meek and mild manner promised to make him a fairly malleable pope.

However, anyone who thought that was very much mistaken. It was true that Pope Calixtus III, as de Borja became known, reigned for only three years. But these were years in which he tied the Catholic Church up in a Borgia stranglehold that prepared the ground for his nephew, Rodrigo who bribed his way to the Throne of St Peter in 1492. And, as Alexander VI, Rodrigo still holds the record as the most infamous pontiff of all time.

This painting shows Enea Silvio Piccolomini, the future Pope Pius II, being made a cardinal by Calixtus III in 1456.

of his nephews – Rodrigo was one of them – became cardinals in 1456. Such positions were normally occupied by mature or elderly men, but these two were had not yet reached 30, which both alarmed and astounded the College of Cardinals. They had agreed

From the start, Calixtus III excelled at nepotism. He set out to pack the Vatican bureaucracy with his relatives and place them in lucrative Church posts.

to the appointments under a false premise, expecting the elderly Calixtus to die soon, before the two young cardinals could be confirmed in their new positions. Instead, Calixtus stubbornly survived long enough for Rodrigo to be made Vice-Chancellor of the Church in 1457, which made him second in importance only to the pope himself. It also provided Rodrigo with the opportunity to acquire considerable wealth.

Another nephew, Rodrigo's brother and Calixtus' special favourite, Pedro Luis Borgia was created Captain-General of the Church, in command of the papal armed forces. Pedro Luis was also made governor of 12 cities. It was a particularly powerful post, because these cities dominated important strongholds in Tuscany and the Papal States, the pope's own territory in central Italy.

CALIXTUS CALLS FOR A CRUSADE

Just as shocking was the means Calixtus adopted to finance his crusade to liberate Constantinople from the Ottoman Turks who had conquered the capital of the Byzantine Empire in 1453 – a situation no self-respecting pope could tolerate. The Ottomans were Muslims and Constantinople, the most Christian of cities after Rome, could not be left in the hands of infidels. A crusade was arguably the most expensive expedition that could be undertaken, and to pay for it, Calixtus sold everything at his disposal, including gold and silver, works of art, valuable books, lucrative offices and grants of papal territories. He also put 'indulgences' up for sale – fees that Catholics paid to set aside punishments for their sins after death.

VATICAN VOCABULARY

INDULGENCES

An indulgence was a pardon or part-pardon granted as remission from eternal damnation in hell for mortal sins committed during life. An important condition, though, was that the Church must first forgive the sin. This meant an indulgence was only granted once a sinner had confessed his wrongdoing and had received absolution (forgiveness). Unfortunately, in time, the system became abused, and an indulgence came to be regarded as a payment made to let a sinner off punishment altogether. When the German priest and theologian Martin Luther made his famous protest in 1517 (a protest that led to the creation of the Protestant church) the Indulgence came under fire as the worst of several abuses.

... Calixtus sold everything at his disposal, including gold and silver, works of art, valuable books, lucrative offices and grants of papal territories.

But the great papal sale was for nothing. The important rulers of Christian Europe, like the kings of France and Germany, were not interested in another holy war. When they declined to contribute troops and weaponry to the pope's crusade that was the end of it. As a result, Constantinople was never retrieved for Christendom. Unsurprisingly, Pope Calixtus III became seriously unpopular in Rome. The situation was so grave that after he died in 1458, the Spanish commanders and administrators he had brought to the Vatican felt seriously threatened and fled from Rome in panic.

AWAITING THE PAPACY

Rodrigo Borgia had to wait for 34 years and the reigns of four more popes before he came within reach of the Throne of St Peter. By then he was 61 years of age and had lost his youthful good looks and slim figure. But what he had retained was much more significant. As a young man, Pope Pius II, the

Calixtus III, pictured here with a cardinal, was also responsible for issuing a papal bull that gave permission for Portugal to engage in the transatlantic slave trade.

successor to Rodrigo's Uncle Calixtus warned him that his penchant for attending orgies was 'unseemly' and urged him to take care of his honour 'with

Rodrigo was not a man likely to follow the saintly path to papal acclaim. To him, the papacy was a business to be milked and exploited for gain, and a great deal of it.

greater prudence'. It was a waste of papal breath: some 40 years later, nothing had changed. Rodrigo's taste for debaucheries, which were euphemistically termed 'garden parties', was as keen as ever. He fathered eight children on three or four mistresses – the last when he was aged 61 – and, as he was once described, he remained 'robust, amiable', with a 'wonderful skill in money matters'. The wealth this 'wonderful skill' brought him both before and after he became pope, was dazzling. One of his contemporaries wrote that

> *... his papal offices, his numerous abbeys in Italy and Spain and his three bishoprics of Valencia, Porto and Cartagena, yield him a vast income and it is said that the office of Vice-Chancellor alone brings him in 8000 gold florins. His plate, his pearls, his stuffs embroidered with silk and gold and his books in every department of learning are very numerous... I need not mention the innumerable bed hangings, the trappings for his horses... nor the magnificent wardrobe, nor the vast amount of gold coin in his possession.*

This was not a man likely to follow the saintly path to papal acclaim. To him, the papacy was a business to be milked and exploited for gain, and a great deal of it. This was certainly the view of Francesco Guicciardini the historian and another contemporary of Rodrigo Borgia who wrote of him as pope:

> *There was in him and in full measure, all vices both of flesh and spirit... There was in him no religion, no keeping of his word. He promised all things liberally, but bound himself to nothing that was not useful to him. He had no care for justice since, in his days, Rome was a den of thieves and murderers. Nevertheless, his sins meeting with no punishment in this world, he was to the last of his days most prosperous. In one word, he was more evil and had more luck than perhaps any other pope for many ages before.*

A portrait of Pope Alexander VI (Rodrigo Borgia) painted by his contemporary, the painter Perugino Pinturicchio (1454–1513).

The papal states had issued their own currency since the ninth century. This is a coin from the reign of Pope Alexander VI.

With a character reading like this, it followed that Rodrigo Borgia's personal ambition knew no bounds and had lost none of its fire in old age. He deliberately set out to create a dynasty that had fingers in all the most vital political pies in Europe. He began as dishonestly as he meant to go on when the conclave of cardinals met to choose a successor to Pope Innocent VIII, who had died in 1492.

Borgia's chance of winning the election appeared bleak even before Innocent was dead. Cardinal Giuliano della Rovere, who detested him, put in the poison by

Rodrigo Borgia's personal ambition knew no bounds and had lost none of its fire in old age.

reminding the pope that Borgia was a 'Catalan', as Spaniards were commonly known in the Vatican, and was therefore unreliable. Rodrigo Borgia was there to hear this slur. He fought his corner with vigour and a range of insults so inflammatory that the rivals were on the brink of a fist fight before they were persuaded to back down out of respect for the dying pontiff.

FIXING THE ELECTION

But already, behind the scenes, the wheeling, dealing and conniving were in full swing as the cardinals sought to outmanoeuvre each other and ensure victory for their personal candidates. Their choices had not been made on the basis of perception of the will of God or the workings of the Holy Spirit – the traditional criteria in papal elections – but on the wishes of the rulers in the city-states of Italy, each wanting a new pope sympathetic to their interests.

There was an enormous amount of money on the table for this exercise. For instance, King Ferrante of Naples offered a fortune in gold to buy the votes of cardinals willing to elect a pontiff who would advance Neapolitan interests at the Vatican. There was no holding back on the dirty tricks, either. For example, propaganda claiming that the Milanese were planning to subjugate the whole of Italy was spread around to scupper the chances of any candidate who came from, or was backed, by the city of Milan.

Rodrigo Borgia was not involved in any of this power play if only because, being a Spaniard, the other, Italian, cardinals deeply distrusted him. This, though, gave Borgia an advantage because it meant

Rodrigo also possessed another advantage that few, if any, of the others had. He was so wealthy he could dispense enormous bribes that could 'buy' votes at the conclave on a grand scale.

he was not tainted by the brute self-interest and venal machinations in which most of the other cardinals at the conclave were embroiled. Rodrigo also possessed another advantage that few, if any, of the others had. He was so wealthy he could dispense enormous bribes that could 'buy' votes at the conclave on a grand scale.

In this 16th-century satire, coins fall like rain while Pope Alexander VI (far right) and his favourites stretch out hands to catch them.

A portrait of Cardinal Ascanio Sforza of Milan by an unknown Renaissance artist. Sforza was a hard-nosed politician, but his ambition for the papacy was no match for the wealth and greed of Rodrigo Borgia.

RODRIGO BORGIA'S PALACE

Created for Rodrigo Borgia over many years by the leading Renaissance artists and artisans of the day, the palace was approached through a courtyard featuring elegantly decorated Tuscan columns. It was no wonder that Cardinal Sforza was unable to resist this wondrous place when it was offered him.
He wrote:

The palace is splendidly decorated. The walls of the great entrance hall are hung with fine tapestries; the carpets on the floor harmonized with the furnishings which included a sumptuous day bed upholstered in red satin with a canopy over it, and a chest on which was laid out a vast and beautiful collection of gold and silver plate. Beyond this, there were two more rooms, one hung with fine satin, carpeted and with another canopied bed covered with Alexandrine velvet; the other even more ornate with a couch covered in cloth of gold. In this room, the central table was covered with a cloth of Alexandrine velvet and surrounded by finely carved chairs.

His chief rivals for the papal succession were Cardinal Ascanio Sforza of Milan and Cardinal Giuliani della Rovere, the latter being bankrolled to the tune of 200,000 gold ducats by the King Charles VIII of France. The Republic of Genoa contributed another 100,000 gold ducats to his campaign funds as well. Della Rovere and Sforza ran neck and neck for the lead in the first three ballots with Rodrigo Borgia coming third. But it was not a distant third, and the deadlock between the other two candidates enhanced Borgia's chances of victory.

These bribes included bishoprics in Spain and Italy, extensive lands and estates, abbeys, castles and fortresses, governorships, Church offices, gold, jewels and treasure of all kinds.

Believing now that he could, after all, slip past della Rovere and Sforza and seize the prize, Rodrigo swamped the cardinals with offers he was sure they would find impossible to refuse. These bribes included bishoprics in Spain and Italy, extensive lands and estates, abbeys, castles and fortresses, governorships, Church offices, gold, jewels and treasure of all kinds.

THE BIGGEST BRIBE OF ALL

Rodrigo reserved the most valuable temptations for Cardinal Ascanio Sforza, the Milanese candidate, to whom he offered his position as Vice-Chancellor and as an additional lure, his fabulous palace, which stood by the River Tiber opposite the Vatican. There were many magnificent mansions in Rome, but none excelled this one.

All this represented possibly the greatest bribe ever offered to a cardinal and Sforza managed to resist it for some five days before finally succumbing. One diarist recorded that, shortly afterwards, a train of four mules loaded with a large quantity of silver left Rodrigo's palace and made its way through the streets of Rome to Sforza's splendid but, by comparison much more modest, mansion.

With Sforza's withdrawal from the papal race, the entire pro-Milanese faction switched their support to Rodrigo Borgia. Cardinal della Rovere, who had made it known that anyone would be preferable to another Borgia pope, was forced to swallow his words and vote for Rodrigo, if only as a gesture to save face. The other cardinals quietly pocketed their own rewards and marked their ballot papers in the same way. It was said that the last of them was a 96-year-old cardinal who was so far gone in senility that he barely knew where he was or what he was doing. Only five cardinals refused the incentives offered by Borgia. Those who accepted, of course, vastly outnumbered them.

The decision was finally reached after an all-night session. It was just before dawn on 11 August 1492

The Palazzo Sforza Cesarini, given to Ascanio Sforza as a bribe to ensure he dropped out of contention for the papacy, still stands in a much altered state today.

that Rodrigo Borgia, now Pope Alexander VI, dressed in papal vestments, appeared on the first-floor balcony of the Vatican before a large crowd to make the traditional pronouncement: 'I am Pope and Vicar of Christ… I bless the town, I bless the land, I bless Italy, I bless the world.'

It was a tradition in Rome to mark papal elections with bouts of rioting and looting and the triumph of the second Borgia pope was no exception. Some 200 people died in the tumult before the result was announced and church bells rang throughout the city to mark the event. What was unique about this election, though, was the astonishment, rage and fear it provoked.

'Now we are in the power of a wolf,' commented Cardinal Giovanni di Lorenzo de'Medici of Florence, himself a future pope as Leo X, 'the most rapacious, perhaps, that this world has ever seen. And if we do not flee, he will inevitably devour us all.'

CORRUPT ELECTION

Several others – Venetians, Ferrarans and Mantuans – vociferously cried 'foul' and there was talk of declaring the election corrupt and therefore void. Cheating on a truly shameless scale had, of course, taken place but the cardinals who fell for the Borgia bribes were giving nothing away and the new pope had himself been very

Cheating on a truly shameless scale had, of course, taken place but the cardinals who fell for the Borgia bribes were giving nothing away ...

careful to leave behind no proof that could be used against him. King Ferrante of Naples wept when he heard how the vast sums of money he had put up for his own candidate had failed to win the papal crown.

But it was not all sour grapes and some of the fears roused by the election of Alexander VI were not justified. Corrupt, immoral and faithless he might be, but the second Borgia pope also possessed qualities that enabled him to cope well with the greedy, materialistic, luxury-loving world of Renaissance Italy that would have flummoxed a more saintly, less worldly pontiff. During the reign of his uncle, Pope Calixtus and the four popes after him, Rodrigo Borgia had become a master diplomat, and administrator. He also knew how to use the amiable approach to personal

An anti-Catholic satire fom the 16th century, showing Alexander VI as the Devil wearing the triple crown of the popes.

THE CORONATION OF POPE ALEXANDER VI

Alexander's coronation, which took place on 26 August 1492, was in such an extravagant vein that even the Triumphs accorded Roman emperors would have been outclassed by it. The procession was more than three kilometres long and comprised 10,000 horsemen, the entire papal household, foreign ambassadors and cardinals on horseback, each of them attended by a 12-man retinue. Pope Alexander himself rode beneath a canopy that shaded him from the intense late August sun. The papal guard and all the officials of the Vatican court followed him.

Making its way slowly through crowds crammed in on both sides, the procession passed under specially erected arches carrying slogans, some of which were frankly blasphemous. 'Alexander the invincible', 'Alexander the most magnificent' and 'The Coronation of the great god Alexander' were among them. But all were outdone by the message inscribed in gold on another of the arches: 'Rome was great under Caesar, greater far under Alexander. The first was a mortal, the latter is a god.'

The heat and the crush were so great that Alexander fainted twice under the strain, but these moments of weakness were moments only. Once the coronation and its attendant celebrations were over, Alexander lost no time asserting himself as a pope who meant business.

relations rather than the 'order from on high' method to get what he wanted. Courtiers at the Vatican were agreeably surprised at the friendly, patient pope they had unexpectedly acquired. They noticed particularly Alexander's willingness to attend to the problems of poor widows and other humble folk, and take action to ameliorate their troubles.

Even more amazing for a man who had surrounded himself in luxury and self-indulgence for several decades, was the careful budgeting Pope Alexander

> Alexander also sought ways and means of keeping his sex life – and its results – out of the public eye. He realized that his children could be an embarrassment to him now that he was pope.

introduced into the Vatican. Once, not too long ago, the Borgia banquets held at Rodrigo's Roman castle had been the talk of the town. They were so lavish they were said to excel the feasts of the emperors of ancient Rome: the richest of rich foods were served on solid gold plates accompanied by the finest wines drunk from extravagantly decorated goblets. Now, as pope, he reduced the Vatican menus from their former lavish size to one course per meal. This reduction was so drastic that invited guests started looking around for excuses to avoid papal dinners.

ALEXANDER'S HIDDEN FAMILY

Alexander also sought ways and means of keeping his sex life – and its results – out of the public eye. He realized, or claimed he realized, that his children could be an embarrassment to him now that he was pope, and at his coronation, he promised Giovanni Boccaccio, the ambassador from the Duchy of Ferrara that he would make sure they remained at a distance from the Vatican and Rome. This was probably impossible for a man as fond of his offspring as Pope Alexander was. Yet, though loving them intensely, he was also determined to use them and his other close relatives to cement his papal powerbase. As a result, the Boccaccio promise ran out after only five days when Alexander appointed his eldest son, Cesare Borgia, to the Archbishopric of Valencia. This made him, at 17 years of age, the primate of all Spain. The pope ignored the fact that young Cesare had not even been ordained a priest. In addition, Alexander appointed another of his sons, the 11-year-old Jofre to the Diocese of Majorca and made him an archdeacon of the cathedral at Valencia.

Cesare and Jofre, together with their sister Lucrezia and another son, Juan, were the children of Alexander's first mistress, the three-times married Vannozza dei Cattani. Two more sons, Giralomo and Pier Luigi and another daughter, Isabella, were born to different mothers and the last, Laura, was the daughter of the pope's final mistress, Giulia Farnese. In 1492, Giulia was in an awkward position and so was her lover, the new pope. As Rome's greatest celebrity and one whose comings and goings were under constant scrutiny, Alexander could not, obviously, continue his habit of visiting Giulia at the Monte Giordano palace where he had installed her. A handy alternative was the palace of Santa Maria in Portico, which lay only a few metres from the steps of the church of St Peter in the Vatican.

Courtiers at the Vatican were agreeably surprised at the friendly, patient pope they had unexpectedly acquired.

The only problem was that a certain Cardinal Zeno already occupied Santa Maria in Portico. This was a minor difficulty, though, and was quickly removed, however, after the venerable cardinal was persuaded that his best interests would be served by loaning his palace to the pope. Giulia, who was pregnant, moved in with the pope's daughter Lucrezia and Lucrezia's nurse Adriana del Mila. Later on in 1492, Giulia gave birth to Laura. But the secrecy Alexander sought eluded him. The little girl, who grew to resemble her father closely, was soon the subject of gossip all over Europe. Diarists wrote of Giulia as 'Alexander's concubine' and one satirist called her 'the Bride of Christ', an appellation that, it was said, amused her greatly.

Alexander VI's family, including his extended family, had a particular value for him because Rome seemed to be full of his enemies. Among them were cardinals he had

Pope Alexander gave a lavish party at the papal palace to celebrate the marriage of his daughter Lucrezia to her first husband Giovanni Sforza in 1493.

superseded at the conclave of 1492, their frustrated backers and the leading families of Rome who feared a strong man like Alexander and would have preferred a pontiff they could manipulate to do their bidding.

> One satirist called her 'the Bride of Christ', an appellation that, it was said, amused her greatly.

Many Italians were suspicious of Alexander because he was a 'Catalan' and therefore a devious foreigner who, despite his years of service in the Vatican, was unlikely to do right by the papacy.

Zampieri Domenichino (1581–1641), who painted this picture of a woman with a unicorn, may have based her face on that of Giulia Farnese, Pope Alexander VI's mistress.

The answer, as Alexander saw it, was to surround himself with his own relatives, the only people he could really trust. This nepotism was, of course, nothing new in the Vatican. Uncle Calixtus had been expert at it in his time and many other popes had seen the papacy as a prime opportunity to enrich and elevate their families by giving them titles, wealth and status otherwise beyond their reach. Even so, Alexander VI outdid them all. In his hands, the workings of this despotic, secretive and exclusive papacy came to resemble those of the Mafia – violent and exploitative where necessary, and propelled by fabulous amounts of money.

The appointments to high office of Alexander's young sons Cesare and Jofre were only the start.

Pope Alexander VI's disagreements with his son Cesare (right) did not stop him appointing him a cardinal at the age of 18.

Alexander filled the Sacred College of Cardinals with Borgias and members of related families. The most important new cardinal was Cesare Borgia, although Alexander had to use trickery to get round the rule that only legitimately born candidates were eligible. Cesare was, of course, illegitimate but he was deftly 'legitimized' by his father who issued a papal bull declaring him to be the son of his mistress Vanozza de'Cattanei and her first husband, the late Domenico Giannozzo Rignano.

But another bull, issued on the same day, reversed the first and acknowledged the truth – that Pope Alexander was Cesare's father. The second Bull was conveniently overlooked and Cesare duly qualified. But more than that, Pope Alexander insisted that all other cardinals of the Sacred College must be there to greet Cesare when he made his formal entry into Rome. It was unprecedented, but the pope was adamant. Predictably, Cardinal Giuliano della Rovere voiced the most strident protest, declaring that he would not stand by and let the College be 'profaned and abused' in this way. Nevertheless, this is precisely what he was forced to do and, with the other cardinals, had to offer to Cesare the homage the pope demanded of them.

The cardinals were already apoplectic with rage over admitting the pope's bastard into their ranks when

Alexander created another, similar, controversy: he proposed that Alessandro, the younger brother of Giulia Farnese, should also become a cardinal. This was seen as a reward for Giulia's sexual services, which served to heighten the temperature at the College of Cardinals even further. Once again, though, Pope Alexander forced the appointment through, this time by threatening to replace all members of the College with more nominees of his own and make Alessandro a cardinal that way.

In addition, the Pope spread Borgia influence both inside and outside Italy by arranging advantageous

unions for his children. The marriage of Alexander's son Jofre to Sancia of Aragon, a granddaughter of King Ferrante of Naples, brought the pope a link with the royal family that ruled both Naples and Aragon. Jofre's sister, Lucrezia Borgia, the only daughter of the pope and his mistress Vannozza dei Cattenei, was more a victim than the vicious purveyor of poison portrayed in so many Borgia legends. Her father, it appears, adored her, but that did not prevent him marrying her off three times for his own political advantage. Her first husband, Giovanni Sforza, who wed the 13-year-old Lucrezia in 1493, was supposed to bring Alexander a valuable connection with Milan. Giovanni, however, proved less than satisfactory. He was more attuned to French interests than to those of his father-in-law and persistently refused to perform the military service in the papal army Alexander required of him.

the Pope spread Borgia influence both inside and outside Italy by arranging advantageous unions for his children.

LUCREZIA'S DIVORCE

Alexander, aided and abetted by Cesare, decided to get rid of the unsatisfactory Giovanni. He was bullied into confessing something that was patently untrue, and totally mortifying for a Renaissance man to admit, that his marriage to Lucrezia had never been consummated, due to his own impotence. The fact that Lucrezia was pregnant at this time was conveniently overlooked. The divorce that followed opened the way for the pope to choose Lucrezia's second husband, the handsome 17-year-old Alfonso of Aragon, Duke of Bisceglie. Alexander had had designs on Naples for a number of years and Alfonso, whose Aragonese family exercised power over the city, seemed like the ideal means for implementing those ambitions.

The marriage took place in 1498, but like Giovanni Sforza, before him, Alfonso soon ran out of usefulness. An assault by French and Spanish forces put an end to Aragonese control of Naples and so made young Alfonso disposable. In July of 1500, probably with the connivance of the pope, Cesare Borgia sent armed henchmen to attack Alfonso as he was walking past the church of St Peter in the Vatican. They failed to kill

Pope Alexander made his son Cesare (second from left) a cardinal at the age of 18. This picture, painted by Giuseppe-Lorenzo Gatteri (1829-86), shows Cesare leaving the Vatican.

Portrait of a woman by Bartolomeo Veneziano (1502–1555), thought to be Lucrezia Borgia, eldest daughter of Pope Alexander. Lucrezia was used as a pawn by her father to conclude advantageous marriages.

him this time, but Cesare completed the job, apparently in person, by strangling his brother-in-law as he convalesced. Lucrezia, a widow at the age of 20, was heartbroken, for she had genuinely loved Alfonso.

Pope Alexander at last achieved what he wanted from a son-in-law when he arranged a third marriage for Lucrezia, with another, but much better, Alfonso.

Giovanni was bullied into confessing that his marriage to Lucrezia had never been consummated, due to his own impotence.

This was Alfonso d'Este, whose family ruled the city-state of Ferrara. At first, d'Este baulked at the idea of marrying into Lucrezia's unsavoury family. This was not surprising when sensational gossip of all kinds, including allegations of murder, incest, immorality, debauchery and virtually every other crime it was possible to commit constantly surrounded the Borgias. Eventually, though, Alfonso came round and the couple were married on 30 December 1501. Unlike Lucrezia's first two husbands, Alfonso and the d'Estes were fully in control of their city, which bordered on the northern boundary of the Papal States, and was able to lend power and influence to Alexander and all his successor pontiffs until the end of the sixteenth century. After that, Ferrara was absorbed by the Papal States.

FAVOURITE SON

But however generous he was towards his other children the lion's share of paternal bounty went to Alexander's favourite, his son Juan Borgia. In 1488, four years before Alexander became pope, the 11-year-old Juan had been gifted the Duchy of Gandia, the Borgia family estate in Spain, in the will left by his half-brother Pedro Luis. Juan's older brother Cesare was infuriated to find himself passed over for the sake

The tomb of Alfonso of Aragon, Duke of Bisceglie, the second husband of Lucrezia Borgia, who was murdered by her brother Cesare in 1500.

of a pampered sibling who was known in the Vatican as 'the spoiled boy' (and lived up to it for most of the time). Cesare was so enraged he swore that he would kill Juan, even though, as a member of the clergy, he

Cesare Borgia sent armed henchmen to attack Alfonso. Lucrezia, a widow at the age of 20, was heartbroken.

was not eligible to take on Juan's essentially secular honours. But Cesare was himself only 13 years old at the time and the threat was not taken seriously.

A portrait painted by Bernardino di Betto, or Pinturicchio (1454–1513) which is said to depict Lucrezia Borgia.

The Duchy of Gandia was not the only bequest Juan received from Pedro Luis. He also inherited Pedro's intended bride, Maria Enriquez de Luna. The 16-year-old Juan set sail for Spain and his Duchy in 1493 and did so in a grandiose style more suited to the travels of an emperor. His doting father had provided him with gold, jewels, silver, coin and a mass of other

Gossips and other observers put it about that the family was in the process of shifting the Vatican treasures to Spain.

booty, which required the holds of four galleys to transport it from Italy to Spain. Gossips and other observers put it about that the family was in the process of shifting the Vatican treasures to Spain.

'They say that he will return within a year,' reported Gian Lucido Cattaneo, an envoy from the Italian city-state of Mantua 'but will leave all that in Spain and come for another harvest.'

A CHIP OFF THE OLD BORGIA BLOCK

Pope Alexander also loaded his favourite son with instructions on how to behave properly, telling him to be 'pious' and 'God-fearing', to refrain from staying out late at night, to shun gambling and take care not to embezzle the revenues of his Duchy. Nevertheless, according to rumour, Juan quickly proved to be a chip off the old Borgia block once he was a safe distance away from his father. He spent his nights in taverns, drinking, gambling and consorting with prostitutes and, worst of all, neglecting his wife Maria. It was even whispered that Juan had been so busy carousing and debauching that he had not found the time to consummate his marriage. This was soon proved untrue for Maria Enriquez quickly became pregnant and Juan, in any case, denied the rest of the gossip as fictions put about by 'people with little brain or in a state of drunkenness'.

But it did not take a great deal of brain or drink to recognize that the young Duke of Gandia had inherited his father's extravagant tastes. One thing Juan failed to understand about Spain was that opulence and excessive show were unwelcome in a country that favoured ascetic Christianity and regarded the luxuriant splendours of Renaissance Italy with disdain.

Pope Alexander also loaded his favourite son with instructions on how to behave properly, telling him to be 'pious' and 'God-fearing'...

Juan, of course, had never known anything but luxury and its gaudy manifestations, so that it was natural for him to create a palace in Gandia that contained magnificent furnishings and brilliantly ornate decor.

When complaints about his son's inappropriate behaviour reached Alexander, he rushed off a furious letter demanding that Juan cultivate greater care for local sensibilities.

However, a while later, in 1497, it became apparent that Juan had roused enmities that needed to be answered by much more than mere grumbling. Despite his protestations, he was a Borgia through and through, leading a decadent life and displaying an excessively arrogant manner. 'A very mean young man,' was how one contemporary described him, 'full of false ideas of grandeur and bad thoughts, haughty, cruel and unreasonable.'

Late in the summer of 1496, Juan came to Rome to be installed by his father as Captain-General of the Church. This was a highly prestigious post that placed Juan in charge of the papal army, even though he had no military experience, training or talent for the task. There were far better qualified nobles in Rome, such as the prominent *condotierre*, Guidobaldo de Montefeltre, Duke of Urbino, to name only one. Naturally they were furious at being upstaged by a callow and overindulged youth. And their worst suspicions were confirmed. Juan's immediate brief was to bring to heel the powerful but rebellious Orsini family who were backed by a strong French presence. After several attempts in which dozens of papal

Pope Alexander VI (first right) and Jacopo Pesaro, Bishop of Paphos (second right) paying their respects to St Peter (seated, left) in an oil painting by Titian (c.1485–1576), leader of the Venetian school of Renaissance art.

soldiers were needlessly sacrificed through Juan's ineptitude, the Orsini were finally brought to heel and their French backers driven off.

The hero of the hour should have been Gonsalvo di Cordova, an aristocrat and renowned general known in his native Spain as *El Gran Capitan* (the Great Captain). It was di Cordova, nominally Juan's 'lieutenant', who masterminded the final, victorious, siege and assault of the 'Orsini wars'. However, Pope Alexander wanted his beloved Juan to take all the credit and gave him the place of honour at the celebration banquet. The infuriated di Cordova refused to take his seat and walked out. The pope, blinded by inordinate love of his favourite son, fooled himself that this hostility was due to jealousy of Juan, and planned new honours for him. One of his ideas was to make Juan King of Naples after the incumbent, Ferrante II, died in 1496. It was only when threatening noises reached him from King Ferdinand of Aragon that Alexander backed off.

MORE PRIZES FOR JUAN

However, favouring Juan did not account for all the ambitions of Alexander at this time. He was, in fact, aiming to use his son as a means of expanding Borgia power throughout Italy. As pope, Alexander already controlled the Papal States, which occupied a large swathe of central Italy. Although he had been thwarted in his plans to absorb Naples, he was able to use papal cities that lay within the Neapolitan boundaries – Benevento, Terracina and Pontecorvo – to make a sizeable new territory for Juan. When this move was announced in June of 1497, a wave of protest swept Rome. Alexander's enemies did not find it difficult to guess its significance. It was, they believed, a preliminary move to absorb the Kingdom of Naples by more furtive means. There was, though, a terrible method by which this expansion, and any

> a highly prestigious post placed Juan in charge of the papal army, even though he had no military experience.

Gonsalvo di Cordova, Duke of Terranova and Santangelo, was the Spanish general who made Spain the premier military power of the 16th and 17th centuries.

THE MURDER OF JUAN BORGIA

On the evening of 14 June 1497, Juan's mother Vannozza held a special dinner at her country village near Rome to celebrate the honours that were being heaped on her son. Juan's elder brother Cesare Borgia was there, together with Jofre and his wife Sancia and their cousin Cardinal Juan Borgia-Lanzel. The environs of Rome could be dangerous at night for wealthy people, who could easily fall prey to marauders, so the party broke up around dusk and Juan rode off with Cesare and a group of friends and their servants. Somewhere along the way, Juan parted company with the others and rode on with two companions, heading for the pope's palace, the Castel Sant'Angelo. Juan never reached the palace, nor was he ever seen alive again.

Juan Borgia, the spoiled darling and favourite son of Pope Alexander VI.

When it was discovered that he was missing, search parties totalling some 300 men were sent out to comb the route Juan had taken. They found nothing. Pope Alexander ordered his Spanish guards to make a fingertip search of the city. They discovered the groom who had accompanied Juan, but he was so badly beaten he was almost dying and could tell them nothing about the fate of his master. They also found Juan's horse whose trappings, particularly the stirrups, showed clear evidence of a violent struggle. Still, Juan was nowhere to be found and the Borgia guards began bullying householders to betray what, if anything, they knew about the missing duke. The Orsini family, recently trounced by the Borgia pope and his upstart offspring, realized they might be prime suspects and barricaded themselves into their homes rather than confront the fury of the pope's 'heavies'.

CONTRACT KILLING

Then, at last, an eyewitness was located. Giorgio Schiavi, a timber merchant who unloaded his wood on an island in the middle of the River Tiber, revealed that around two o'clock in the morning, he had seen two men, acting furtively, throw a body into the water. The searchers dragged the river all night and for half the following day, until at noon, a corpse clad in rich brocade and carrying the insignia of Captain-General of the Church was discovered. It was Juan. He had been brutally hacked about as many as eight times and his throat was cut. His hands were tied together and a stone had been hung about his neck to make sure he sank to the bottom of the river. The murder had all the hallmarks of a contract killing.

A modern illustration of Juan's murder, showing his body about to be thrown into the River Tiber.

others Alexander had in mind, could be halted in its tracks – assassination.

Pope Alexander was devastated when he heard how horribly Juan had been killed. It was said that he let out a great roar like an injured animal when he saw Juan's bloated, muddied body. The diarist Johann Burchard, Master of Ceremonies to Pope Alexander, wrote:

The pope, when he heard that the duke had been killed and flung into the river like dung, was thrown into a paroxysm of grief, and for the pain and bitterness of his heart shut himself in his room and wept most bitterly.

GUILT AND GRIEF

Alexander refused to let anyone in for several hours, and neither ate nor drank anything for more than three days. In his overwhelming grief, he imagined that Juan had been killed because of his own sinful excesses. He said:

God has done this perhaps for some sin of ours and not because he deserved such a cruel death... We are determined henceforth to see to our own reform and that of the church. We wish to renounce all nepotism. We will begin therefore with ourselves and so proceed through all the ranks of the church till the whole work is accomplished.

It was the grief talking, of course. Alexander was too much of a dyed-in-the-wool sinner, too far gone in excess and pleasure to convert himself in the overnight manner he seemed to suggest. Instead, he reverted to

The pope, blinded by inordinate love of his favourite son, fooled himself that this hostility was due to jealousy of Juan.

type and to his long-established immoralities and his intrigues in politics. His cardinals and other clergy did not mind too much for they, too, were loath to give up their own pleasures.

Juan was buried in the family chapel a few hours after he was found. He was accompanied to his grave by 120 torchbearers. As the procession reached the place on the shore of the River Tiber where the body was found, men of the Borgia's own private army unsheathed their swords and swore vengeance on whoever had perpetrated the crime. Despite the offer of a generous reward, the murderer was never found, but there were plenty of suspects. One of the noble Roman families, deprived by Juan and his father of the honours they believed were their due, might have done the deed. In particular, Cardinal Giuliano della Rovere, the great enemy of the Borgias, who had links with the Orsini family, could have contrived the killing.

AN INVESTIGATION IS HALTED

Another possible culprit may have been closer to home, too close, in fact, for comfort. Pope Alexander had ordered an investigation shortly after the murder, but this was suddenly closed only three weeks later. It was never reopened. This mystery fed the speculation that surrounded Juan's death and it was whispered that the investigation had already done its job and revealed a murderer whose name the pope did not want publicized. The most likely candidate, according to the gossip, was his son, Cesare Borgia, who had been one of the last to see Juan alive. Juan's young widow, Maria Enriquez de Luna and her family seemed certain that Cesare had murdered his brother. Nine years after

When the procession reached the place where the body was found, men of the Borgia's own private army unsheathed their swords and swore vengeance.

swearing to kill Juan, they believed, he had made his threat come true, and there appeared to be evidence to support this theory.

For one thing, Cesare's ruthless, rapacious nature and his penchant for intrigue were already well known. Murder, it was said, was well within his compass. Besides that, Cesare had everything to gain from Juan's death. Ever since 1488, Cesare had coveted the Duchy of Gandia and all the other honours and riches their father had conferred on Juan. Now, with Juan removed from the scene, he had his chance but was checked at first by his father's protests. Alexander had taken a great deal of trouble to place Cesare in the College of Cardinals and was convinced that from this springboard, his son would one day become pope. But Cesare was too much a man of the world and in particular, a man of the sensual Renaissance world. He was more interested in hunting than in prayer, coveted wealth and women rather than spiritual integrity and preferred land and estates to a life of humility and sacrifice.

> Juan's young widow, Maria Enriquez de Luna and her family seemed certain that Cesare had murdered his brother.

Ultimately, Cesare got his way, if only because Jofre, the son Pope Alexander planned would take Juan's place, proved too weak and diffident to face up to the challenges involved. Cesare, an inspiring military leader and a first-class strategist, was much more the vigorous strong man required to realize his father's ambitions. This was why, however reluctantly, Alexander allowed Cesare to resign holy orders in 1498, the first cardinal ever to do so.

CESARE SUCCEEDS JUAN

Now, Cesare's secular aims were within his reach. He was created Captain-General of the Church in his brother's stead and in 1499, acquired a wife – the 16-year-old Charlotte d'Albray, who was the ideal daughter-in-law for a pope who aspired to all-embracing political power. Charlotte, the sister of King John III of Navarre, belonged to an aristocratic Gascon family related to the royal family of France and according to Italian envoys at the French court, was 'unbelievably beautiful'.

But the two-month honeymoon Cesare and his unbelievably beautiful young wife spent at a castle in his duchy of Valentinois created for

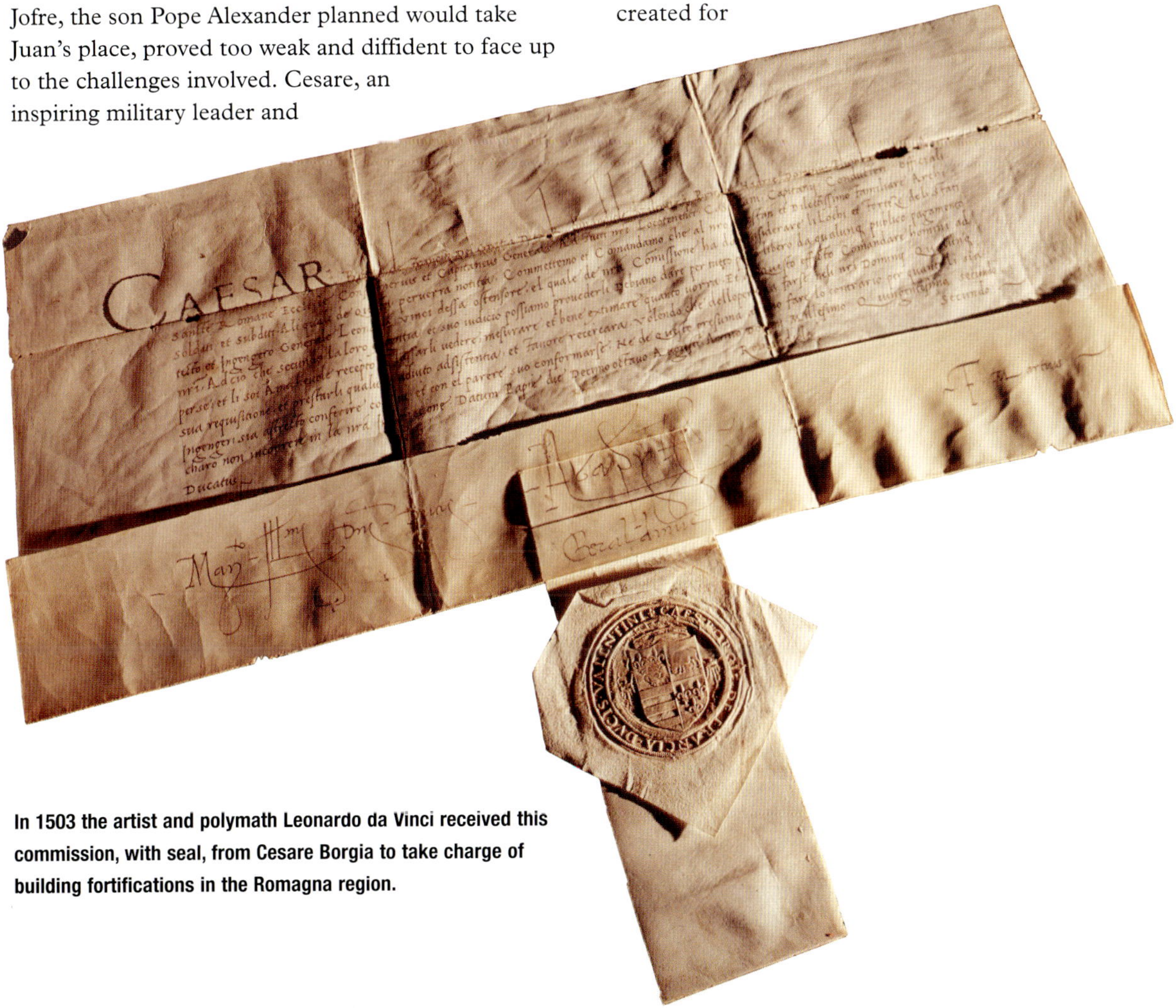

In 1503 the artist and polymath Leonardo da Vinci received this commission, with seal, from Cesare Borgia to take charge of building fortifications in the Romagna region.

him in 1498 by Pope Alexander, was the only time the newlyweds spent together. After July 1499, when he left the castle for the wars, Cesare never saw Charlotte again, nor their daughter, Luisa, who was born in the spring of 1500. Cesare fought first in support of his ally King Louis XII of France in the siege and capture of Milan and next at the head of the papal army against rebellious feudal lords in the Romagna, which lay adjacent to the Papal States in the northeast of Italy. Tribute to the pope was overdue and Alexander sent Cesare to teach the lords of the Romagna a lesson.

One story told of a supper hosted by Cesare Borgia at the end of October 1501 where 50 courtesans danced naked with 50 servants.

Both campaigns were extremely successful and in Jubilee year, 1500, Cesare and his father provided Rome with the greatest bonanza celebration the Borgias had ever staged. It featured, for a start, a bloody spectacle reminiscent of the gladiatorial games of ancient Rome, in which Cesare, resplendent on horseback, cut off the heads of six bulls in St Peter's Square to wild applause from the watching crowd. According to rumours and stories circulating in Rome, and supported by the diaries of Johann Burchard, the celebrations continued with a session of debauchery that exceeded virtually all other acts of depravity the Borgias had so far committed.

NAKED REVELS

One story told of a supper hosted by Cesare Borgia at the end of October 1501 where 50 courtesans danced naked with 50 servants. This was followed by an orgy in which whoever made love to the prostitutes the most times or produced the 'best performances' received prizes. The onlookers, who included Pope Alexander, Cesare and Lucrezia, selected the winners. Foreign diplomats in Rome, who regularly transmitted salacious gossip about the Borgias to

Lucrezia dances for her father, Pope Alexander VI, and his guests at one of his infamous parties.

CESARE BORGIA AND NICCOLÒ MACHIAVELLI

The adjective 'machiavellian', which is synonymous with cunning, scheming or unscrupulous, comes from the name of an Italian writer, Niccolò Machiavelli. He wrote a book entitled *The Prince,* published in 1532, which made a case for unethical methods of acquiring and exercising power. One of Machiavelli's models for this exercise was Cesare Borgia, Duke of Gandia.

Machiavelli met Cesare when he went to his court as Secretary of the Florentine Chancellery in 1502, and remained at the court for more than three months. This meant Machiavelli had plenty of time to study how Cesare conducted himself and his business. He used several of Cesare's exploits and strategies as examples of how to gain and retain power and advised politicians and rulers to emulate him.

In Chapter Seven of *The Prince,* Machiavelli cited one event that had particularly impressed him. It showed Borgia asserting his power by the most brutal means and told how he handled a difficult situation in Romagna, northern Italy. After he had conquered the region, Cesare found that it was wild, disorganized and almost ungovernable. Machiavelli wrote:

> *... wishing to bring back peace and obedience to authority, he* [Cesare Borgia] *considered it necessary to give it a good governor. Thereupon he promoted Messer Ramiro d'Orco de Lorqua, a swift and cruel man, to whom he gave the fullest power. This man in a short time restored peace and unity with the greatest success. Afterwards the duke considered that it was not advisable to confer such excessive authority... And because he knew that the past severity had caused some hatred against himself, so... he desired to show that, if any cruelty had been practised, it had not originated with him, but in the natural sternness of* [Ramiro]. *Under this pretence he took Ramiro, and one morning caused him to be executed and left on the piazza... with the block and a bloody knife at his side.*

Niccolò Machiavelli took Cesare Borgia as the model for his celebrated book *Il Principe* (The Prince).

their masters at home spread the news that the papal apartments had been turned into a private brothel where at least 25 women came into the Vatican each night to provide the 'entertainment' at parties attended by Pope Alexander, Cesare and large numbers of cardinals. Pope Alexander had increased membership of the Cardinals' College by nine new candidates, each having paid thousands of ducats for the privilege.

The money went to line the pockets of the pope and Cesare who were already rich enough to make the fabled King Croesus of Lydia envious. Probably the most scurrilous purveyor of gossip about the Borgias was one of their greatest enemies, a certain Baron Silvio Savelli, whose lands had been confiscated by the pope. Savelli hated Alexander with savage intensity. After receiving an anonymous letter from Naples that overflowed with the most scandalous details about the pontiff and his family,

Savelli had it translated into every European language and circulated it around the royal courts of Europe. The letter named Pope Alexander as 'this monster' and 'this infamous beast' and continued:

> *Who is not shocked to hear tales of the monstrous lascivity openly exhibited at the Vatican in defiance of God and all human decency? Who is not repelled by the debauchery, the incest, the obscenity of the children of the pope… the flocks of courtesans in the palace of St Peter? There is not a house of ill fame or a brothel that is not more respectable!*

Although the case was overstated in order to defame the Borgias to the maximum, these accusations hit the target for many more of the family's enemies in Rome. For years, cardinals, clerics and nobles had been crushed under the wheels of Pope Alexander's ambition, his flagrant nepotism, his greed for lands and estates, the presence in the Vatican of his mistresses and bastard children, and the insults his debauched life had offered to the Church. But it was not until 1503, when he died at the papal palace in Rome, probably of malaria, that they were able, at last, to hit back. Cesare, too, contracted the disease that had been spread through the city by clouds of mosquitoes, but he was younger and healthier and survived.

Despite, or maybe because of, his physicians' efforts, which included bleeding him regularly, Pope

A painting of the death of Pope Alexander VI by the German realist painter Wilhelm Trübner (1851–1917). Rumour had it the pope was poisoned, but it is more likely that he died of malaria.

Alexander expired after almost a week, on 18 August. The news was kept secret for several days. Nevertheless, panic gripped members of the Borgia family still in the Vatican, for they knew, as Cesare did, that with the pope gone all guarantee of their safety had disappeared with him. Some of them fled Rome immediately. Others remained behind only long enough to loot Alexander's treasury and ransack the papal apartments for gold, silver, jewels, gold and emerald cups, a gold statue of a cat with two large diamonds for eyes and the mantle of St Peter, which was covered in precious stones. The loot was hidden in the Castel Sant'Angelo and only then was the announcement made that the pope was dead. Death and the sweltering August weather had so distorted Alexander's body that it became a thing of horror to look upon. Johann Burchard recorded:

> *Its face had changed to the colour of mulberry or the blackest cloth and it was covered in blue-black spots. The nose was swollen, the mouth distended where the tongue was doubled over and the lips seemed to fill everything.*

Even when the grossly swollen corpse had been forced into its coffin, no one wanted to come near or touch it. A rumour had gone round that Pope Alexander had made a pact with the Devil in order to make himself pope in 1492, and that demons had been seen in the exact moment he had died. This may have been one of the reasons why priests at the church of St Peter refused to accept the pope's body for burial. Others were disgusted at the condition of the corpse, or the disrepute the Borgia pontiff and his family had brought on the Catholic Church. Frightening threats were required to make the priests give in, and do their funerary duty.

> For years, cardinals, clerics and nobles had been crushed under the wheels of Pope Alexander's ambition, his flagrant nepotism, his greed for lands and estates, the ... mistresses and bastard children, and the insults his debauched life had offered to the Church.

UNMOURNED BY THE CHURCH

The black reputation of the Borgias also kept most prelates in the Vatican away from the Requiem Mass normally said for departed popes, and only four made an appearance. Francesco Piccolomini, who succeeded him as Pope Pius III, banned another Mass, for the repose of Alexander's soul. 'It is blasphemous,' Pius proclaimed 'to pray for the damned.' Eventually, Alexander was buried in the Spanish national church of Santa Maria di Monserrato in Rome.

The Borgia 'empire', which had taken Alexander so many years and so much intrigue and effort to build, soon fell apart after his death. While her father lived, Lucrezia had enjoyed some importance as a link with the pope that was used by ambassadors, envoys and other hopefuls seeking papal favours. Alexander's cousin, Adriana del Mila performed a similar function, for as one contemporary diarist wrote of the house in Rome the two women shared: 'The majority of those wishing to curry favour with the pope pass through these doors.' All that came to an abrupt end once Alexander died.

CESARE AND LUCREZIA: THE END

Cesare's power vanished just as quickly. Old enemies – the Orsini, Guidobaldo da Montefeltre, Cesare's sometime brother-in-law Giovanni Sforza, the feudal lords of the Romagna – all came back to reclaim the rights and territories he had taken from them. In 1503, Alexander's greatest and most enduring enemy, Giuliani della Rovere became pope as Julius II and at once set about making it impossible for the Borgias to retain their

> Panic gripped members of the Borgia family. Some of them fled Rome immediately.

hold over the Papal States. Captured and imprisoned by Gonsalvo di Cordova, another vengeful foe with ample reason to hate all Borgias, Cesare managed to escape and ended his life in 1507 as a humble mercenary fighting for his brother-in-law, King John III of Navarre. Cesare's much misused sister, Lucrezia, died in 1519 from complications caused by her eighth pregnancy.

With Lucrezia, the last major player of the infamous Borgia era was gone, but neither she, nor her father, nor her brother Cesare have ever been forgotten. The legend of Borgia nepotism, simony debauchery, murder and dirty dealings of almost every other kind lives on and their name has become a byword for infamy that persists to this day.

The bedroom of Lucrezia Borgia in the castle at Sermoneta, in which she lived from 1500–1503, has been preserved as a museum.

THE GALILEO AFFAIR

The most fateful event in the life of Galileo Galileo actually occurred 21 years before he was born at Pisa in 1564. *De Revolutionibus Orbium Coelestium (On the Revolutions of Celestial Spheres)* by the Polish mathematician, astronomer and cleric Nikolaus Copernicus was published in 1543, the year of its author's death.

Soon the implications of the book went off like a stick of dynamite in the history of both science and the Church. Copernicus' book contradicted virtually everything the Church believed – and taught – about the Heavens and the way the Earth, the planets and the Sun operated. Galileo, to his great cost, later became a Copernican, convinced that *De Revolutionibus* stated the truth, while the Church was wrong. This was very dangerous thinking in Galileo's time. In endorsing and then spreading ideas that fundamentally challenged the teachings of the Church, Copernicus and his followers were vulnerable to charges of heresy. The Church and the papacy could be utterly ruthless in their efforts to suppress any opinion on any subject that diverged from the truth as they upheld it. This attitude had noticeably hardened since the middle of the sixteenth century, when the breakaway Protestants confronted the Catholic Church with the most fundamental threat it had ever faced.

Galileo Galilei (left) made astronomical observations that persuaded him of the veracity of the theories of Nikolaus Copernicus (above). Copernicus's book on planetary movements, *De Revolutionibus,* revolutionized the science of astronomy.

This may have been a reason why Copernicus took the precaution of flattering Pope Paul III by dedicating

THE CHURCH VS THE COPERNICANS

The beliefs championed by the Church derived from the theories of two astronomers of ancient Greece, Aristotle who lived in the fourth century BCE and Ptolemy, who lived in the second century CE. Within the medieval Church, their theories were held to be immutable truths confirmed by Holy Scripture. According to the Aristotelians, as the supporters of Aristotle were known, these truths were, therefore, impossible to change and heresy to challenge. The ancient, geocentric theory held that Earth was sited, motionless, at the centre of the Universe while the Sun revolved round it. One of the 'proofs' for this Earth-centred theory could be found in the Bible, where in Psalm 104, verse 5, it says: 'He set the earth on its foundations; it can never be moved.'

Copernicus' heliocentric (Sun-centred) theory disputed this statement, maintaining that it was the Sun that occupied the centre of the Universe, and was circled by the Earth and the other planets of the Solar System, which were then known as 'wandering stars'. The Sun might appear to move across the sky during the day, but this, Copernicus maintained, was an optical illusion: the appearance of movement came from the motion of the orbiting Earth.

De Revolutionibus to him and also why he held back from having his book published in his lifetime. The decision was prescient. The heliocentric theory escaped religious condemnation for only three years after the death of Copernicus, until 1546, when a Dominican monk, Giovanni Maria Tolosani, denounced his ideas

> In endorsing and then spreading ideas that fundamentally challenged the teachings of the Church, Copernicus and his followers were vulnerable to charges of heresy.

and strongly asserted the unquestionable truth of Scripture. Criticism went little further than that for the moment, but in around 1609, when official action was taken to suppress the work of Copernicus, it was Galileo Galilei who first came into the firing line.

GALILEO IN VENICE

In Pisa, Galileo was considered an arrogant upstart for consistently seeking to prove that concepts of science approved by the Church were mistaken. He became so unpopular that, in 1592, he left for another university, in Padua, located in the rich and powerful Republic of

An engraving of Pope Paul III. Copernicus dedicated his book *De Revolutionibus* to the pontiff as a means of flattering him and hopefully averting criticism from the Church.

PROTESTANTS V CATHOLICS

Since its earliest days, the Christian Church had had its breakaway groups, dissenters, sects and schisms. But none of them equalled the major shift in faith that occurred during the Reformation, when the Protestant movement broke away from the Catholic Church, renounced the jurisdiction of the Pope and set up its own beliefs and style of Christian worship. This greatest schism of them all is still in evidence today. The fundamental break between the Protestant and Catholic faiths was set off on 31 October 1517 by Martin Luther, a German monk, theologian and university professor. Luther wrote to Albrecht, the archbishop of Mainz and Magdeburg criticizing the activities of Peter Tetzel, a Dominican friar and Pope Leo X's commissioner for indulgences. Tetzel was in Germany to sell indulgences as a means of raising money to rebuild St Peter's Basilica in Rome.

Catholics classed donating money to the Church, through indulgences or any other means, as 'good works', but Luther did not agree. In his Disputation *...on the Power and Efficacy of Indulgences,* later known as *The 95 Theses,* which he attached to his letter, Luther insisted that only God could grant forgiveness for sins and that salvation could not be acquired by buying indulgences.

But the dispute over indulgences was only the start. Luther also attacked the Catholic practice of barring Christians from reading the Bible for themselves, and instead insisting that they must have 'ignorant' and 'wicked' priests explain it to them. Instead of the Catholic concept of the pope as the mediator between God and Jesus Christ on behalf of humanity, the Protestants maintained that Jesus was the only mediator. The only means of obtaining eternal salvation, the Protestants asserted, was through faith in Christ, rather than charitable works, as the Catholics believed.

The Reformation and the Catholic response, known as the Counter-Reformation, eventually changed the map of Europe, with the north turning largely Protestant and the south remaining Catholic. In Galileo's time, the dispute between the two churches remained a controversial issue and, as Galileo himself discovered, the much-feared Inquisition and its horrifying methods were put in place to crush any sign of heresy or dissent which might lead to further fracturing.

Venice. This proved to be a beneficial change of scene. The Venetian Republic had a much more tolerant attitude towards dissent than other Italian city-states and vastly more than Rome, where police-style methods were used to stamp it out. In Padua, Galileo mixed with highly ranked, influential Venetians and was able to discuss his ideas with much greater freedom than the situation in Pisa had allowed. In this healthier intellectual atmosphere, Galileo explored the science of ballistics and invented the thermoscope, an early form of the thermometer, and the geometric compass, a type of pocket calculator.

INVENTION OF THE TELESCOPE

Then, in 1609 Galileo heard talk of a spyglass, later renamed the telescope, a new invention pioneered by a German optician, Hans Lipperhey. At once, Galileo recognized the telescope as a huge leap forward in optics that could revolutionize the practice of astronomy. He set about constructing his own telescope, which was much more powerful than Lipperhey's original, magnifying objects two or three times over. Subsequently, Galileo built another telescope with 32-times magnification, which he believed could show him the true magnificence of the heavens, and open the way to new discoveries.

On an icy night in January 1610, Galileo wrapped himself in a thick cloak, climbed to the highest room of his house in Padua and spent the hours until dawn surveying the sky. He did the same the next night, and the next, until he had recorded a full month of observations. The record was a revelation. Almost everywhere he looked, Galileo found that the Heavens differed fundamentally from the sky according to Aristotle, Ptolemy and the popular notions that stemmed from their theories. The Moon was not

GALILEO CHALLENGES THE POPE

Galileo had argued against the official papal line on astronomy and the sciences ever since he was in his mid-twenties and gave public lectures in mathematics at Bologna in 1588. The following year, he moved on to teach the subject at the University of Pisa. The mathematics Galileo was supposed to impart to his students was, of course, the sort that had been handed down from ancient times. What he taught instead was that the theories of Aristotle and Ptolemy were not always correct. For one thing, Galileo challenged Aristotle's ideas about falling objects. Heavy objects, he said, did not fall faster than lighter ones, as Aristotle maintained. Galileo proved his theory by dropping two different-sized cannon balls from the top of the bell tower at Pisa, commonly known as the Leaning Tower of Pisa. The cannon balls reached the ground at virtually the same time, although one hit the ground measurably later than the other. Despite the small discrepancy, Galileo maintained that Aristotle's ideas had been disproved.

The scene at the Leaning Tower of Pisa in around 1589 when, according to his secretary, Galileo disproved the theory that heavy objects fall faster than lighter objects.

GALILEO'S SUPERNOVA

In 1604, Galileo witnessed a supernova, an exploding star, which led him to challenge Aristotle's view that the state of the heavens as seen from Earth was permanent and unchanging. A supernova, Galileo believed, proved beyond doubt that this idea was false. For a start, it showed that the lifetime of a star was finite.

One way in which a supernova occurs arises after the core of an ageing star ceases to generate energy. After that, it collapses into a neutron star or black hole, heats up to explosion point and blows up, driving its outer layers deep into space. At that juncture, the supernova can illuminate the entire sky with a massive burst of radiation and may remain in view for several weeks or months before fading away.

Galileo was fortunate to witness this most spectacular display because supernovae occur only once in a half-century and being in the right place at the right time in order to witness one of them usually requires regular night-time surveillance of the stars. In addition, Galileo observed his supernova without the aid of a telescope, which was not invented until 1609.

An intriguing aspect of this event is that the supernova Galileo saw in 1604 must have exploded thousands or even million of years previously: the Universe is so unimaginably vast that the explosion could take all that time to travel through space until it came within sight of Earth. By then, of course, the star itself was long dead and gone.

Galileo drew diagrams of planets, including Earth, in motion around the Sun. This was contrary to church teachings which held that the Sun orbited the Earth.

Galileo spent many hours observing the stars and planets through his telescope.

smooth, as Aristotle had taught, but rough and pitted with craters. Earth was not the only planet to have a satellite: Galileo observed four moons orbiting the planet Jupiter. He also saw proof that Venus, like Earth, orbited the Sun.

MESSENGER OF THE STARS

Galileo wrote a short book, *The Messenger of the Stars,* about Jupiter and its newly discovered moons. It was an instant bestseller and all 550 copies printed sold out within a week of publication in March of 1610. The book created great excitement, for Galileo had revealed a vast new area of knowledge and understanding. One of Galileo's admirers at this time was Cardinal Maffeo Barberini, a member of a very rich, very powerful family that was influential in Rome and Florence. Barberini first met Galileo in 1611 and appreciated the astronomer's punchy manner and his skill in debate. His admiration was so great that he once wrote to Galileo: 'I pray the Lord God to preserve you, because men of great value like you deserve to live a long time to the benefit of the public.'

However, Barberini was very much a man of the world and was too astute not to know a dissenter when he saw one. He was also wary enough of the direction Galileo's work was taking to make sure that he kept up to date with his research. At some point,

SIDEREVS
NVNCIVS
MAGNA, LONGEQVE ADMIRABILIA
Spectacula pandens, suspiciendaque proponens
vnicuique, præsertim verò
PHILOSOPHIS, atq; ASTRONOMIS, quæ à
GALILEO GALILEO
PATRITIO FLORENTINO
Patauini Gymnasij Publico Mathematico
PERSPICILLI
Nuper à se reperti beneficio sunt obseruata in LVNÆ FACIE, FIXIS INNVMERIS, LACTEO CIRCVLO, STELLIS NEBVLOSIS,
Apprime verò in
QVATVOR PLANETIS
Circa IOVIS Stellam disparibus interuallis, atque periodis, celeritate mirabili circumuolutis; quos, nemini in hanc vsque diem cognitos, nouissimè Author depræhendit primus; atque
MEDICEA SIDERA
NVNCVPANDOS DECREVIT.
VENETIIS, Apud Thomam Baglionum. M DC X.
Superiorum Permissu, & Priuilegio.

The frontispiece of Galileo's book *Sidereus Nuncius* (*The Messenger of the Stars*), published in 1610. The book contained his observations of the night sky, made over a full month.

the Cardinal was sure, he would have to warn Galileo away from taking his discoveries too far and so treading on territory where the Inquisition would be waiting for him.

> At some point the Cardinal was sure, he would have to warn Galileo away from taking his discoveries too far ...

Partly, the Cardinal's caution was sparked by a change of heart in papal circles about the value and veracity of *De Revolutionibus*. The publication of Copernicus' groundbreaking book had been pioneered by less conservative churchmen who had pressured Pope Paul III to accept the author's dedication to him.

Subsequently Paul III, who served as pope between 1534 and 49, and another pontiff, Gregory XIII, who was elected in 1572, gave their approval to some of the doctrines, which *De Revolutionibus* contained.

But Paul was not really happy about sanctioning Copernicus' ideas. In 1542 he revived the Inquisition for a reason that had nothing to do with the Polish astronomer and his theories: it was aimed at suppressing the Protestants who were fracturing the Church with their own revolutionary concept of Christianity. But as time was to prove, Paul's new Roman Inquisition would serve for any other charge of heresy that popes, present or future, might care to bring.

The Inquisition was used for precisely this purpose after 1614, when a priest called Father Tommaso Caccini denounced Galileo and his 'heretical' opinions concerning the motion of the Earth, as set out in *The Messenger of the Stars*. The import of Galileo's book

Galileo demonstrates his telescope to Venetian nobles in 1610. This telescope was able to magnify 32 times and was more powerful than any that preceded it.

and the observations it recorded were clear for all to see: it inferred that the Church had been peddling inaccuracies and, far from revealing God's truth to the people, they had been concealing it.

By this time, Galileo had gathered a degree of support for his Copernican ideas in the universities, among the intelligentsia and even in the Church. This popularity, combined with the perils of Protestantism, made Galileo's teachings appear all the more dangerous.

Galileo's book inferred that the Church had been peddling inaccuracies and, far from revealing God's truth to the people, they had been concealing it.

Galileo's position was not helped by the publication of a pamphlet written by one of his acquaintances, the Carmelite cleric Paolo Antonio Foscarini, in which he defended Copernicus and his heliocentric theory. Foscarini tried to have it both ways, stating that it was possible to justify Copernicus with quotations from the Bible. Cardinal Robert Bellarmine, a Jesuit and one of the few to hold the title Doctor of the Church, soon saw through Foscarini's device and wrote to him in very stern terms:

> *To want to affirm that in reality the Sun is at the centre of the world and only turns on itself without moving from east to west, and the Earth...revolves with great speed about the sun...is a very dangerous thing, likely not only to irritate all scholastic philosophers and theologians, but also to harm the Holy Faith by rendering Holy Scripture false.*

Foscarini's book was considered so seditious and heretical it was soon placed on the Index of Prohibited Books. The Foscarini affair, widely viewed as a scandal in papal circles, prompted virulent anti-Copernican feeling still simmering by the time Galileo arrived in Rome. In this atmosphere, there was little chance Galileo could obtain an unbiased hearing for his own views. Even so, he did get a warning from his friend Cardinal Barberini. Barberini did not confront Galileo personally but instead sent a secretary, Giovanni Ciampoli, who idolized the astronomer, to tell him:

> *Signor Cardinal Barberini who, as you know from experience, has always admired your qualities, said to me yesterday evening that he would appreciate greater caution in this issue, to avoid going beyond the reasoning of Ptolemy or Copernicus or finally that you should not pass beyond the limits of physics or mathematics, because the theologians claim that interpreting Scripture is their prerogative.*

Cardinal Roberto Bellarmine, an eminent theologian, treated Galileo far less tactfully. Bellarmine was a Jesuit, a member of an organization that made loyalty to the teachings of the Catholic Church its first rule of obedience. Bellarmine, therefore, had never deviated from the Church's view that the positions and

An engraving of Cardinal Bellarmine, who warned Galileo that he must not support or defend the 'heretical' theories of Copernicus.

GALILEO'S LETTERS

Galileo wrote numerous letters to high-ranking churchmen, and also to his own students in which he justified his Copernican-influenced theories. In one of his letters, originally written in 1613, but later expanded into the Letter to the Grand Duchess Christina of Tuscany, he pointed out the vast difference between the faith-led mentality and the scientific approach. Galileo wrote:

> *Some years ago I discovered in the heavens many things that had not been seen before our own age. The novelty of these things…stirred up against me no small number of professors…. Showing a greater fondness for their own opinions than for truth, they sought to deny and disprove the new things, which, if they had cared to look for themselves, their own senses would have demonstrated to them. To this end, they hurled various charges and published numerous writings filled with vain arguments…. Men who were well grounded in astronomical and physical science were persuaded as soon as they received my first message. Well the passage of time has revealed to everyone the truths that I previously set forth…*

This was a case of irresistible force meeting immovable object, for, as the wording of his letter shows, Galileo was arrogantly confident that he was in the right while his opponents, the so-called Aristotelians, were equally certain that the truth was on their side. But Galileo should not have been so sure that 'everyone' agreed with him. In 1616, when he made a special journey to Rome to defend himself against Caccini's allegations, he encountered the full might of the Church and the papacy as they set their faces implacably against him.

The Grand Duchess Christina of Tuscany, born in 1565, was a grand-daughter of Catherine de' Medici. Galileo wrote his Letter to Christina on the relationship between religious revelation and science in 1615.

functions of the Sun and the Earth were as the Bible stated. According to the Cardinal, all scholars who studied the Scriptures 'agreed in interpreting them literally as teaching that the Sun is in the Heavens and revolves around the Earth with immense speed and the Earth is very distant from the Heavens at the centre of the universe, and motionless. Consider, then,' Bellarmine continued, 'whether the Church can tolerate that the Scriptures should be interpreted in a manner contrary to that of the Holy Fathers and of all... commentators, both Latin and Greek.'

Galileo was never going to get past a cast-iron attitude like this, any more than he could dissuade those priests who looked through his telescope at the Moon and concluded that since the instrument was artificial, then the heavily cratered surface they saw through it must be artificial, too.

COPERNICUS'S BOOK IS BANNED

It was not surprising then, that Bellarmine went much further than Barberini's kindly meant, softly worded admonition and told Galileo bluntly that an edict had been promulgated in February of 1616 utterly condemning the heliocentric doctrine as heretical. A month later, on 5 March 1616, *De Revolutionibus* was listed on the Index of banned books. From then on, anyone who sought to promote or even discuss Copernicus' theory of the stationary Sun and the moving Earth was a heretic and, Bellarmine added, the Inquisition knew very well how to deal with them.

Bellarmine's warning thoroughly alarmed Galileo, which was precisely the Cardinal's intention. Galileo was well aware of the punishments for heresy – interrogation, torture and incarceration and, for those found guilty, death by burning at the stake. There was, for instance, the precedent of a Dominican friar, Giordano Bruno, who was burned to death in 1600 for suggesting, like Copernicus and Galileo, that the Earth moved around the Sun. Bruno compounded his 'heresy' by suggesting that there were other worlds in the Universe like Earth, with their satellites and Sun. With such an example of the extreme dangers of heresy staring him in the face, Galileo seems to have thought twice about promoting Copernicus' theories as blatantly as he had done before. Galileo was, in any case, now 52 years old, which was considered quite elderly in the seventeenth century, and his health had been poor for some time. It seemed prudent, therefore, to lie low for a while.

A Dominican friar, Giordano Bruno, was burned to death in 1600 for suggesting that the Earth moved around the Sun.

HOME TO ARCETI

After he returned from Rome, Galileo lived at Arceti, his house near Florence and appeared to have been tamed by his unpleasant encounter with Bellarmine and the threats of the Inquisition. He studied three comets that appeared, flashing through the sky over Florence, in the autumn and early winter of 1616 and wrote a book about his findings entitled *The Assayer*, which was published in 1623. For the rest, Galileo assumed the leisurely life of a country gentleman, taking rides through the countryside on his mule, or hawking with his falcon

This statue of the Dominican monk Giordano Bruno was erected in the Campo de Fiori, Rome where he burned at the stake in 1600 for supporting Copernicus' theory and other heretical ideas.

A portrait by Gian Lorenzo Bernini (1598–1680) of Pope Urban VIII: sometime friend, but ultimately bitter enemy of Galileo.

FACT DISGUISED AS FICTION

Fact dressed up as fiction or, in the case of Galileo's *Dialogo,* as imaginary discussion, had already been used in 1611 by Johannes Kepler, the German mathematician and astronomer who was a contemporary of Galileo and another adherent of Copernicus' heliocentric theory. Kepler's *Somnia, (The Dream)* made a treatise on interplanetary travel read as if it were a fantasy about a journey to the Moon, and has since been called the first work of science fiction. There was, of course, no guarantee that the Inquisition would fall for the trick the likes of Galileo or Kepler was playing on them, and *Somnia* led to alarming consequences for Kepler's mother Katherina. In 1617, she was accused of witchcraft on the basis of her son's book. Fortunately, the old lady was acquitted and released in 1621, mainly due to Kepler's vigorous arguments in her defence.

Nevertheless, the danger involved was all too evident and Galileo wanted to take no chances. He decided to deliver the finished manuscript of his *Dialogo* to Rome in person and see it through the approval and printing processes. He was asked to make small changes – nothing too drastic – and the book was finally published in February of 1632. It was an instant success and sold out a very short time after it went on display in the bookshops.

Johannes Kepler, born in Germany in 1571, was an astronomer, astrologer and mathematician. A key figure in the 17th-century revolution in astronomy, he was best known for his laws of planetary motion.

The frontispiece of Galileo's *Dialogo Dei Massimi Sistemi* (*Dialogue concerning the Two Chief World Systems*) the controversial book that destroyed his lifelong friendship with Pope Urban VIII.

on his wrist. At other times, he tended the vines he grew in his garden. But this backwater existence provided precious little stimulation for Galileo's lively mind. The situation could not go on for much longer.

In 1623, Cardinal Barberini had been elected pope as Urban VIII. This seemed to be a piece of good fortune for Galileo because, despite the showdown in Rome in 1616, he had remained close friends with Barberini and the two had exchanged an ongoing correspondence ever since. As a compliment to the new pope, Galileo dedicated his book *The Assayer* to him. Urban was so impressed with it that he ordered

The universe according to the Ancient Greek astronomer and mathematician Ptolemy, showing Earth at the centre with the Sun orbiting around it.

extracts from the book read at public meetings. He also invited Galileo to visit him in Rome but ill health prevented the astronomer from taking up the invitation until the spring of 1624.

Pope Urban came to meet Galileo when he arrived and the friends soon made up for lost time with regular meetings – six over the next five weeks. Together they strolled through the Vatican gardens spending many hours talking and exchanging ideas, including Copernicus' heliocentric theory. Galileo left Rome at the end of his visit on 8 June 1624, taking with him a letter to the Grand Duke Ferdinando II in which Pope Urban eulogized his friend as 'a great man whose fame shines in the Heavens and goes on Earth far and wide'. Praise indeed, and it encouraged Galileo to believe that the debate about the heliocentric theory, so savagely closed down in 1616, could be safely reopened.

> Galileo assumed the leisurely life of a country gentleman, taking rides ... hawking with his falcon on his wrist. At other times, he tended the vines he grew in his garden.

GALILEO'S *DIALOGO*

Galileo now planned to write another book, *Dialogo Dei Massimo Sistemi (Dialogue Concerning the Two Chief World Systems)*, this time in the form of a three-way conversation, with two characters discussing the theories of Copernicus and the third putting forward the views of Ptolemy. By using fictional characters reciting lines as in a stage play, Galileo imagined he might get round objections from the Inquisition and the Sacred Congregation of the Index. (The Sacred Congregation was the body within the Catholic Church that decided on which books were 'heretical' and should therefore not be read by Catholics.)

This painting by Joseph-Nicolas Robert-Fleury (1797–1890) portrays the 68-year-old Galileo Galilei (centre) on trial for heresy in Rome in 1633.

Even so, his experience in Rome in 1616 had made him wary of upsetting the papal authorities. They had it in their power to destroy any idea with which they did not concur, and do the same to whoever put forward or supported that idea. Galileo took the precaution of testing the content of the *Dialogo* on the Jesuit jurist Francesco Ingoli, who had once criticized his Copernican views. Galileo wrote to Ingoli, putting the arguments in favour of Copernicus' and the heliocentric theory, but he was careful to add: 'I do not undertake this task with the aim of supporting as true a proposition that has already been declared suspect and repugnant.' Instead, Galileo continued, he wanted to set out all the arguments for and against Copernicus so that all might be fairly judged.

Ingoli received Galileo's letter in Rome in December 1624. Galileo waited anxiously for a furious reaction from Pope Urban, but there were no fireworks, no irate demands that the astronomer return to Rome immediately and explain himself and no rumblings from the Inquisition. Believing the

> Using fictional characters reciting lines as in a stage play, Galileo imagined he might get round objections from the Inquisition…

coast was clear Galileo went ahead with the *Dialogo.* It proved to be a monumental work, running to some 500 pages and taking six years to complete. It was a painful process, too. Galileo was 66 years old by the time the task was finished and suffered badly from arthritis, which made writing difficult for him.

Pope Urban could never play the game in which authors used verbal trickery to avoid censure by the religious authorities while still disseminating their heretical ideas.

In producing his *Dialogo,* Galileo resorted to a device often used by scientists in Catholic Europe, which was to disguise controversial information by presenting their theories as nothing but intellectual exercises or giving them the appearance of fiction.

Galileo was understandably pleased with himself when *Dialogo* was approved, but there was one important thing he had overlooked. He failed to realize that Pope Urban could never play the game in which authors used verbal trickery to avoid censure by the religious authorities while still disseminating their heretical ideas. In this, Galileo may have mistaken the latitude Urban had allowed him as a cardinal: friend or no friend, this was not possible for Urban as pope. It had grown even more impossible because in 1625 news reached Rome that the German Protestants, the great enemies of the Catholic Church, had accepted the heliocentric theory.

In supporting the theories of Ptolemy, like all popes before him, Urban was peddling the brainstorms of a fool.

The pope's new hard-line attitude became all too clear to Galileo after he presented Urban with a copy of the *Dialogo.* Urban was incandescent with rage when he saw what Galileo had done with Simplicius, the character who voiced the opinions representing Ptolemy. Whereas the other two voices, Salviati, a scientist and Sagredo, an intellectual, made sense when they spoke for Copernicus and his theories, Simplicius, as the name suggested, expressed himself like an idiot and a buffoon. As one of Galileo's admiring friends, Tomasso Campanella put it:

> *Simplicius seems to be the plaything of this philosophical comedy, which at one and the same time, shows up the foolishness of his sect, the empty words, the instability and obstinacy and whatever else you like to mention.*

Not only was Simplicius ridiculed throughout the book, Galileo managed to get in a sly dig at the Aristotelians, writing that they were 'content to adore shadows, philosophizing not with due circumspection but merely from having memorized a few ill-understood principles'. Even worse was the notion, put about by infuriated Aristotelians, that Simplicius was a caricature of Pope Urban himself.

END OF A LONG FRIENDSHIP

Whether or not that was Galileo's intention, Urban, it seems, believed it was. Galileo's message was obvious. In supporting the theories of Ptolemy, like all popes before him, Urban was peddling the brainstorms of a fool. No wonder Urban was so incensed and sadly, his friendship with Galileo died there and then. Understandably, Urban felt betrayed and just as he could be an effusive friend, he could also be an implacable enemy. As Francesco Niccolini, the Tuscan ambassador in Rome, wrote of Pope Urban:

> *When his Holiness gets something into his head, that is the end of the matter, especially if one is opposing, threatening or defying him, since then he hardens and shows no respect to anyone.... This investigation is really going to be a troublesome affair.*

Niccolini was right. Towards the end of 1632, Galileo was summoned to Rome where he was ordered to appear before the Inquisition. Galileo tried desperately to postpone the evil hour, pleading ill health and the outbreak of plague in Florence, which would make it dangerous for him to move. But Urban was adamant. The astronomer, now 68 years old, was medically

A suspected heretic being tortured by the Inquisition in the 17th century. The Virgin Mary and the baby Jesus 'watch' the scene from an adjacent wall.

examined and judged fit to travel. Urban decreed that unless he was found to be gravely ill, virtually dying in fact, he should be arrested and forcibly brought to Rome. Rather than suffer such humiliation at the hands of his former friend, Galileo left Florence of his own volition on 20 January 1633. He spent a short time in quarantine at Acquapendente 198km (123 miles) from Florence, and after being cleared, arrived in Rome three weeks later, on 13 February. There, he stayed at the Villa Medici as a guest of Francesco Niccolini, a concession he was allowed, despite Urban's enmity, because of his age and his parlous state of health.

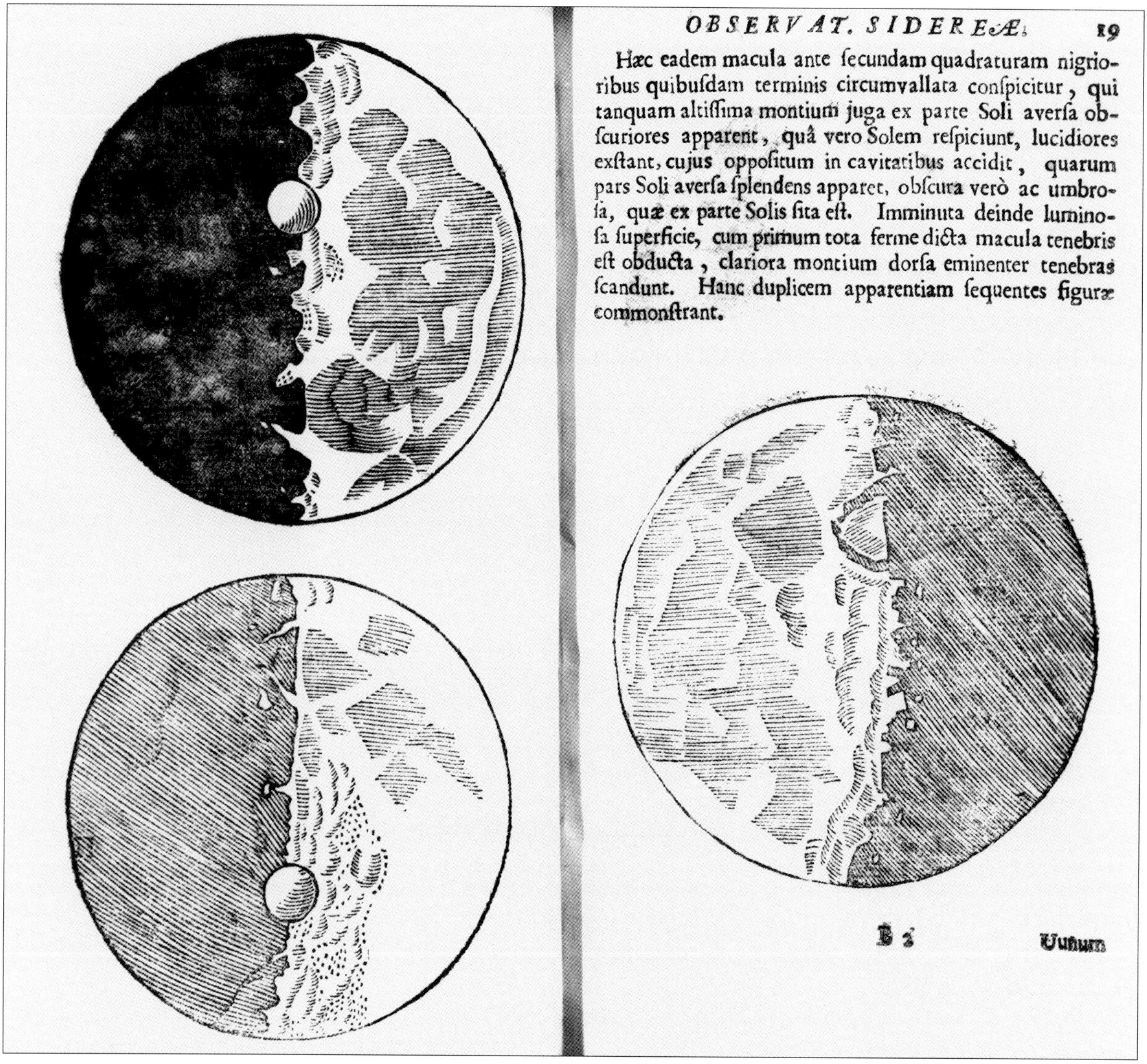
OBSERVAT. SIDEREÆ. 19

Hæc eadem macula ante ſecundam quadraturam nigrioribus quibuſdam terminis circumvallata conſpicitur, qui tanquam altiſſima montium juga ex parte Soli averſa obſcuriores apparent, quâ vero Solem reſpiciunt, lucidiores exſtant, cujus oppoſitum in cavitatibus accidit, quarum pars Soli averſa ſplendens apparet, obſcura verò ac umbroſa, quæ ex parte Solis ſita eſt. Imminuta deinde luminoſa ſuperficie, cum primum tota ferme dicta macula tenebris eſt obducta, clariora montium dorſa eminenter tenebras ſcandunt. Hanc duplicem apparentiam ſequentes figuræ commonſtrant.

B 2 Uunum

This page from a 1653 edition of *The Messenger of the Stars* shows Galileo's sketches of the cratered surface of the moon. His discovery of earth-like mountains and valleys on the moon challenged the view that the heavens were perfect and unchanging.

Galileo was obliged to wait two months before he was finally interrogated. The reason for the delay was that the Inquisition could not make up its mind how his case should be handled. Urban had always been sure that there could be no scientific or theological proof for the heliocentric theory, but others at the Holy Office were not so certain, and feared that if such proof were actually forthcoming, it might result in the revelation that God, the Bible, the pope and the Catholic Church had made a fundamental mistake. That would be embarrassing to say the least but, at worst, it could have detrimental consequences for the credibility of the Holy See.

As if this were not enough, there was also the problem of how to prosecute a man as famous and admired as Galileo, who was also the author of a book, the *Dialogo,* approved by the Friar Master of the Sacred Palace, the papal court at the Vatican. Pope Urban, it seemed, knew nothing about it and denied ordering a licence to be granted for the publication. Yet, the book had been published and scored a great success. Much as he wanted to come down hard on his one-time friend and bring the *Dialogo* into court as prosecution evidence, even Pope Urban could see that using the book to discredit Galileo was not an option.

After weeks of agonizing over these problems, the Holy Office of the Inquisition at last decided to proceed with the trial. Galileo was interrogated on

the Holy Office ... feared that if such proof were actually forthcoming, it might result in the revelation that God, the Bible, the pope and the Catholic Church had made a fundamental mistake.

12 April 1633. Under questioning, he stoutly maintained that he not deviated from the ban on *De Revolutionibus* or the opinion against Copernicus' heliocentric theory as set out in the Edict of 1616. Furthermore, he had presented the Copernican theory as a hypothesis only and denied that he had ever said it was true.

GALILEO IN DANGER

Galileo's dogged line of defence put the Holy Office in a quandary. If the Inquisition were to save face, as they must, it could not simply let Galileo go unpunished. One possible alternative was simply to ban the *Dialogo* and place it on the list of prohibited books, like Copernicus' *De Revolutionibus,* but that, of course, would amount to letting Galileo off the hook. Pope Urban came out firmly against the idea that the book should be condemned, but not its author. Nothing would do but to prosecute and reach the guilty verdict Galileo's former friend clearly desired.

Normally, at this stage, suspected heretics were handed over to the Inquisition to be tortured until they confessed. The inquisitors gave the accused a last chance to recant by showing them the instruments of torture, which were often blessed by priests before they were used, regarded as they were by the Church as holy tools by which God enabled the Inquisition to return deviants to the one 'true' faith.

It was highly likely that Galileo knew about these instruments and the agony they could inflict. It was not normal practice for the Inquisition to torture the elderly though it remains unknown just how far Galileo, nearly 70 years old in 1633, believed that he would be excused torture on account of his age. However, for a frail and frightened old man, worn down by ill health and anxiety, the mere threat of torture could have sufficed in order to achieve the only other alternative open to the Inquisition: pressurizing Galileo to wear him down until at last he gave in out of sheer fright and exhaustion.

The instruments of torture... were often blessed by priests before they were used. [They were] regarded by the Church as holy tools.

Nearly three weeks after his first appearance before the Inquisition, Galileo returned to the court on 30 April and admitted that in writing the *Dialogo,* his judgement had been bad. He said:

> *I freely confess that in several places, it seemed to me that I set forth in such a form that a reader ignorant of my real purpose might have reason to suppose that the arguments on the false side, and which it was my intention to confute, were so expressed as to be calculated rather to compel conviction by their cogency than to be easy of solution.*

A HUMILIATING CONFESSION

Galileo went further and humiliated himself by confessing to 'vainglorious ambition'. After being forced to make this craven statement, Galileo was taken down to the dungeons of the Holy Office where he spent three weeks before appearing again in front of the Inquisition. He was there formally to renounce Copernicus and his theory and present the inquisitors with a written admission of his wrongdoing. He now realized, he said, that the *Dialogo* had 'accidentally' supported the Copernican view of the heavens whereas the Church had correctly ruled that this view was wrong. Afterwards, on the orders of Pope Urban, Galileo's renunciation was disseminated throughout Catholic Europe, where it was read out in all churches so that all Catholics would know that the great Galileo Galilei had been broken by the will of the Inquisition.

His humiliating submission and the pope's vindictiveness hurt Galileo deeply. He was furious and bitter at his treatment by the Inquisition and his erstwhile friend, who had forced him to make a truly painful sacrifice. He had, after all, been forced to deny

the work and the beliefs of a lifetime for the sake of a mistaken theory he knew in his heart was totally wrong. Galileo was still defiant, despite his abject recantation. Niccoloni, together with Galileo's other friends, had to work hard to persuade him to be amenable, even acquiescent, for if he persisted Pope Urban and the Inquisition could unleash upon him their armoury of punishments. If that happened, it was unlikely that the old astronomer could escape a second time. It took Niccolini some time to get through to him. He wrote:

> *He claimed, nevertheless, that he could defend his opinions very well, but I exhorted him, with the aim of getting things over quickly, not to struggle to uphold them, but to submit to whatever the (Inquisition) might desire him to believe.... He was greatly afflicted by this, and for myself, I have seen what he has landed in as a result of this, and I have great doubts about the safety of his life.*

PRONOUNCED GUILTY

On 22 June 1633, Galileo returned for the last time to the Inquisition, this time to hear his fate. He was dressed for the occasion in long white robes and the conical hat of a repentant sinner and knelt before his judges to hear his sentence. The Inquisition pronounced Galileo guilty of 'heinous crimes' and ruled that he was 'vehemently suspected of heresy'. Galileo replied,' I curse and detest (my) errors and heresies.'

Galileo had, after all, been forced to deny the work and the beliefs of a lifetime for the sake of a mistaken theory he knew in his heart was totally wrong.

His book, *Dialogo* was banned and remained on the Index of Prohibited Books for nearly 200 years. Galileo himself was sentenced to lifelong imprisonment. Afterwards, he was taken down to the dungeons beneath the Holy Office once again and might have stayed there but for the intervention of the young Cardinal Francesco Barberini, the nephew of Pope Urban VIII. Barberini was a great admirer of

John Milton, (right) the English author and poet best known for *Paradise Lost*, visited a rather unwell Galileo (second from left) in 1638, while the astronomer was under house arrest at Arceti, near Florence.

VATICAN VOCABULARY

LIMBO AND PURGATORY

Although Limbo is not an official feature of the Roman Catholic religion, it is connected to it. The word is taken from the Latin *limbus*, meaning edge, and describes a condition experienced in the afterlife by people who die in original sin, but have not been assigned to Gehenna, the Hell of the damned. Purgatory is frequently taken to describe a place of fearful suffering where the souls of sinners atone for their wrongdoings and undergo terrible punishments. In fact, the Catholic Church views purgatory in a much more optimistic light, as a situation where souls of those who die in a state of grace are purified and given temporary punishment, where appropriate. This process prepares them to go to Heaven. Buying an indulgence during life could lessen the length of time a sinner had to spend in limbo or purgatory before their soul was allowed to go on to heaven in the afterlife.

Galileo, and he managed to persuade his uncle to allow the astronomer to return to the Tuscan Embassy. Ambassador Niccolini was alarmed at the state Galileo was in. 'It is a fearful thing,' he wrote, 'to have to do with the Inquisition. The poor man has come back more dead than alive.'

> Galileo ... remained under house arrest, a prisoner of the Inquisition, forbidden ... to return to teaching.

Niccolini agitated for Galileo to be allowed to go home to Florence. Pope Urban refused but did permit the disgraced astronomer to move to the home of Ascanio Piccolomini, Archbishop of Siena, where he suffered a nervous breakdown. Galileo remained with Piccolomini in order to recover for the next five months. It was not until the end of 1633 that Galileo was allowed to return home to Arceti. Even there, though, he remained under house arrest, a prisoner of the Inquisition, forbidden to receive fellow scholars or scientists as visitors or to return to teaching.

But he could still write and at Arceti he worked on a new book he had started while staying with Piccolomini entitled *Two New Sciences,* about the sciences of mechanics and motion. However, his disgrace at the hands of the Inquisition made Italian publishers afraid to print it. The Inquisition stood in Galileo's way in Venice and Jesuits ruined his chances of publication in Germany. Eventually, Galileo's friends resorted to smuggling the manuscript over the Alps into the Protestant Netherlands, where papal writ did not extend. The book finally appeared in June of 1638. By this time, Galileo had so ruined his eyes gazing at the stars through his telescopes he had become blind. He was never able to read the printed copy of his last book.

> Galileo had so ruined his eyes gazing at the stars through his telescopes he had become blind.

THE DEATH OF GALILEO

Towards the end of 1641, the fever that had afflicted Galileo every winter returned once more, but this time there was no recovery. Galileo died on 8 January 1642 a few weeks before his seventy-eighth birthday. Even in death, Pope Urban remained vengeful. He refused to allow his one-time friend to be accorded a public funeral and sat firmly on the pleas of the great astronomer's friend, the mathematician Vincenzio Viviani that Galileo deserved a monument. Urban's reasons were that through his sins against God and the Catholic Church, Galileo had given rise to 'the greatest scandal in Christendom'. Instead, Galileo was hidden away in a modest grave in the cellar of the church of Santa Croce in Florence.

Almost a century later, in 1737, Pope Clement XII ordered a proper tomb and monument built for Galileo in Santa Croce. But another 350 years were to pass before Pope John Paul II in 1992 reversed the judgments of 1616 and 1633 and confirmed that Galileo had been right.

Galileo's tomb and monument were constructed in 1737 at the Santa Croce church in Florence by Pope Clement XII. By this time, more than a century had passed since Galileo's death.

GALILAEVS GALILEIVS PATRIC. FLOR.
GEOMETRIAE ASTRONOMIAE PHILOSOPHIAE MAXIMVS RESTITVTOR
NVLLI AETATIS SVAE COMPARANDVS
HIC BENE QVIESCAT
VIX. A. LXXVIII. OBIIT. A. CIↃ. IↃ. C. XXXXI.
CVRANTIBVS AETERNVM PATRIAE DECVS
X. VIRIS PATRICIIS SACRAE HVIVS AEDIS PRAEFECTIS
MONIMENTVM A VINCENTIO VIVIANIO MAGISTRI CINERI SIBIQVE SIMVL
TESTAMENTO F. I.
HERES IO. BAPT. CLEMENS NELLIVS IO. BAPT. SENATORIS F.
LVBENTI ANIMO ABSOLVIT.
AN. CIↃ. IↃ. CCXXXVII.

VII

THE POPES

THE PRISONER OF THE VATICAN, PART ONE

The year 1848 was the most terrifying ever experienced by the authoritarian monarchs of Europe. The pope in Rome, who exercised similarly absolute rule over the Papal States in central Italy, was not immune and was, in fact, affected even more fundamentally than his fellow despots.

✦

For the first time ever, their power and the total control they exerted over their subjects was under serious threat. The threat originated from the rise of new, liberal ideas as expressed in the slogan of the French Revolution, which had convulsed the continent some 60 years before: Liberty, Equality, Fraternity. These novel concepts spread across Europe in subsequent years, giving hope of a freer life to downtrodden millions.

Paris was just one of the European cities which saw violent clashes during the Europe-wide uprisings of 1848, in which ordinary people claimed new rights and freedoms. Even Pope Pius IX suffered the consequences, changing his views from liberal to autocratic almost overnight.

Pope Pius IX, who had been elected two years previously in 1846 seemed at first an unlikely casualty of this 'revolutionary wave', as some historians have labelled the events of 1848. His predecessor, the ultra-conservative Gregory XVI, believed that modernity in all its forms was innately evil. This applied especially to technological advances such as lighting the streets by gas or the new, faster form of travel introduced by railways, which Gregory viewed as works of the Devil and contrary to the way God meant life on Earth to be. Pius, who was nearly 30 years younger than his predecessor, welcomed progress and was one of the few European rulers with a liberal cast of mind. Among Pius' innovations on becoming pope were gas street lighting and railways, the very advances Gregory had condemned. He also freed political prisoners from the papal jails and set out to reform the inefficient and corrupt bureaucracy of the Vatican. Plans were laid to curb the activities of the Inquisition, abolish the Index of Prohibited Books and to free newspapers and books from heavy censorship. New civil liberties and the introduction of democracy were on the cards. But Pope Pius never implemented them and just how much further the liberal pope would have gone in modernizing the papacy was never revealed. By January 1849, exactly a year after the revolutions, Pope Pius had abandoned his liberal ideas and become as reactionary and authoritarian as his fellow despots.

REMORSELESS CHANGE

What had happened to bring about such a total U-turn? The short answer is that the revolutionary drive towards 'Liberty, Equality and Fraternity' became so remorseless it promised to sweep away the 'old order' and do so with utmost violence and bloodshed. In the Papal States alone, popular disorder was so widespread it made the streets dangerous. Demands for a new constitution were so strident that Pius' probable agenda – to introduce liberal change gradually and under his own direction – became utterly unworkable. A climax was reached when Pope Pius' strongman Prime Minister, Pellegrino Rossi, was stabbed to death on Vatican Hill on 15 November 1848. The murder was witnessed by numerous

Pius freed political prisoners from the papal jails and set out to reform the inefficient and corrupt bureaucracy of the Vatican.

The first Vatican Council, called by Pope Pius IX, took place in 1869–1870 and had two main purposes: to confirm papal infallibility and to reinforce his anti-modern policy.

REVOLUTIONARY DEMANDS

Revolts, riots, revolutions and popular discontent were, of course, nothing new in European countries, but the uprisings that began in January 1848 were different. The grievances they advertised were neither local nor specialized, but ran right across the board. Extending from France (again), and the German and Italian states to the Austro-Hungarian Empire, Switzerland, Greater Poland in west-central Poland and Wallachia in southern Romania violent demonstrations seriously frightened the governing élites of Europe. They came with demands for new, liberal constitutions, democratic voting rights, freedom of speech and other concessions. All of this revealed a new mood of defiance to established authority and marked an end to the deference that had once kept despotic rulers safe from popular unrest. The principle of 'Us against Them' arose on an international scale and as the French liberal historian, Alexis de Tocqueville, noted, 'Society was cut in two. Those who had nothing united in common envy. Those who had anything united in common terror.'

passers-by but no one, it seems, did anything to prevent it. The killer was never apprehended.

Rossi's death left Pius severely shaken. Popes, after all, had been assassinated before, though not in the last nine centuries, but even so, Pius feared he could be next. To avoid this fearful fate, he resolved to escape from Rome and got away dressed as an ordinary priest, wearing sunglasses as a disguise. Fortunately, no one recognized the anonymous figure entering the Bavarian ambassador's carriage and travelling south into the Kingdom of the Two Sicilies to Gaeta, a fortress on the coast north of Naples. Meanwhile, the Papal States were convulsed by revolts in Bologna and all points south as far as Rome. Throughout this area, the pope's representatives, his legates, were driven out and replaced by local committees that lost no time

The liberal reforms Pope Pius promoted soon after his election, such as civil rights and freedom from censorship, were greeted with joy, but did not last long.

The murder of the Pope's Prime Minister Pellegrino Rossi in 1848 made Pius IX fear for his own life. He fled to a hideaway near Naples.

proclaiming the end of papal rule. This was confirmed in January 1849 when an Assembly in Rome, which had been elected by popular vote, introduced a new Constitution in which the first Article stated that the temporal power of the papacy was abolished. From now on, the Constitution also proclaimed, the government of the Papal States would be democratically elected.

THE POPE'S ARMED GUARD

Foreign intervention came to the aid of the pope, though, so rule by the liberal Assembly never got that far. Austria and France, both Catholic countries that had dominated Italy between them from 1713–1814, dispatched troops, sent the Assembly packing and restored Pius to the place and powers he had briefly lost. But it was something of a charade for the pope to have to rely entirely on his armed guards to maintain his presence. The Austrians, who occupied Lombardy northwest of the Papal States and Veneto in the northeast, now policed the pope's territory. They, and the French troops who patrolled the streets of Rome, were all that stood between Pope Pius and further disaster.

> Pius resolved to escape from Rome and got away dressed as an ordinary priest, wearing sunglasses as a disguise.

Pius was not made welcome when he returned to the Vatican, though his restoration created glad tidings for devout Catholics all over Europe. But the pope who came back to Rome was not the same pope who

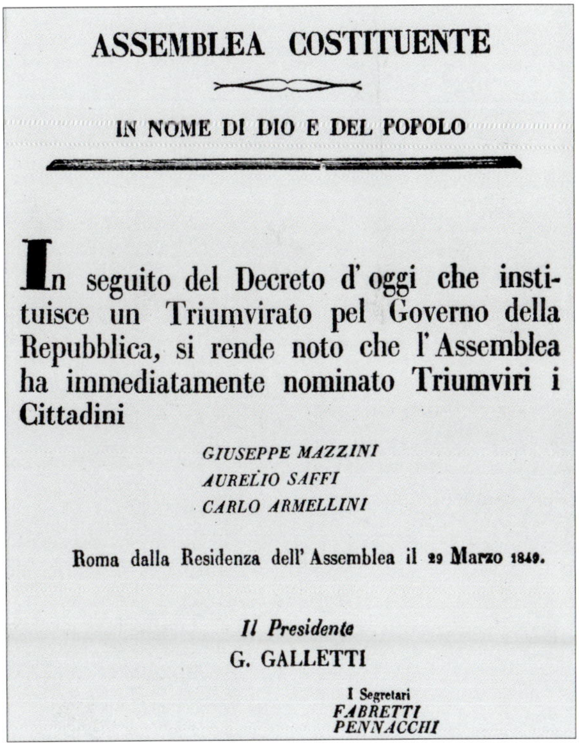

ASSEMBLEA COSTITUENTE

IN NOME DI DIO E DEL POPOLO

In seguito del Decreto d'oggi che instituisce un Triumvirato pel Governo della Repubblica, si rende noto che l'Assemblea ha immediatamente nominato Triumviri i Cittadini

GIUSEPPE MAZZINI
AURELIO SAFFI
CARLO ARMELLINI

Roma dalla Residenza dell'Assemblea il 29 Marzo 1849.

Il Presidente
G. GALLETTI

I Segretari
FABRETTI
PENNACCHI

A printed announcement proclaims that a triumvirate has been chosen by the democratically elected Assembly to govern the short-lived Italian Republic in March 1849.

The year of revolutions 1848 was a dangerous time for Pope Pius IX, as demonstrations against his rule took place in Rome.

had left the city under such dangerous circumstances. Pius had been thoroughly disturbed by the vigorous and, in his opinion, impudent attempts to displace him from the role God had intended for all popes – the temporal rule over the Papal States and the spiritual rule of the Church. Pius IX felt that he had come far too close to losing both, and that made him all the more determined to re-impose the powers of the papacy but this time in autocratic form.

THE LIBERAL CONSTITUTION

Meanwhile, other despotic rulers in Europe had also been knocked sideways by the intensity of the 1848 risings. However, by 1849 they had managed to restore their positions by dint of draconian suppression. Liberals were arrested, tortured and killed, and their followers were cowed and threatened into submission. The liberal constitutions the despots had been forced to grant, if only to play for time, were summarily withdrawn and absolute rule was re-introduced. Even so, life was never quite the same again for Europe's autocrats. Their sense of security had evaporated and they felt bound to suffocate themselves in security. Life was never the same again for Pope Pius either, but for different reasons. Although the short-lived Assembly in Rome was defunct, the liberal constitution its members had passed into law remained intact. The pope had no power to withdraw it, as other despots had withdrawn theirs, and it remained the only new constitution to survive the brute-force retribution that destroyed the uprisings of 1848. And unlike other parts of Europe where the revolutions had failed, the Papal States and the rest of Italy had the means, the will and the people to make liberal dreams into reality.

The focus of liberal hopes was also, of course, a nemesis for Pope Pius IX. It was the Kingdom of Sardinia, which, despite its name was centred on

In a traditional papal pose, Pope Pius IX raises his fingers to give a blessing. With a reign of almost 32 years, Pius was the longest-lasting pope in history.

INRI

Piedmont in northwest Italy where Turin was its capital. The Kingdom included the nearby region of Liguria as well as Sardinia, the second-largest island in the Mediterranean after Sicily. Under its sovereign, King Vittorio Emanuele II of the House of Savoy, Piedmont–Sardinia had used its constitution to turn what had once been an authoritarian state into a parliamentary democracy. The Church no longer controlled the schools, there was freedom of religion and the Jesuits, who were thought to be in league with the pope to the detriment of the kingdom, were thrown out. All this boded very ill indeed for Pius IX, who watched developments in Piedmont–Sardinia with great apprehension. Even worse, as far as the pope was concerned, Vittorio Emanuele was popular among his subjects through his support and encouragement of liberal reforms and they, in their turn, had turned away from the Church and, in particular from Rome, as the focus of power.

The Church no longer controlled the schools, there was freedom of religion and the Jesuits were thrown out.

In 1861, Vittorio Emanuele II of Piedmont-Sardinia became the first of the three kings of Italy.

As if this were not sufficient disadvantage for the beleaguered pope, Vittorio Emanuele was also that invaluable figurehead, a great patriotic war hero, having personally fought in four battles of the first Italian War of Independence against Austria in 1848–49. The purpose of the war had been to put an end to Austrian and other foreign control of Italy. What it actually proved was that no single Italian state could defeat the foreigners on its own. Even though Piedmont–Sardinia lost the war, the youthful 29-year-old Vittorio Emanuele emerged as an inspiring leader and symbol of the *Risorgimento,* the movement for the unification of Italy.

As the warrior king rose in eminence and popular regard, the peril he posed to Pope Pius increased. Before long, the dream of transforming Italy from a collection of small separate states into a single monarchy, first mooted more than 30 years earlier, began to take more concrete shape, and nowhere more potently than in the ambitious mind of Vittorio Emanuele. Evidently, there would be little space for a pope, much less an autocratic one, in this scheme of things.

Vittorio Emanuele's first chance to make his bid for rule over all

RISORGIMENTO: THE UNIFICATION OF ITALY

The *Risorgimento* (which translates as resurgence) was the name given to the movement behind the unification of Italy. For centuries Italy had been fragmented into the city-states and small kingdoms that began to develop after the fall of the Western Roman Empire in around 476 CE. One such small realm was the Papal States in central Italy, ruled by the popes in Rome.

This situation persisted for almost 1400 years and latterly resulted in foreign rule in some parts of Italy by the French or the Austrians. The process of unification took place gradually, between 1814 and 1870 when Italian forces occupied Rome and the Papal States. Further territory, including Trentino, South Tyrol and Trieste, was added to Italy in 1919, after World War I.

Italy did not arrive until 1859, when another war with Austria broke out. This time, the King acted in partnership with the French, who wanted the Austrians, their great enemy, out of Italy. The decisive action of this new war came when Vittorio Emanuele triumphed against the papal army at the battle of Castelfidardo in the Papal States. Afterwards, the King drove the papal forces all the way southwest to Rome, some 200 kilometres away. The outbreak of hostilities was accompanied by revolts in the Papal States and once again the papal legates were driven out.

> Evidently, there would be little space for a pope, much less an autocratic one, in this scheme of things.

With that, nationalists in Naples and Sicily began clamouring to unite with Piedmont–Sardinia and by 18 February 1861, the unified Kingdom of Italy was officially inaugurated. At that early stage, though, the whole of Italy had yet to be involved for there were two large areas still outside the new domain. One was in the northeast, where Veneto and its capital Venice were still controlled by Austria. The other, more significantly, was Rome and the Papal States, where the pope was fully geared up to fight all or any intrusion onto his sacred patch.

VATICAN VOCABULARY

PAPAL INFALLIBILITY

The Catholic dogma of Papal Infallibility which was established by the First Vatican Council on 18 July 1870 declares that the Holy Spirit actively preserves the pope from even the chance that he will make an error when promulgating statements on faith or morals. These statements derive from divine revelation or are at least, connected to divine revelation.

In order to be accounted infallible, the pope's teachings have to be based on sacred tradition and sacred scripture, or should, at least, not contradict either of them. However, Papal Infallibility does not suggest that the pope is incapable of sin or wrongdoing.

Since the doctrine was introduced 138 years ago, it has been used only once. In 1950, Pope Pius XII defined the Assumption of Mary as an article of faith in the Roman Catholic religion. It has, therefore, been 'assumed' that after her death, Mary, the mother of Jesus, was transported to Heaven with both her body and her soul intact.

Apart from this single use of infallibility, the Church relies on the idea that the pope decides what will, and will not, be acceptable as a formal belief in the Roman Catholic religion.

To this end, Pius deployed a weapon only he possessed. In a Papal Encyclical issued in January 1860, he excommunicated Vittorio Emanuele and everyone else who had been involved in the desecration of papal territory. Pius went on to inform the offenders that God was on his side, not theirs, and would undoubtedly act against them to reverse the outrage that had been dealt to His Church and to himself as His representative on Earth. It would therefore be wise, Pope Pius warned, if there were a 'pure and simple restitution' of the Papal States to their rightful owner.

EXCOMMUNICATING THE KING

Centuries earlier, in medieval times, excommunication and threats of God's punishment had been quite enough to terrify all but the most recalcitrant into instant obedience. But this effect had long been fading in Italy, where many people, particularly among the educated classes, had become alienated from Rome, if not yet from the Roman Church and no longer trembled at the very thought of God's vengeance. In this context, Pius was out of his political depth. He was not addressing impressionable devotees, but worldly men with little regard for shielding their immortal souls against penalties from Heaven. They were more concerned with political advantage and how to seize it for themselves.

> Pius went on to inform the offenders that God was on his side, not theirs, and would undoubtedly act against them.

Several private agendas were in play. Vittorio Emanuele and his government set aside the capture of Rome for the moment while they concentrated first on ejecting the Austrians from Veneto. Giuseppe Mazzini and Giuseppe Garibaldi, two of the three nationalist leaders who spearheaded unification (the third was Camillo Benso, Conte di Cavour, Vittorio Emanuele's erstwhile prime minister) held the opposite view. For them, the seizure of Rome was of primary importance because the *Risorgimento* could not be complete without Rome as the capital of Italy. The French emperor Napoleon III teamed up with Vittorio Emanuele for his own purposes – not only to eject the Austrians from Italy, but in the long term to ensure that instead of a unified Italy, there would be only a gaggle of weak states that could never rival France for influence in Europe.

VATICAN VOCABULARY

PAPAL LEGATE

A papal legate was a personal representative of the pope, a post usually given to a cardinal. Legate were sent to foreign governments, monarchs or churches outside the Vatican with the pope's instructions to take charge of important Catholic events, such as an ecumenical council or to make decisions on matters of faith. Papal legates might also take charge where there were problems with heresy, as they did during the struggle between the papacy and the heretic Cathars in Languedoc.

GARIBALDI CAUSES A PROBLEM

A more important rivalry in the short term arose between Vittorio Emanuele and his government and the great military hero of the *Risorgimento*, Garibaldi, who attempted to upstage the King and seize Rome in 1860 and then in 1862. On both occasions, Garibaldi was thwarted but Vittorio Emanuele could not afford to leave it at that. Not only was Garibaldi a republican, he was a hugely popular figure among Italian nationalists. For them, Rome was the Holy Grail of the *Risorgimento* and Garibaldi's ambition to capture the city was a great patriotic endeavour. Not only that, the continuing presence of French troops guarding the pope in Rome was a national disgrace that had to be erased.

> The educated classes had become alienated from Rome, if not yet from the Roman Church, and no longer trembled at the very thought of God's vengeance.

In these circumstances, Vittorio Emanuele's ambitions to become King of all Italy were at stake. He could not afford to allow Garibaldi's private, ragbag army to 'liberate' Rome and, as Vittorio suspected they would, declare a republic. He needed to take the initiative and remove the French himself. This, apparently, is what the King and his government aimed to do when they concluded the Convention of

On 20 May 1859, at Montebello in Lombardy, the forces of France and Piedmont thrashed the Austrians in what would come to be known as the Second War of Italian Independence.

Though a republican, Giuseppe Garibaldi (left) hails Vittorio Emanuele II (right) as King of Italy at a historic meeting at Teano, between Rome and Naples, on 26 October 1860.

September with the French in 1864. Under this agreement, the French promised to evacuate Rome by 1866, unknowingly leaving Vittorio Emanuele free to implement his own clandestine plan – to manufacture some excuse to annex the city to his Kingdom of Italy and make it a royal rather than a republican capital. As a smokescreen for this aim, the King made what looked like major concessions: his government would transfer his capital from Turin in Piedmont–Sardinia to Florence in Tuscany, well away from Rome, and he would undertake not to attack the Papal States again.

HOPE FOR THE POPE

On the face of it, these new arrangements afforded Pope Pius some welcome reassurance and filled him with a new sense of security. The pope's optimism spread to his cardinals, who were just as convinced as their pontiff that Emperor Napoleon III would never depart Rome and leave Pius 'in a helpless condition to the Piedmontese and the tender mercies of his subjects. The Catholics of France and of the whole world,' the Cardinals maintained, 'would not stand (for) it.'

Vittorio Emanuele's ambitions to become King of all Italy were at stake. He could not afford to allow Garibaldi's private, ragbag army to 'liberate' Rome and declare a republic.

The new mood of confidence in the Vatican was encouraged by events outside Italy that were moving towards a war in which Prussia was squaring up to Austria and both were in opposition to France. However, these three powers were linked by the belief that a united Italy could prove a rival to each and all of them when it came to exerting influence in Europe. It followed that all three meant to do their utmost to prevent Italian unification. This, inevitably, was greeted

PAPAL RIGHT-HAND MAN

Giacomo Antonelli, one of the last laymen to be created a cardinal, was papal secretary of state to Pope Pius IX from 1848 (the year of revolutions across Europe), until his death in 1876. Antonelli made it his life's work to preserve the Pope from his enemies and to defend the papacy from all or any attempt to liberalize it. For example, in November 1848, after the assassination of Prime Minister Pellegrino Rossi, it was Antonelli who made the arrangements when Pius left Rome and fled to Gaeta for safety. The following year, when Liberals seized the Papal States, it was Antonelli who requested the French and Austrians to send armed forces to restore the territory – successfully as it turned out – to Pius's control. Antonelli's anti-liberal activities and his many efforts to frustrate the Risorgimento made him a marked man. In 1855, he only just escaped being killed by assassins.

But Antonelli also became notorious for some behind-the-scenes chicanery. After his death, it was found that there was a deficit of some 45 million lire in the finances of the Vatican, which had been under Antonelli's control. Antonelli's personal fortune, however, was found to be substantial, and he had bequeathed almost all of it to members of his family. Despite his obvious devotion to Pope Pius, Antonelli left the pontiff only a very small amount in his will.

Cardinal Giacomo Antonelli acted as Pope Pius IX's secretary of state for nearly 30 years. He consistently championed the papal cause, but all the same appears to have embezzled the papal treasury while in power.

as great news in the Vatican, which had by far the most to fear from the *Risorgimento.* Nothing would have made the pope and his cardinals happier than the promise that the nascent Italian state was going to be put in its proper, backwater, place.

In January 1865, Odo Russell, the British envoy in Rome, reported home to London a conversation between himself and Cardinal Giacomo Antonelli, the pope's formidable Secretary of State. 'Like the pope,' Russell wrote, 'Antonelli hopes for a European war to set matters right again in the Holy See!'

> ... these new arrangements afforded Pope Pius some welcome reassurance and filled him with a new sense of security.

HOPES DASHED

But like other hopes engendered by the Convention of September, this turned out to be so much pie in the sky. The war between Austria and Prussia, which began in June 1866, failed to go the way the Vatican hoped. The pope had been certain that Austria would crush the Prussians, who had allied themselves to the Kingdom of Italy, and that the Austrians would soon occupy his own lost provinces.

VATICAN VOCABULARY

PAPAL OR APOSTOLIC NUNCIO

'Nuncio' derives from the Latin *nuntius*, meaning 'envoy'. A papal nuncio, officially known as apostolic nuncio, is an ambassador who acts as the diplomatic representative of the Vatican to foreign states or to international organizations, such as the United Nations. The nuncio has the same rank and privileges of an ambassador from any other state and usually holds the rank of archbishop for as long as he remains in the post. (Until such time as the Roman Catholic Church ordains women, all papal nuncios will be male.)

But the opposite was the case. The Prussians and their Italian allies triumphed, and quickly, for the war ended by October after only four months. The timing could not have been more inauspicious. By December 1866, under the Convention of September, the French were making preparations to leave Rome. Before the year was out, their flag had been taken down from its mast at the Castel Sant'Angelo and the French troops embarked at Civitavecchia, the port of Rome, bound for home. In the Vatican, all the earnest hopes, the optimism and the certainty that the French would never leave sailed away with them.

> There were several subversive groups in the city who, given half a chance, would be only too willing to manufacture a rebellion.

PANIC IN THE VATICAN

With this, a sense of abject terror began to pervade the Vatican. Pope Pius' advisors pleaded with him to get away to safety while he could, and seek sanctuary in Spain or Austria. Their fear was increased even further by the fact that Pope Pius and his autocratic rule had roused strong resistance within Rome. Even worse, there were several subversive groups in the city who, given half a chance, would be only too willing to manufacture a rebellion, with all the mob fury and destruction that implied. Undoubtedly, his aides were convinced, the pope was in deadly danger, but the prime source of that danger was not as they envisioned it.

The source was not malcontents and mobs, but the Italian government of King Vittorio Emanuele. The retreat of the French from Rome had painted them into an awkward corner. By signing the Convention of September in 1864 they had guaranteed papal rule in Rome, together with the security of the Papal States, which they had promised not to attack. For the sake of his honour and future credibility as monarch of all Italy, Vittorio Emanuele could not afford to renege openly on these commitments. What he could do, though, was to renege behind the scenes.

> The pope had been certain that Austria would crush the Prussians, ... But the opposite was the case.

For quite a while, Emanuele's government had been secretly financing the subversive, anti-papacy groups active in Rome in the hope that they would foment a 'spontaneous' uprising. Giuseppe Garibaldi, a virulent anti-papist, stoked up the temperature by calling the papacy 'the most noxious of all sects' and demanding the removal of the Catholic priesthood, which he believed encouraged ignorance and superstition. Once the fires of rebellion were lit, Emanuele could play saviour and rush his own troops into Rome to retrieve the situation. Then, taking over the city and the Vatican and neutralizing the pope would be a piece of cake.

THE REVOLUTION THAT NEVER WAS

But it was not. Events turned out very differently. Despite all persuasions, generous handouts and Garibaldi's revolutionary fervour, Rome stubbornly refused to rise. Partly this may have been due to the presence in the city of Pope Pius' personal guard, most of them foreigners and many of them thugs. Another force, comprising papal irregulars, patrolled the city's streets and had an even more fearsome reputation for violence. Emperor Napoleon III carefully watched these events, or rather non-events, from Paris. No

Today, the revolutionary Giuseppe Garibaldi remains a great Italian hero for the military campaigns he fought in the cause of Italian independence.

mean intriguer himself, the crafty Napoleon easily recognized the signs of deceit and double-dealing and towards the end of 1867, he ordered French troops back into Rome where they were soon policing the streets once again.

Pope Pius, his cardinals and the rest of the Vatican were overcome with joy at what they saw as a timely rescue. The British envoy in Rome, Odo Russell, held a more sombre, realistic view. The presence of the French forces, he wrote 'tends to make of Rome a fortified city and of the pope a military despot'. But there was no doubting the jubilant mood that had gripped Rome when the French returned. The pope's supporters, the clerical party, Russell continued:

> *rejoice with great joy in their present turn of fortune and believe in their future triumph. [They] pray devoutly that a general European war may soon divide and break up Italy.*

When Russell had an audience with the pope in the spring of 1868, the pontiff told him that, as a proportion of Rome's population, the papal army was now the largest in the world and if the interests of the Church ever required it, 'he would even buckle on a sword, mount a horse and take command of the army himself'. Pope Pius was 75 years old at the time.

But for Pius, the interests of the Church required much more than bravado and military display. As a European ruler, he was unique in having a spiritual hold over millions of devout Catholics who were dispersed throughout the continent and prepared to obey his every pronouncement and follow his every lead. There were also other Catholics who had slipped into 'error' by

A splendid scene of colourful pageantry as the papal procession passes through the streets of Rome at the inauguration of Pope Pius IX in 1846. Pius would see many changes in his long and eventful reign.

PAPAL CONDEMNATION OF 'CURRENT ERRORS'

Quanta Cura revealed just how far the pope had retreated from his previous liberal views to condemn virtually every progressive idea in which he had once believed.

This encyclical came with a catalogue of wrongdoings entitled *Syllabus of Errors,* which listed some 80 errors all good Catholics must avoid. None of them should subscribe to freedom of speech, freedom of the press, or freedom of religion and, like Pius himself, must reject the notion that 'the Roman Pontiff can and should reconcile himself to progress, liberalism and modern civilization'. This was an agenda that sought to take the Church and its adherents back to medieval times, the heyday of absolute Church influence over the minds and beliefs of the faithful, when dissent could often mean death. Naturally enough, conservatives within the Church, particularly the ultra-reactionary Jesuits, greeted *Quanta Cura* with jubilation. But by so clearly distancing himself from the realities of late nineteenth-century life, which had already absorbed many of the freedoms the pope condemned, Pius was making himself and the papacy look anachronistic, if not ridiculous. This left many Catholics, who were loyal to the Church but still valued progress and its benefits, confused and in some cases horrified.

Envoy Odo Russell went further. He believed that *Quanta Cura* and its *Syllabus* would prove catastrophic for the pope, the papacy and especially for the Catholic clergy who, he wrote, would have to take part in 'a vast ecclesiastical conspiracy against the principles that govern modern society'. If they refused, then they would find themselves 'in opposition to the Vicar of Christ whom they are bound to obey'. The only result, as Russell saw it, was complete disaffection between the Holy See and the modern, progressive nations of Europe.

embracing the modernity Pius had once supported himself. Such deviants needed to be drawn back into the fold. In 1864, Pius had already outlined the way he meant to do it, by forging a narrower path of permitted belief than any pope before him had ever devised.

NO RELIGIOUS FREEDOM

Pius' first targets were religious freedom and equal rights for all religions, which he rejected outright as 'the greatest insult imaginable to the one true Catholic faith'. This equality, the pope told Emperor Franz Josef of Austria in a letter written in 1864 'contains an absurdity of confusing truth with error and light with darkness, thus encouraging the monstrous and horrid principle of religious relativism, which... inevitably leads to atheism'. These deeply reactionary and conservative ideas found their way into the papal encyclical called *Quanta Cura (Condemning Current Errors)*, which was proclaimed by Pope Pius on 8 December 1864.

Quanta Cura created a furore of protest across Catholic Europe, but Pope Pius seemed entirely unaware of it. Instead, he staged a grand jubilee in Rome to affirm his iron resolve to steer the Church away from insidious modernity. Early in March 1866, vast, colourful processions wound their way through the streets of Rome. Taking part were cardinals in brilliant red robes followed by a throng of monks and friars bearing sacred images and a blaze of candles to light the awe-inspiring scene. At several of Rome's most historic churches, the processions halted while priests piled up books banned by the papal Index and set them on fire.

Pius' first targets were religious freedom and equal rights for all religions, which he rejected outright as 'the greatest insult imaginable to the one true Catholic faith'.

But Pius kept the best, or as his enemies saw it, the worst, revelation till last. The First Vatican Council, attended by a huge gathering of cardinals and bishops, opened at St Peter's Basilica on 8 December 1869. The Council had two purposes: to ratify the *Syllabus of Errors* of 1864 and to endorse a new principle in Church doctrine, the infallibility of the pope. This applied when the pope spoke officially on the subjects of faith and morals after God had revealed them to him.

PAPAL INFALLIBILITY APPROVED

Even *Quanta Cura* and its *Syllabus of Errors* had not administered a shock as great as this, and both critics and supporters voiced strongly worded opinions on the subject. However, the opinion that really mattered was Napoleon III's. Thus far, he had been willing to bolster the pope, if only as a concession to French Catholic sensibilities. But now, His Holiness was proposing to throw over every civic freedom that had been gained in the last 80 years since the French Revolution, and make himself the divine arbiter of Europe's future. It was too much. Napoleon made it known that if papal infallibility were voted into being at the Vatican Council, he would withdraw French troops from Rome.

The ballot took place on 18 July 1870. The pro-infallibility lobby won by 547 votes to two against. However, Pope Pius did not have things entirely his own way. His powers of infallibility were not nearly as

His Holiness was proposing to throw over every civic freedom that had been gained in the last 80 years since the French Revolution.

comprehensive as he had wanted. They had been watered down by the opposition, which managed to detach the basic principles of civil liberties from the condemnations set out in *Quanta Cura* and its *Syllabus of Errors*. It was, however, significant that the ambassadors of the principal Catholic countries in Europe – France, Austria, Spain and Portugal – were conspicuously absent when the vote took place.

French troops pack up, ready to depart from Rome in 1866, leaving the city without its former protection.

In this early photograph, Pope Pius IX blesses his troops before the battle of Mentana which took place on 3 November 1867. The papal forces, with the French, routed the volunteer army of Giuseppe Garibaldi, preventing them from capturing Rome.

Fate, however, had a curious twist in store for both the Emperor Napoleon and Pope Pius IX. On 27 July 1870, the French announced they were going to remove their troops from Rome because, it was said, they were 'needed elsewhere'. This had nothing to do with Napoleon's threat or with papal infallibility. 'Elsewhere' lay along the border between eastern France and Prussia, the largest and most powerful of the German states. Tensions had been growing for some time and, on 19 July, the day after the ballot in Rome, the French declared war.

FRANCE AND PRUSSIA AT WAR

The Franco-Prussian War, which lasted less than a year until it ended in decisive Prussian victory on 10 May 1871, was a complete disaster for France. The hostilities ruined Napoleon III, who was captured by the Prussians, and afterwards exiled in England. This brought an end to monarchy in France, and as a final insult to a defeated opponent, the Prussians declared the unification of the German states under their leadership in the spectacular Hall of Mirrors at the Palace of Versailles, built by the French King Louis XIV some 150 years earlier.

... the French announced they were going to remove their troops from Rome because, it was said, they were 'needed elsewhere'.

For Pope Pius, the war was a disaster of another kind: the defeat of his erstwhile French ally meant there was nothing to prevent Vittorio Emanuele and the Italian government seizing Rome and declaring the city the capital of united Italy. This gave rise to fearful rumours that the pope was about to desert Rome and leave its already panic-stricken inhabitants to their fate at the hands of the terrible nationalists. It was whispered that the Jesuits were urging Pius to get away at once, ask the British for protection and move to the

THE INFALLIBLE POPE

Papal infallibility caused more of a shock and furore than anything else Pope Pius had done so far. Popes could legitimately claim many privileges and powers, but nothing as extreme as this. Needless to say, papal infallibility polarized opinion.

The influential French bishop Félix Dupanloup wrote approvingly to Cardinal Antonelli: 'The Council will be a great force against Piedmont [and the Italian government]. Our strongest argument against Rome capital of Italy is Rome capital of Catholicism… the pretensions of [Vittorio Emanuele and the] Piedmontese will become not merely impossible, but the object of ridicule.' Above all, Dupanloup asserted, the Council would serve as a demonstration of strength that would make it impossible for the French to abandon Rome again.

Charles-Émile Freppel, Bishop of Angers in western France, expressed a contrary view. He saw the infallibility question in a more personal, human light. 'We are at the end of the pontificate of a tired and discouraged old man, who views everything through the misfortunes he has suffered,' Freppel wrote. 'For him, everything that takes place in the modern world is, and must by necessity be, an "abomination".'

Other critics were much more forthright, in some cases brutally so. Ferdinand Gregorovius, the German historian and theologian wrote:

> *Many seriously believe that the pope is out of his mind. He has entered with fanaticism into these things and has acquired votes for his deification.*

Authoritarian Catholic rulers in Europe were horrified by the concept of papal infallibility because it impinged upon their own positions. They believed that through the Divine Right of Kings they had been appointed by God and were answerable only to Him. But here was a pope who could override them by going one step further and claiming that he was the voice of God.

British-ruled island of Malta. The only hope seemed to be for the pope to negotiate with Vittorio Emanuele and his government and prevent the occupation of Rome that way. Even the stalwart Cardinal Antonelli begged the pope to take this course, but no amount of pleading or panicking had any effect.

SUPPORT FOR THE POPE

This was not just the reaction of a stubborn old man entombed in his own arrogant world. He had – or thought he had – much more than that on which to fall back. First of all, Pope Pius was relying on the promises he had received from Count Otto von Bismarck, the 'Iron' Chancellor of Prussia, the Prussian King Wilhelm I and the Italian government itself that there was no prospect that papal territory would be invaded. This was why Pius grew so angry when army officers and the papal police seemed unable to get the message. For example, when the papal commissioner of police came to him and asked for instructions about what to do when the invaders came, Pius, in spite of his age, leapt from his seat in a fury and shouted, 'Can't you understand? I have formal assurances that the Italians will not set foot in Rome! How many times must I keep repeating myself?'

What the pope did not seem to understand, though,

The only hope seemed to be for the pope to negotiate with Vittorio Emanuele and his government and prevent the occupation of Rome that way.

was that in the everyday world outside the Vatican, assurances vanished when a change in circumstances warranted. This is what threatened to happen a month after the French left Rome. On 20 August 1870, in the House of Deputies (the Italian 'parliament'), the

Pope Pius IX announces papal infallibility on matters of faith or morals. This new 'power' polarized Catholic opinion, gratifying some, but horrifying others.

Count Otto von Bismarck, the so-called 'Iron Chancellor' of Prussia and great enemy of Napoleon III who fulfilled his ambition of unifying the states of Germany under Prussian leadership in 1871.

government won a vote of confidence that came with a significant condition: the King's ministers must find a way 'to resolve the Roman question in a manner in keeping with national aspirations'.

The message was coded, but it was easy to see what it inferred: if 'national aspirations' were to be fulfilled, the 'Roman question' could not be resolved in favour of the pope. The leader of the Catholic Church in England, Cardinal Henry Edward Manning, certainly read danger in this new situation and had an urgent meeting with the British Prime Minister, William Gladstone, to arrange aid and, if necessary, rescue, for the Holy Father. Soon afterwards the British warship HMS *Defence* sailed into Civitavecchia. It was under instruction to embark the pope if he wished to leave.

'SPONTANEOUS' UNREST

It was a shrewd precaution. Behind a façade of reassurances that there would be no assault on Rome, the Italian government was desperately searching for a pretext that would enable them to seize the city. Despite the fact that the idea had failed before, the Italians fell back on the 'spontaneous' unrest that could be caused inside Rome to give them a 'duty' to intervene. There could be heavily armed attacks on military barracks, hopefully leading to a popular uprising. The papal troops, who were chiefly foreigners, might be bribed into quarrelling with each other, creating brawls in the city streets that would soon be joined by the inhabitants.

Guns could be fired at night while Italian flags were raised here and there. This would give the impression, as Prime Minister Giovanni Lanza put it to a group of young conspirators, 'that Rome was in the throes of anarchy and that the pope's government could no longer control the situation with its own forces'. Lanza went on to sound a note of caution. 'See that as many disorders as you like break out in Rome,' he told the conspirators 'but not revolution'.

This was a risky, impetuous policy and one that earned no approval from the cautious Minister of Foreign Affairs, Emilio Visconti-Venosta, who had hoped that a compromise could be reached between the pope and the Italian government. Chancing his arm was not part of Visconti's nature and to the last, he hoped that somehow, 'the pope's independence, freedom and religious authority could be preserved'.

NO NEGOTIATIONS

But the greatest obstacle to this ambition was Pope Pius himself. He had no intention of negotiating with the Italian government because this would give it recognition and legitimacy, something he would never allow. Even the reasonable, emollient Visconti was unable to penetrate papal resistance. Neither did a government plan, revealed in September 1870, to give the pope the so-called Leonine City, a section of Rome that included the Vatican and lay on the right bank of the River Tiber.

Predictably, Pope Pius dismissed the idea. As far as he was concerned the forces of God were struggling with the forces of the Devil for control of Rome, and the Devil, in the form of the government of King Vittorio Emanuele was going to lose. In less apocalyptic terms, perhaps, this was also the general opinion in the Vatican.

Emperor Napoleon III of France, whose troops policed Rome and protected the Vatican and the pope.

This, though, was before the capture of Napoleon III by the Prussians, the abolition of the monarchy in France and, finally, the resounding victory of Prussia in the war of 1870–71. Although he was stunned by these events, in particular the departure of Napoleon from the scene, Pope Pius persisted in turning down more last-minute proposals for settling the dispute without war. One of them, delivered on 10 September 1870 by a Piedmontese nobleman, Count Panza di San Martino, came from King Vittorio Emanuele, pledging that the independence and prestige of the Holy See would be protected.

Pius read the King's letter, but refused to answer it directly. Instead, he sent a short missive to the King. He wrote, 'Count Panza di San Martino has given me a letter that Your Majesty wished to direct to me but

The war of 1870–1871 between France and Prussia ruined Napoleon III, who was captured by Prussian forces in September 1870 and went into exile.

one that is not worthy of an affectionate son who claims to profess the Catholic faith.' To respond to the King's proposals, Pius asserted, would be to

> *... renew the pain that my first reading caused me.... I bless God who has seen fit to allow Your Majesty to fill the last years of my life with such bitterness. I ask God to shed his grace on Your Majesty, protecting you from danger and dispensing his mercy on you who have such need of it.*

Better, the pope was sure, to stand firm, tough it out, and ... die rather than compromise and hand over the papal lands that rightfully belonged to God.

PRISONER OF THE VATICAN

The underlying message was, of course, the same as before. There were to be no craven concessions to the Devil and his hordes. Better, the pope was sure, to stand firm, tough it out and, if necessary, die rather than compromise and hand over the papal lands that rightfully belonged to God. In the event, Pope Pius did not die in the defence of Rome. Instead, his stubborn stand made him what he himself described as the 'prisoner of the Vatican'. He never left the enclave until his death in 1878 and over the following 50 years, neither did three of the four popes who came after him.

Giovanni Lanza was President of the Council of Ministers of Italy (equivalent to Prime Minister), between 1869 and 1873. He was instrumental in establishing a government of united Italy in Rome.

VIII THE POPES

THE PRISONER OF THE VATICAN, PART TWO

The Kingdom of Italy declared war on the Papal States on 10 September 1870. Two days later, Italian forces crossed into papal territory. Four days after that, they captured the port of Civitavecchia.

From there, they advanced slowly towards Rome, some 60 kilometres (37 miles) distant, hoping that some compromise could be reached to save them from having to take the city by force. To this end, they plastered propaganda posters on walls with a message expressing goodwill and peaceful intentions.

Inside Rome, the Vatican authorities had no faith in propaganda. Instead, following the pope's own lead, they remained certain that divine intervention would produce a last-minute rescue. It failed to materialize. By 19 September, the Italians had reached the Aurealian Walls, a structure 18 metres high and 19 kilometres long that surrounded Rome. Now, Rome truly *was* under siege. So too was Paris, which was ringed by the Prussians on the same day. It was clearly impossible for the Vatican to expect help from the French, but Pope Pius anticipated a move from Austria, the most powerful Catholic state in Europe.

Cardinals pray (left) as Pope Leo XIII lies dying in 1903. Pope Leo was as convinced of his infallibility as his predecessor, Pius IX. Pope Benedict XV (above) reigned as pope from 1914 until 1922.

THE AUSTRIANS HOLD OFF

The Austrians, however, were reluctant to take a pro-Vatican stand in case it led them into a war with the

RIVAL PROPAGANDA

Both sides in the struggle for Rome – the Italian nationalists and the Vatican authorities – used propaganda to present their cause to the inhabitants. From the nationalists, there was a message from Raffaele Cadorna, head of the army division heading for Rome. But the Vatican opposition got there first and put up posters carrying a dread message. It read:

Romans! A horrendous evil is being attempted! The Holy Father, in the peaceful possession of His capital and of the few provinces spared from usurpation from His dominion is threatened without any reason by the troops of a Catholic king. Rome is therefore in a state of siege.

Cadorna's posters, which were pasted over this apocalyptic statement, read more mildly and included a dig at the French:

Italians of the Roman Provinces! The independence of the Holy See will remain inviolable, as will the freedom of the citizens, both more fully guaranteed than they ever were under the protection of foreign forces.

Italians, something the Austrian Emperor Franz Josef wanted to avoid at all costs. The best the Austrians could do was express their devotion to Pope Pius and offer him shelter in any city within the Austro-Hungarian Empire should he decide to leave Rome.

Monsignor Scapinelli, the apostolic nuncio in Vienna, exploded with rage when he received this message. 'It takes some nerve,' Scapinelli told the Austrian foreign minister Count Friedrich Ferdinand von Beust, 'to invite me to move into your house while you do nothing to prevent me from being thrown out of my own!'

Vittorio Emanuele, meanwhile, tried diplomatic pleas to persuade the pope to change his mind and settle the 'Roman question' by agreement. He had no luck. Pius refused to yield to humanitarian arguments citing the loss of life the use of force would incur.

The army of the Kingdom of Italy assaulted Rome (top) and captured it in September 1870, The walls of Rome (bottom) were peppered with bullet holes.

Instead, he turned the argument on its head and told the Italians and their king that they, not he, would be responsible for any fatalities and would have to take the burden of immense responsibility before God and before the tribunal of history.

THE END OF THE LINE

Both sides had clearly reached the final impasse. After this, there was nothing left but for the Italian forces to prepare their entry into Rome and for the pope to make a public demonstration of faith in God. For this purpose, Pope Pius, now 78 years old, knelt down and on his knees climbed the 28 Holy Steps near the church of St John Lateran. On reaching the top, he prayed to God imploring Him to protect his people. Many people in the crowd watching were moved to tears.

The best the Austrians could do was offer him shelter in any city within the Austro-Hungarian Empire should he decide to leave Rome.

The attack by the Italian army began at five in the morning of 20 September 1870. Dr Maitland Armstrong, the American consul in Rome described what happened:

The old walls generally proved utterly useless against heavy artillery. In four or five hours, they were in some places completely swept away, a clear breach was made near the Porta Pia 50 feet [15 metres] wide and the Italian soldiers in overwhelming force flowed through it and literally filled the city, simultaneously, the Porta San Giovanni was carried by assault. A white flag was hoisted over from the dome of St Peter's. After the cannonading ceased, the papal troops made but a feeble resistance and they, who a moment before, ruled Rome with a rod of iron were nearly all prisoners or had taken refuge in the Castle of St Angelo or St Peter's Square.

The struggle for Rome, such as it was, was not nearly as brutal as Dr Armstrong suggested. The papal forces were under orders to put up enough resistance to show their willingness to defend the Holy See and the Italians were under strict instructions to limit the damage they wrought, refrain from firing at non-combatants and to leave the Leonine City untouched. Even though Pius had rejected the offer of the City, the Italian government still intended it to serve as the pope's own territory.

Another factor that may have dampened the proceedings was the prevailing mood in Rome. The pope had his devotees, who were terrified that he was going to leave the City and abandon them, but many other Romans appeared to regard the invading troops as liberators, freeing them from authoritarian papal rule. Even more alarmingly, there were popular demands that all monasteries and nunneries be removed from Rome and the monks and nuns thrown out.

A political cartoon showing Pope Pius IX (foreground), his powers gone after 1871, gloomily departing the scene as the triumphant King Vittorio Emanuele II (background, second right) receives the acclaim of the Roman crowd.

SANCTA SCALA – THE HOLY STAIRS

It is believed that the 28 white marble steps of the *Sancta Scala* (also called the Holy Stairs) originally came from the staircase that led to the *praetorium* or guardroom, in Jerusalem where Jesus appeared before Pontius Pilate, the Roman governor of ancient Judea. The steps were considered to have become sacred as the blood of Jesus fell on them as he climbed the stairs to his trial almost two thousand years ago. Tradition has it that the *Sancta Scala* were removed from Jerusalem in around 326 CE and transported by the Empress Helena, later St Helena, to Italy, then re-erected in the complex of palaces occupied by the popes in Rome. St Helena was the mother of the Emperor Constantine I, who adopted Christianity as the religion of Rome and its empire in around 330 CE.

In 1589, Pope Sixtus V had the *Sancta Scala* removed to their present site, in front of the ancient chapel, the *Sancta Sanctorum* (Holy of Holies) in the old Lateran Palace in Rome. Sixtus ordered elaborate decorations and extensive frescoes to be painted onto the surrounding walls and ceilings by a number of eminent Renaissance artists. In Catholic tradition, pilgrims who visit the *Sancta Scala* may climb them only on their knees. For this act of devotion, they can earn remission of sins.

Visitors to the Vatican climb the Sancta Scala on their knees, the only way they are permitted to reach the top.

668 HARPER'S WEEKLY. [OCTOBER 15, 1870.

POPE PIUS IX.

The observer who once called the *basso popolo,* (the lower-class Romans), 'wild and bloody' had not been exaggerating. If these people had been minded to rise up to join the Italians, the occupation of Rome would have been a great deal more gory and destructive than it was, so it was in the interests of both sides to accomplish the task quickly and cleanly. Once that was done, terms of surrender were soon organized and the whole of Rome, apart from the Leonine City, became the realm of Vittorio Emanuele II, the first King of Italy.

Terms of surrender were soon organized and the whole of Rome, apart from the Leonine City, became the realm of Vittorio Emanuele II, the first King of Italy.

Rome was now transformed. One of the city's newspapers published on 23 September put it in jubilant terms while listing the many ways in which life was restricted by papal rule:

> *After 15 centuries of darkness of mourning, of misery and pain, Rome, once the queen of all the world, has again become the metropolis of a great State. Today, for us Romans, is day of indescribable joy. Today in Rome freedom of thought is no longer a crime and free speech can be heard within its walls without fear of the Inquisition, of burning at the stake, of the gallows. The light of civil liberty that, arising in France in 1789, has brightened all Europe now shines as well on the eternal city. For Rome, it is only today that the Middle Ages are over!*

The Italian foreign minister, Emilio Visconti-Venosta wanted reconciliation between his government and Pope Pius IX, but realized that the pontiff would never contemplate it.

This celebration of modernity and the freedoms Pope Pius had tried so hard to suppress set his attitude even more firmly in stone than ever before. The Italians tried to cede the Leonine City to the pope. He refused. An offer of homage was suggested but was also turned down because it would involve the pope receiving a representative of the 'usurper king', Vittorio Emanuele and this he would not do.

NEVER GIVE IN

Eventually, it dawned on those who hoped for reconciliation, such as Emilio Visconti-Venosta or Prime Minister Lanza, that Pius would never accept any proposal, suggestion or even hint from the Italian government. Each and every approach the Italian government made to the pope met the brick wall of resistance, creating apprehension in the Italian government and poisoning the atmosphere at the Vatican.

A pall of gloom prevailed, with cardinals afraid to walk out in the streets, or drive in the splendid carriages that identified them as servants of the pope. Priests could be seen slinking along, obviously afraid of being recognized and harassed by hostile roving gangs. Perhaps worst of all, shouts of 'Death to the pope!' could be heard from outside the walls of the Vatican. Freedom of the press allowed seditious and blasphemous books to be sold openly in Rome, which stoked even further the hatred for the papacy, which was growing more and more apparent throughout the new Italian kingdom.

According to the pope's indefatigable Secretary of State, Cardinal Antonelli, the government's repeated claims of respect for the pope, concern for his welfare and safety and their desire to find a compromise

Cardinal Giacomo Antonelli was a major figure in the Vatican during the 1848 liberal revolution and stoutly defended Pope Pius IX's conservative reaction to it.

that would enable him to function freely were nothing but a cynical cover for some terrible abuses. Antonelli's list comprised a fearful indictment, including, he wrote:

> *...the complete stripping of the august Head of the Church of all his dominions, of all his income, the bombardment of the capital of Catholicism, the impieties that are being spread through the population by newspapers, the violent attacks against religion and the monastic orders, the profanation of the Catholic cult, which is being labelled superstition, the stripping of all public schools of every sacred image, which has been ordered by government authorities and already cried out, the removal of the name of Jesus from above the grand portal of the Roman College.*

It was against this dangerous background that Cardinal Antonelli was busy trying to encourage papal nuncios in European capitals to rouse to action governments that were friendly to the pope. His efforts produced a few, though not nearly enough, positive returns. In Germany, for example, princes, noblemen and lawyers in several states signed a petition condemning the occupation of Rome and the destruction of the pope's secular power in the Papal States. In Belgium and several other countries, Catholics were encouraged to hold protest meetings at which they declared the seizure of Rome a sacrilege

In Germany, for example, princes, noblemen and lawyers in several states signed a petition condemning the occupation of Rome.

and the threats to the pope as virtual patricide. Protest processions were held and hundreds of masses were sung. Individual bishops in Germany and Belgium bombarded Vittorio Emanuele and his government with their personal protests. Much was made of the pope's new appellation, the 'prisoner of the Vatican' and a great deal of hot air was expended on angry denunciation of the 'heretic' Italians and the punishments that awaited them for their 'crimes'.

ANTONELLI FRUSTRATED

But what Antonelli most fervently wanted – a concerted, Europe-wide campaign by Catholic governments, clergy and congregations that was vast and vocal enough to put real pressure on the Italians to withdraw from Rome and the Papal States and restore the pope to his rightful heritage – was not forthcoming. In his genuine desire to rescue Pope Pius from a desperate situation, Antonelli had overlooked a vital fact about late nineteenth-century Europe. The continent had moved on a long way from the days when rulers could stand on their autocratic rights and expect unquestioning obedience from their subjects. The revolutions of 1789 and 1848 had destroyed the Europe in which such attitudes prevailed. This was confirmed even more recently by an aftershock – the Paris Commune of early 1871 – in which workers, variously classed as anarchists or socialists, rose up against the French government, which had just been forced into accepting a humiliating peace by the Prussians.

The lukewarm response of the Austrians and Belgians to Antonelli's pleas were indicative of this new situation, whereas Pius and his devoted Secretary of State were in denial about it. In reality, restoring an

In reality, restoring an infallible pope who had publicly set his face against the modern world would create havoc.

infallible pope who had publicly set his face against the modern world would create havoc. Newly enfranchised populations would be bound to rise in defence of their own hard-won civic rights and the freedoms that came with them. Besides, Pius was not interested in protests, demonstrations, reassurances or the wringing of hands. For him, the only acceptable outcome was that the Italian state should be dismantled. Vittorio Emanuele must be sent back to Piedmont, where he came from. Rome and the Papal States had to be retrieved and, as Antonelli himself put it, 'the full and absolute restoration of the pope's dominions and powers' should be implemented.

THE DEATHS OF BOTH KING AND POPE

This amounted to a total impasse and it was still there in 1878 when both chief protagonists, King Vittorio Emanuele and Pope Pius, died. The King went first, on 9 January, aged 57, from pneumonia, after Pope Pius had acceded to his final request, which was to receive the Sacraments. The pope followed just over four weeks later, on 7 February. He was 85 years old and had served what is still the longest pontificate in papal history.

But while the Catholic world mourned, others took advantage of the pope's demise to express their

The Communards who fought for the socialist Paris Commune in 1871 are photographed around the base of the Vendôme column, erected by Napoleon Bonaparte to commemorate his victory at Austerlitz in 1805.

fury at his actions and attitudes. The Church and the Catholic clergy were persecuted in both Germany and Switzerland. In Austria, Pius was reviled for his refusal to receive a member of the imperial family who had come to Rome for the funeral of the late King. A secular, anti-Catholic party with a virulent hatred of the papacy now ruled France, the one-time protector of the Holy See. Spain and Belgium, though Catholic countries, were no friends of the Vatican, either.

The future of the papacy in relation to the Italian state did not look promising.

Against this background, the future of the papacy in relation to the Italian state did not look promising. What was needed was a pair of protagonists – king and pope – who were willing to work out a compromise. Above all, both needed to see the wisdom of moving off square one, which was where the deaths of Vittorio Emanuele and Pius IX had left them. Furthermore, both were backed by intransigent supporters so virulently opposed to their enemy's cause that they reached for their strongest adjectives to heap appalling insults on each other.

POPE LEO AND KING UMBERTO

In this context, neither Leo XIII, who succeeded Pius IX as pope, nor Umberto I who became King of Italy on his father's death, looked like working the miracle that was required to bring about a peaceful solution to the 'Roman question'. Pope Leo was a cultured, gentle

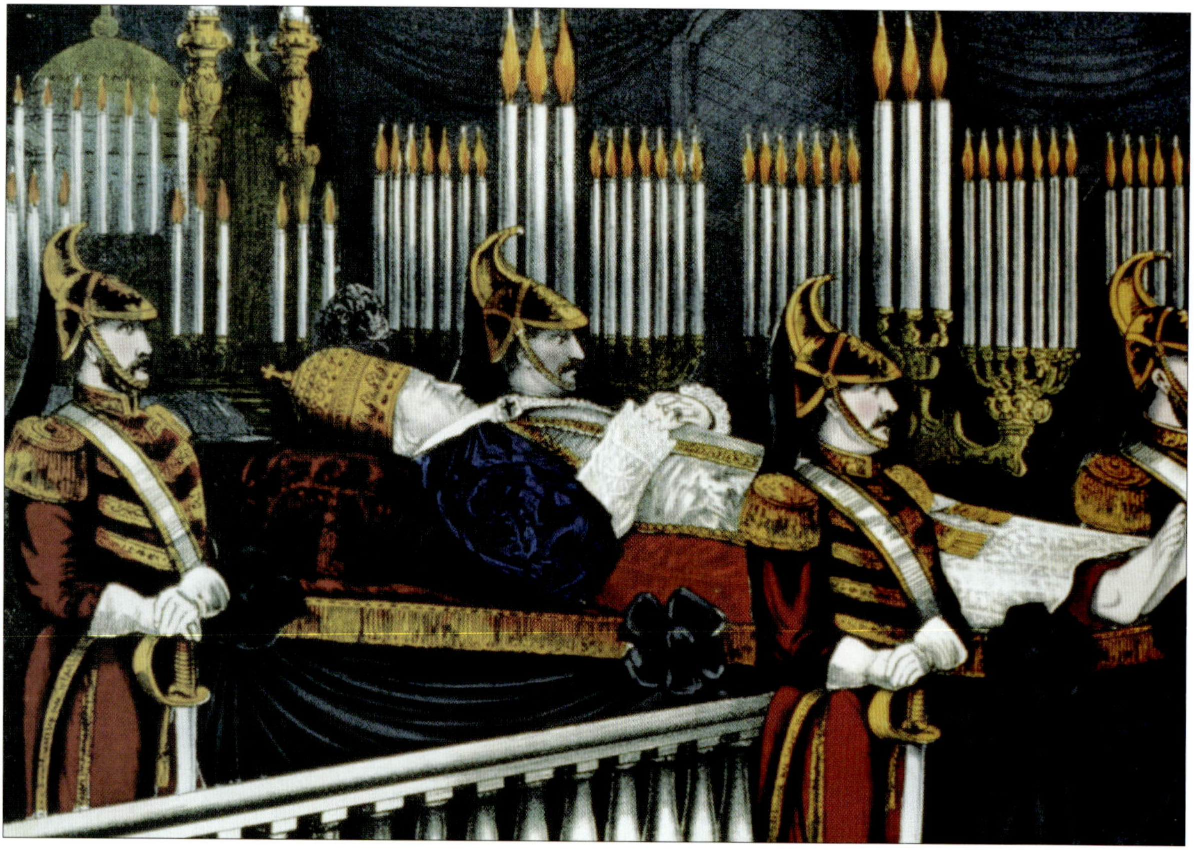

The funeral cortège of Pope Pius X who wears the triple crown of the popes as his body is taken in procession through the streets of Rome in 1914.

man. He was a diplomat and never indulged in the emotional fireworks favoured by his predecessor. He never spoke impetuously or acted without careful thought. Unlike Pius, Leo XIII understood the modern world and appreciated the benefits of democracy, though not all the way. He rejected equality and unconditional freedom of thought as unsuitable for ordinary people, who, he believed, were too immature and undisciplined to handle them properly.

But the inescapable sticking point was Leo XIII's belief in his infallibility as pope and with that, his inalienable right to retrieve and rule the whole of Rome and the Papal States. As always, the Kingdom of Italy stood immovably in the way of such ideas, as did its sovereign, Umberto I, who was firmly wedded to the principle that Rome was, and would remain, the capital of his kingdom. In any case, the times were too far out of joint for Umberto

Umberto I, the second King of Italy who was loathed by liberals and left wingers for his hardline conservative policies. Umberto was assassinated by an anarchist in 1900.

Leo XIII rejected equality and unconditional freedom of thought as unsuitable for ordinary people...

even to attempt an accord with the Pope. Throughout his reign, Italy was convulsed by the spread of socialist ideas and public hostility to various crackdowns on civil liberties. The upheavals this caused culminated in the assassination of King Umberto in 1900 by an anarchist, Gaetano Bresci, in Monza, in the north of Italy. Pope Leo XIII died three years later at the age of 93 years, still a prisoner of the Vatican. During the quarter-century his pontificate lasted, Leo never once set foot outside the precincts of the Holy See.

Reconciliation was even less likely between Pope Leo's successor, Cardinal Giuseppe Sarto, who was elected as Pius X, and Vittorio Emanuele III, who became the third king of Italy on his father's assassination. It had long been the custom for popes to choose the name of a predecessor they particularly admired and Pius X gave notice of his deeply conservative credentials when he chose the same name as the first 'prisoner of the Vatican', Pius IX. The tenth Pius proved to be a vociferous critic of 'modernists' and 'relativists' whom he classed as dangerous to the Catholic faith and its adherents. To emphasize these ideas, Pius X formulated an Oath against Modernism, which began in a truly uncompromising manner:

> *I firmly embrace and accept each and every definition that has been set forth and declared by the unerring teaching authority of the Church, especially those principal truths which are directly opposed to the errors of this day.*

Those clerics who refused to take the Oath – there were about 40 who were courageous (or foolhardy) enough to do so – faced possible excommunication and so did scholars or theologians who strayed over into secular or modernist research during the course of their work. Although still 'imprisoned' in the Vatican, Pius X was not afraid to punish foreign heads of state who recognized the Kingdom of Italy and therefore, by inference, the Italians' 'theft' of Rome and the Papal States. This stance could have embarrassing consequences, for when the President of France, Émile Loubet, made an official visit to King Vittorio Emanuele III, Pius X refused to receive him. The

French retaliated by breaking off diplomatic relations with the Vatican.

The diminutive, timid Vittorio Emanuele III was not the man to deal with the righteous determination of Pius X, who towered over him both intellectually and physically. The tiny, delicate Cardinal Giacomo della Chiesa, a nobleman who was elected as Benedict XV on Pius' death in 1914, was much more the king's stature. Even the smallest of the three cassocks made for a new pope was still far too large for him. In consequence, he was nicknamed *Il Piccolino* (the little man) but there was nothing diminutive about his personal convictions.

Benedict strongly reiterated Pius X's stand against the Italian 'occupation' of Rome and the Papal States.

Vittorio Emanuele III, the third king of Italy, was a tiny man of shy disposition who, unlike Pope Pius X, approved of liberal policies. But he never sought to promote his ideas in the face of Pius' deeply conservative stance.

He also opposed modernism and those modernist scholars who had been excommunicated by his predecessor. The most dominant event of Benedict's pontificate was World War I. He referred to this as 'the suicide of Europe' and tried desperately, but unsuccessfully, to halt it. But an even greater preoccupation and one that had a direct bearing on the safety, even the continuation, of the papacy emerged after the war came to an end in 1918.

Benito Mussolini's followers barricade the Fascist Party building in Milan in 1922, the year Mussolini seized power in Italy.

The Russian Revolution of 1917, the slaughter of the Romanov royal family the following year, and the professed aim of the new Bolshevik rulers to spread their communist creed across Europe struck fear and apprehension right across the continent. The danger seemed especially acute to the Vatican, for the communist government was atheist and would soon set about dismantling the Orthodox Church in Russia. The spectre of godlessness being spread across Europe in the wake of a communist victory was too fearful to contemplate. Yet, contemplating it was necessary. In Rome, the danger assumed proportions far greater than those behind the struggle with the Kingdom of Italy or the occupation of the Papal States. Already, in 1919, a terrifying future seemed to be unfolding in Italy, where socialist activists were fighting right-wing fascists in street battles of the most violent intensity and taking Italy to the brink of anarchy.

AGAINST COMMUNISM

For all his innate conservatism, Benedict XV was able to read the writing on the wall and his insights produced the first chink in the armour of papal resistance to the Italian state. In 1919, Benedict took a step that would have been anathema to his immediate predecessors: he sanctioned the setting up of the Catholic Popular Party, led by a priest, Luigi Sturzo. Previously, popes had barred Catholics from even voting in elections and certainly from holding elected office. Now, they were officially fighting elections and, in fact, did well on their first outing, coming second to the Italian Socialist party, with 21 per cent of the vote to the Socialists' 32 per cent. Better still, to Pope Benedict's considerable relief, the Popular Party, in coalition with the liberal government, shut the socialists out of power. But a much more fundamental upheaval was already on its way. Industrial strikes – 2000 of them in 1920 alone – together with unrest and violence from both the right and left of the political spectrum continued unabated until civil war in Italy seemed inevitable.

At this juncture, an unexpected saviour arrived on the scene. The Fascist movement formed in 1919 and led by a one-time socialist, Benito Mussolini, began to deploy gangs of thugs in the streets of towns and cities with the aim, quite literally, of battering their socialist

THE LATERAN TREATY OF 1929

The negotiations took many years, but on 11 February 1929, Cardinal Pietro Gaspari, representing Pope Pius XI and Benito Mussolini, representing Vittorio Emanuele III, King of Italy, used a gold quill pen specially provided for the purpose to sign the Lateran Treaty in the Popes' Room at the Lateran Palace in Rome. The Treaty created the world's smallest sovereign state, Vatican City, which measured only 44 hectares. This was the new much smaller, but undoubted domain of the pope who became its acknowledged ruler.

The argument that had alienated the Vatican from the Kingdom of Italy for nearly 60 years was now settled. The first four of its 27 Articles set out the major points on which the two sides were now, at last, agreed:

Article 1: Italy recognizes and reaffirms the principle established in the first Article of the Italian Constitution dated 4 March 1848, according to which the Catholic Apostolic Roman religion is the only State religion.

Article 2: Italy recognizes the sovereignty of the Holy See in international matters as an inherent attribute in conformity with its traditions and the requirements of its mission to the world.

Article 3: Italy recognizes the full ownership, exclusive dominion, and sovereign authority and jurisdiction of the Holy See over the Vatican as at present constituted, together with all its appurtenances and endowments, thus creating the Vatican City.

Article 4: The sovereignty and exclusive jurisdiction over the Vatican City, which Italy recognizes as appertaining to the Holy See, forbid any intervention therein on the part of the Italian Government, or that any authority other than that of the Holy See shall be there acknowledged.

Once the Treaty was signed, the bells of St John Lateran rang out. There was much to be celebrated. Under the Treaty, the Vatican agreed to recognize the Italian state as legitimate and Rome as its capital. Italian schools were now duty bound to provide Catholic instruction, and the religious imagery removed after the Italian state was proclaimed was restored. The clergy, however, would not be allowed to participate in politics and the Catholic Popular Party was disbanded.

Mussolini (left) pays his respects to King Vittorio Emanuele III (right) after the fascist leader's March on Rome in 1922 brought him to power in Italy.

and other rivals to defeat. The police, the military, the liberal right wing, wealthy businessmen and anyone else with a vested interest in peace for the sake of profit quietly approved, or at least turned a blind eye to the Fascist violence.

MARCH ON ROME

Pope Benedict, who died early on in 1922, did not live to see the final outcome of these events. In October of that year, Mussolini made his 'March on Rome' where a thoroughly cowed King Vittorio Emanuele III, appointed him Prime Minister. Mussolini soon expanded his powers, abolishing all other political parties, the trade unions and all democratic freedoms. He replaced them with a totalitarian state with himself in charge as *Il Duce* (the leader).

Meanwhile, in the Vatican, a new pope had been elected to succeed Benedict and though he did not approve of the terrorist tactics Mussolini used to gain and keep hold of power, he saw in him a man with whom he could do business. Cardinal Achille Ratti, Archbishop of Milan, was a man of strong will and fervent belief. He was elected Pope Pius XI on 6 February 1922, in the last of 14 ballots. His first act as pope – restoring the blessing *Urbi et Orbi* (to the City and the World) – gave notice of a more international outlook than previous popes who had refused to make the blessing after the loss of Rome and the Papal States as part of their protest against the intrusions of the secular outside world on holy Vatican soil.

A MODERN POPE AT LAST

Above all, Pope Pius XI was aware that in the twentieth century the world was driven by new imperatives now that four Empires and their absolute rulers in Germany,

Mussolini watches as Cardinal Gaspari signs the Lateran Treaty of 1929. This momentous event brought nearly 60 years of papal isolation to an end.

THE PRESS REACTS TO THE TREATY

The Lateran Treaty made big headlines. 'Mussolini and Gaspari sign historical Roman pact!' declared the *San Francisco Chronicle*. 'Historic Scene in the Lateran Palace!' trumpeted *The Catholic Advocate*. 'Long Church strife in Italy ended' announced the *Wisconsin Rapids Daily Tribune* in an issue dated 7 June 1929, the day the Treaty was ratified. The article continued:

All Rome resounded to the pealing of joyous church bells today as (Italian) Prime Minister Mussolini and Cardinal Gaspari solemnly exchanged ratifications of the historical Lateran Treaty...There were no speeches and the ceremony was brief and simple. One of its most striking and symbolical moments was when the great bronze doors opening out upon the colonnade of St Peter's Square, which had remained half shut for 59 years, were once more opened wide.

Russia, Austro-Hungary and Ottoman Turkey had been dethroned following World War 1. In this context, old rivalries grew outdated and needed to be cast aside if new challenges – communists versus democrats, religion versus secularism – were to be effectively met. In accordance with this new reality, Pius XI accepted that the Kingdom of Italy was not going to go away, and that the Papal States had gone forever. From this, it followed that papal isolation had to end so that the Church could resume its missionary work and once more exert a global influence.

Benito Mussolini, for his part, cared little for the Catholic faith, the pope or anything else that did not bolster his own power. But he *was* an opportunist who knew perfectly well that his dictatorship labelled Italy as a rogue state and cast him as an enemy of democratic liberties. For these reasons, Mussolini welcomed the headline-making value of reconciliation with the pope and the esteem it would lend his regime, particularly among the millions of Catholics across the world.

THE LAST PRISONER OF THE VATICAN

On 25 July 1929, Pope Pius XI celebrated mass. Afterwards, he led a procession through the doors of St Peter's Basilica and out into the midsummer sunshine that blazed down on the public square beyond, where a crowd of around one-quarter million was waiting to receive his blessing. The fifth and final prisoner of the Vatican had at long last been released from his self-imposed confinement and, for the first time in nearly 60 years, rejoined the outside world.

A smiling Pope Pius XI leaves the Vatican to make a splendid re-entry into Rome after the signing of the Lateran Treaty.

THE POPE AND THE NAZIS

If ever a pope was handed a poisoned chalice on his election to the Throne of St Peter, it was Eugenio Maria Giuseppe Giovanni Pacelli, who became Pius XII on 2 March 1939, his sixty-third birthday. Only six months later, on 3 September, the invasion of Poland by the forces of Nazi Germany initiated World War II, placing Pius in a unique – and deeply uncomfortable – position.

As the only ruler whose power had global reach, Pius was expected to make a strong moral stand over the issues surrounding World War II. The conflict was not merely a struggle for power or territorial gain and influence. The British and their allies believed they were fighting Nazi Germany and its Führer, Adolf Hitler in order to liberate Europe and the world from a racist and expansionist dictatorship. The Nazis, for their part, believed just as fervently that the 'thousand-year Reich' they sought to establish in Europe – and maybe the world – was their rightful destiny.

The tall figure of Cardinal Eugenio Pacelli, the papal nuncio to Germany, strides down the steps of the presidential palace in Berlin on 12 December 1929.

Pius XII's troubles began when both sides in the war expected his endorsement and support. Both were infuriated when neither got what they wanted. Pius chose the middle way, adopting neutrality as the stance from which he felt he had the best chance to exert his influence for peace and, hopefully, bring the conflict to an end. Unfortunately, it proved to be a big mistake. Virulent accusations were unleashed, condemning the pope of moral 'cowardice' and culpable 'silence'.

Above all, Pius was charged with the innate anti-Semitism that allowed him to abandon the hapless Jews of Europe to persecution and extermination in the death camps set up by the Nazis. The Germans, on the other hand, saw the pope as an implacable foe and one prominent Nazi, *SS Obergruppenführer,* (Senior Group Leader) Reinhardt Heydrich commented that

Pius was charged with the innate anti-Semitism that allowed him to abandon the hapless Jews of Europe to persecution and extermination.

Pius XII was a greater enemy of the Third Reich than either British Prime Minister Winston Churchill or US President Franklin D. Roosevelt.

The controversy over the wartime role of Pope Pius XII continued after the end of World War II in 1945 and far beyond that into the twenty-first century. A collection of books and documentaries grew up around the subject, but the greatest single boost the debate received was sparked off by a sensational stage play premièred in Berlin on 20 February 1963. It was entitled *The Deputy: a Christian Tragedy* and it was written by the German playwright Rolf Hochhuth, who later went on to make a name for himself specializing in controversial political dramas. However, Hochhuth's picture of a cold-eyed collaborator with a heart of stone did not ring true with anyone who knew Pope Pius and his longstanding record as a diplomat of charm and skill. He certainly looked the monkish aesthete who kept himself aloof from the world, with his tall, stick-like frame, parchment-pale face and air of holy detachment. But the impression he made in public was quite different. James Lees-Milne, the British writer and diarist wrote:

His presence radiated a benignity, calm and sanctity that I have certainly never before sensed in any human being. All the while, he smiled in the sweetest, kindliest

THE DEPUTY – LIBEL OR LICENCE?

In *The Deputy,* Hochhuth castigated Pius for wilful neglect and moral turpitude, depicting him as a ruthless, avaricious character who was more concerned with the Vatican finances than the fate of the Jews or, in fact, any other victims of the Nazis, such as gypsies, homosexuals, freemasons and Jehovah's Witnesses. The play, Hochhuth's first, was also staged, in English, at London's Aldwych Theatre by the Royal Shakespeare Company later on in 1963. It was performed on Broadway in New York in 1964 and again in the UK in 1986 and 2006. The influence exerted by *The Deputy* was immense. It revived the debate about the guilt or otherwise of the papacy and the pope in the Nazi's 'Final Solution to the Jewish Question'.

In 1963, German playwright Rolf Hochhuth created a sensation with his first play, *The Deputy* which depicted Pope Pius XII as a Nazi collaborator during World War II.

way... I was so affected I could scarcely speak... and was conscious that my legs were trembling.

Lees-Milne was not the first to feel wobbly during a close encounter with a famous celebrity, but the rulers and ministers with whom Eugenio Pacelli negotiated during his long diplomatic career were made of sterner stuff.

Theobald Bethmann-Hollweg, chancellor to Kaiser Wilhelm II of Germany, was anxious to make a negotiated peace to bring World War I to an end.

PACELLI IN BAVARIA

His first major appointment outside the Vatican came in 1917, the third year of World War I, when Pope Benedict XV sent him to Bavaria as papal nuncio or ambassador. Monsignor Pacelli's first task was to lay Pope Benedict's plan for peace and an end to World War I before the King of Bavaria, Ludwig III and the aggressive, autocratic Kaiser Wilhelm.

Pacelli seems to have made enough of an impression on the two monarchs and also on Wilhelm's chancellor, Theobald von Bethmann-Hollweg, to raise hopes that there was a real prospect for peace. But he was 'extraordinarily disappointed and depressed' when the German military intervened and escalated the fighting by introducing unrestricted submarine warfare. But if he could not halt the war, Pacelli moved on to the next best thing – promoting the humanitarian approach, as formulated by Benedict, a pope well known for his compulsive charity towards the poor and needy.

After World War I ended on 11 November 1918, Pacelli remained in Bavaria after most other diplomats departed. They had been wise to leave, for in April 1919 the so-called Spartacist revolutionaries seized power and formed the short-lived Bavarian Soviet Republic. The Republic, which was modelled on the atheistic revolution in Russia, lasted only four weeks, but for as long as it survived Pacelli, as a churchman and representative of the pope, was in a delicate position. Calm composure and nerves of steel were required, and the nuncio proved he had plenty of both.

Eugenio Pacelli's chief task as papal nuncio was to conclude a concordat (an agreement between the Apostolic See and a government of a certain country on religious matters) with various European

Spartacist radical socialists commandeer a car during the brief revolution in Germany following the end of World War I.

Eugenio Pacelli's chief task as papal nuncio was to conclude a concordat with various European governments.

governments to ensure the safety and freedom of the Catholic churches in their countries. A concordat gave the Church several important rights. One was the entitlement to organize youth groups, another to make Church appointments. The Church was allowed to run its own schools, hospitals and charities and could conduct religious services. All these enabled the Church to function and ensured the continuation of the Catholic religion.

Yet, concluding these complex agreements was fraught with one overriding difficulty, for the immediate post-war period offered a real chance that, after Bavaria, more soviets would be created to realize the Bolshevik dream of spreading communism throughout the continent. Pacelli, however, was undeterred. Once an invading German army had destroyed the Bavarian Soviet Republic, the nuncio concluded a concordat, his first, with Bavaria, which was now a state within the Weimar Republic.

RETURN TO ROME

After his frustrating encounters with the Soviets, Eugenio Pacelli was recalled to Rome in 1929 where, despite his failure in Russia, both Catholics and

OUTWITTING REVOLUTIONARIES

On a day in 1919, a small group of youthful revolutionaries broke into the building occupied by the Vatican embassy and tried to steal Pacelli's motorcar. Although his frail physique and 43 years made him unlikely to win a fistfight with the intruders, Pacelli went out to confront them and demanded that they leave the grounds, which were technically Vatican territory. The intruders, all Spartacists, agreed to go but only if they could take the car with them. Pacelli knew they were not going to get far because he had already seen to it that the starter motor was disconnected, and had received a guarantee from the Bavarian government that the vehicle would be immediately returned to him. The Spartacists towed the car away, but to their chagrin soon found the papal nuncio had outsmarted them.

Cardinal Pacelli leaves the presidential palace in Berlin in 1927 after meeting the president, General Paul von Hindenburg.

Protestants greeted him as a great hero of the Christian cause. Pope Pius rewarded him with a cardinal's hat and he achieved a further promotion, in 1930, to Cardinal Secretary of State. In this exalted position, Pacelli agreed concordats with several countries where the Catholic Church needed to be bolstered after the upheavals of World War I. A concordat with the German state of Baden was finalized in 1932, and in the following year, others were signed with Austria and in July 1933, six months after Adolf Hitler attained power as Chancellor, with Nazi Germany. Yugoslavia followed, signing concordats in 1935 and in Portugal in 1940.

The most fateful of these agreements was, of course, the *Reichskonkordat* with Germany. The Nazis

THE CARDINAL AND THE SOVIETS

After Bavaria, Pacelli moved on to Berlin as papal nuncio in Germany and then in 1925 embarked on negotiations with the Soviet Union. There, eight years after the Bolshevik victory, vicious and systematic persecution of the Russian church was already well under way. Priests and bishops were flung into prison, where many were murdered. Russian clergy and laity were rounded up and transported to the gulag at Solówki on the Black Sea. Churches were plundered and destroyed. Religion was vilified in schools and in the press. God, and teaching about God, became forbidden subjects.

Even so, Pacelli was determined to follow his orders from Pope Pius XI, which were to set up diplomatic relations between the communists and the Vatican. To help the process along, he organized desperately needed shipments of food to Russia where thousands, if not millions, had been left hungry and destitute after World War I. But even Pacelli could go so far and no further. The men he had to deal with, such as Foreign Minister Georgi Chicherin, made it virtually impossible to broker an agreement. Chicherin was a thoroughgoing atheist who despised religious education and refused to allow the ordination of priests and bishops. In this dangerous atmosphere, Pacelli believed he had a chance to come to terms in secret, but there was no meaningful progress. In 1927 Pius XI ordered him to break off negotiations.

Georgi Chicherin was the atheistic Russian foreign minister who destroyed Cardinal Pacelli's attempts in 1925 to set up diplomatic relations between the Vatican and the Soviet Union.

The devastating Reichstag fire of 1933, pictured here, may have been started by the Nazis themselves to provide an excuse to persecute German communists.

VIOLATING THE CONCORDAT

In the six years until 1939, the Nazis committed more than 50 violations of the *Reichskonkordat,* starting with a round-up of Jews within a mere five days of the agreement being signed. They continued by passing a law enforcing the sterilization of Germans considered to be 'life unworthy of life' such as criminals, dissidents, the feeble-minded, homosexuals, the insane and others who had to be stopped from reproducing themselves and so passing on their weaknesses to future generations. Cardinal Pacelli registered protests, the first of them concerning another infringement of the *Reichskonkordat,* a boycott of Jewish businesses. This was one of 45, which the Nazis never answered, but the protests did form the substance of an encyclical, *Mit Brennender Sorge* (With Burning Concern), which Pacelli prepared for the Pope. The encyclical was proclaimed on 10 March 1937 but unlike his carefully diplomatic nuncio, Pius XI did not mince his words. He wrote:

> *Whoever exalts race, or the people, or the State... or the depositories of power or any other fundamental value of the human community... whoever raises these notions above their standard value and divinizes them to an idolatrous level, distorts and perverts an order of the world planned and created by God; he is far from the true faith in God and from the concept of life which that faith upholds.*

were well aware that much of the outside world believed they had come to power by thuggery and chicanery. But an agreement with the papacy, the most ancient and venerable polity in the whole of Europe, would provide the missing piece in the jigsaw of their victory by giving their regime respectability and a standing in the world that was not available from any other source. In addition, it was an effective way to silence opposition to the Nazis from the Catholic Church in Germany.

THE FAITHLESS FÜHRER

Whether or not Pacelli realized that this was the nefarious purpose behind his negotiations with Hitler remains unknown, but it would be surprising if the idea did not cross the mind of such an experienced and intelligent diplomat. Pacelli's aim was, of course, to strengthen the position of the Catholic Church in Germany, protect Catholic organizations and ensure that Catholic education, Catholic schools and Catholic publications would not be molested. But this was where Cardinal Pacelli was under a misapprehension.

In 1933 Adolf Hitler had not yet established his reputation for making agreements to obtain a short-

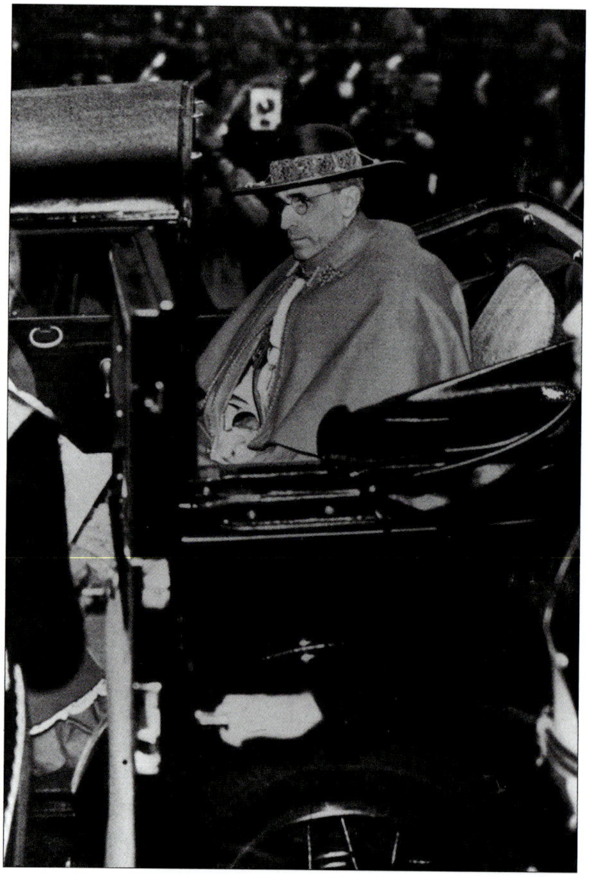

This photograph shows Cardinal Pacelli in early 1939, before he was elected pope.

This official portrait of Pope Pius XII, as Pacelli became on the eve of World War II, reflects his pensive and steely character.

term gain and, when they were no longer of use, reneging on them. So the negotiations went ahead and Pacelli, acting on behalf of Pope Pius XI, played his part in good faith. By the time the Nazis broke the *Reichskonkordat,* the deed was done and the papacy found itself joined to a faithless and cynical partner.

Cardinal Pacelli learnt the horrific details of *Kristallnacht* when the papal nuncio in Berlin contacted him.

The Vatican responded to the perfidy of the Nazis with its own unique weapon, the encyclical. Papal encyclicals were normally written in Latin. But this time, Cardinal Pacelli enlisted several German cardinals to help him write *Mit Brennender Sorge* entirely in German. Pacelli was well aware that the Nazis would make every effort to prevent its distribution, and precautions were taken to ensure that it reached all Catholic churches in Germany. The text was smuggled into the Nazi state where it was printed and secretly distributed. Finally, the encyclical was read in all Catholic churches at Mass on Palm Sunday, 14 March 1937.

When the Nazis realized what had happened, their reaction was typically heavy-handed. All available copies of *Mit Brennender Sorge* were confiscated, the printers and distributors were arrested and the printing presses were seized. Trumped-up charges of dishonest currency dealings were laid to imprison Catholic priests and put them on trial.

Adolf Hitler made his position brutally plain when he described the Nazi opinion of the Pope's encyclical with the following statement:

PIUS XII – NAZI AND ANTI-SEMITE?

The presumed failure of the new pope, Pius XII, to speak out against the depredations of the Nazis have been taken as a first signs of his 'cowardice' and 'silence' on subjects that might give offence to Hitler and his totalitarian regime in Germany. From that, among other things, has sprung the theory that the pope was himself pro-Nazi and anti-Semitic. What this theory failed to address, though, was first of all, the adverse Nazi response to the election of Cardinal Pacelli as pope. A complaint in the *Berlin Morgenpost* (Berlin Morning Post) accused the new pope of 'prejudiced hostility and incurable lack of comprehension. [Pius XII] is not accepted with favour in Germany because he was always opposed to Nazism and practically determined the policies of the Vatican under his predecessor.'

'Eugenio Pacelli had little understanding of us; little hope is placed in him,' commented the Nazi *Schutzstaffel,* the official publication of the SS, Hitler's personal bodyguard. Elsewhere, in Britain, France and the United States, the new pope was cordially welcomed, but Nazi Germany was the only major power that failed to send a representative to the papal coronation.

Despite his severe, ascetic looks, Pius XII was a man of great charm. humour and compassion. Acting mainly in secret, he saved the lives of an estimated 860,000 Jews during World War II.

NAZI WARTIME ATROCITIES

In 1942, Reinhard Heydrich, the Reich 'Protector' of Bohemia–Moravia (in what is today the Czech Republic) was assassinated when the Czech resistance bombed his car. Heydrich's successor, Karl Hermann Frank, resolved to stage 'special repressive action to give the Czechs a lesson in propriety'. The SS 'Blackshirts' applied this lesson by taking a fearful revenge on a village called Lidice, in Bohemia, where 172 men and boys were shot and the women and children were transported to Ravensbruch concentration camp.

Also, in 1942, the Catholic Archbishop of Utrecht wrote a pastoral letter protesting against the persecution of the Jews in the Nazi-occupied Netherlands. What the Nazis termed a 'countermeasure' followed five days later, when large numbers of Dutch Jews and Catholics were arrested and sent to concentration camps. There, they served as hostages for the pope's 'good behaviour', to be mistreated again if and when Pius XII spoke out against Nazi rule.

A repeat performance of Lidice took place in 1944, when the activities of the French resistance hampered the movement of German troops urgently needed to help stem the advance of Allied forces after the D-Day invasion in northern France. At Oradour-sur-Glane, a village in southwest France, all the male inhabitants were shot, the women and children were herded into the village church where they were burnt to death and the village was razed to the ground. At least 1000 villagers died.

SS General Karl Hermann Frank surrendered to the US Army at Pilsen (Plzen) in 1945. He was tried before a Czech court for war crimes and the obliteration of the Czech village of Lidice. Found guilty, he was executed before 5000 onlookers in 1946.

> *The Third Reich does not desire a* modus vivendi *with the Catholic Church, but rather its destruction... in order to make room for a German Church in which the German race will be glorified...*

MALEVOLENT NAZI INTENTIONS

Cardinal Pacelli, for one, was not surprised. Even before Hitler and the Nazis came to power, he had never doubted their intentions. The years before 1933 had seen plenty of 'rehearsals' for their totalitarian state, its racism and its brutality. Nazi thugs in the paramilitary SA or SS were used to break up communist and other political party meetings. Other opponents were beaten up or murdered. Nazi rallies and their pageantry were openly militaristic. All this set the scene for a reign of terror that began after Hitler became Chancellor of Germany on 30 January

> Pope Pius XII preferred quiet diplomacy and persuasion to dramatic gestures and fiery pronouncements.

A small boy, one of only seven survivors of the Nazi massacre at Oradour-sur-Glane, France, takes part in a memorial service held at the mass grave of the victims five months after the event, in November 1944.

1933 with the setting up of the first Nazi concentration camp at Dachau in Bavaria where the first inmates – Jews, socialists, trades unionists and other political opponents – were tortured, terrorized and brutalized.

Several notorious sequels followed, including the Reichstag fire of 1933, the Nuremberg laws of 1935/6 stripping German Jews of their civil rights and *Kristallnacht* (Crystal Night). This took place on 10 November 1938, when attacks on Jews, their synagogues and their property broke out all over Germany and Austria. *Kristallnacht* resulted in the murders of 91 Jews and the arrest of another 25,000 to 30,000, all of whom were later deported to concentration camps.

As a neutral state, the Vatican City could implement clandestine rescue work on a scale that only a pope could achieve.

Cardinal Pacelli learnt the horrific details of *Kristallnacht* when the papal nuncio in Berlin contacted him. At that time, Pope Pius XI was dying and some historians have suggested that Pacelli persuaded him to refrain from making an official protest. Pius XI died three months later, on 10 February 1939. Pacelli was elected pope in his place. At that point, its publishers had not yet sent the last encyclical of Pius XI's reign *Humani Generis Unitas* (On the Unity of Human Society), which had been prepared the previous September, to the Vatican. By the time it finally arrived, Pius XI was dead. Though Pacelli had succeeded him, he did not proclaim Pius's final encyclical, which raised several controversial issues, expressed in Pius XI's usual forthright fashion, condemning racism, colonialism, and anti-Semitism, all of them features central to Nazi policy.

A second misunderstanding about Pope Pius XII centred on his personal style. He had never been a barnstormer, making free with purple prose and emotional delivery. He preferred quiet diplomacy and persuasion to dramatic gestures and fiery pronouncements. In addition, his diplomatic

Ernst von Weizsacker was the German ambassador to the Vatican who warned the Vatican of Adolf Hitler's plans to kidnap Pope Pius XII. Here he is seen being questioned at Nuremberg.

experience had given him a sound idea of the nature of the Nazi beast. Pius knew perfectly well that the Nazis would respond to any criticism or act of defiance by raising the level of their own brutality. This, in fact, was a major concern among Jewish leaders and those prisoners in the concentration camps who were able to communicate their fears to the outside world. They constantly begged the pope to soft-pedal any condemnations he might make about Nazi atrocities.

As an eyewitness at the Nuremberg Trials of Nazi war criminals in 1945–46 put it:

A PLOT TO KIDNAP THE POPE

The Nazis' belief that Pope Pius XII was hand in hand with the Jews was in line with the anti-Semitic propaganda that for years had been the staple diet fed to the German people by Dr Josef Goebbels. Even though Pope Pius was still refusing to directly condemn the Nazis' treatment of the Jews in 1943, it seems that Hitler had lost patience with the pontiff and was considering a daring plan to punish him. The Führer's intention was to kidnap Pope Pius and imprison him somewhere in Upper Saxony, in East Germany. But that was not all. Minutes of a meeting dated 26 July 1943 revealed that Hitler was not going to stop at seizing the pontiff. He was contemplating an invasion of the Vatican and dispatched orders to one SS chief in Italy, General Karl Otto Wolff, telling him to

occupy as soon as possible the Vatican and Vatican City, secure the archives and the art treasures which have a

Pope Pius XII blesses the crowd in 1943, a year in which public appearances could have been dangerous due to Adolf Hitler's plan to kidnap him.

unique value, and transfer the pope, together with the Curia [the papal court] for their protection, so that they cannot fall into the hands of the Allies and exert a political influence.

General Wolff, together with Nazi officials and diplomats, many of them Catholics, were aghast when they learnt that the Führer was willing to go to such lengths to get his hands on the most prestigious leader in the world. Pope Pius himself was rather more charitable. He believed that Hitler was possessed by the Devil and on several occasions attempted to exorcise the Führer and so release him from the Devil's wicked influence. As for Hitler, he had a megalomaniac's view of the pope as 'the only human being who has always contradicted me and who has never obeyed me'. He was resolved to eliminate this blot on his autocratic record.

Defying the Führer had long been a dangerous, usually lethal business, but the plot to kidnap the Pope was not the time to be content with obeying orders and setting aside the dictates of conscience. It took considerable courage, but there were Germans willing to take risks to thwart their Führer's plans. One of them was Ernst von Weizsäcker, the German ambassador to the Vatican. He warned the Holy See of the danger in which Pope Pius stood and suggested they refrain from doing anything that might provoke the volatile Führer into action. The Nazi ambassador to Italy, Rudolf Rahn, together with several other German diplomats, also worked to foil the kidnap plan. So did General Wolff, who managed to talk Hitler out of it by the end of 1943.

Or so the General thought. According to a detailed report in an issue of the Catholic daily paper *Avvenire d'Italia* (which loosely translates as *Events in Italy*) published in January 2005, Wolff realized to his horror that in 1944, the projected kidnapping had resurfaced when he received new orders to that effect from Hitler. At this juncture, around the end of May 1944, Wolff was the SS Commander in Nazi-occupied Rome. The Allied Fifth Army, which had invaded mainland Italy eight months previously was advancing fast on the city and was only days away from capturing it. The German *Wehrmacht* was preparing to withdraw so Hitler seemed to think this would be a convenient moment to seize the pope and take him along.

General Karl Friedrich Wolff of the Waffen SS took great personal risks to warn Pope Pius XII of the kidnap plot.

Wolff resolved to act quickly and before May was out, he had set up a secret meeting with the pope. He arrived in disguise, wearing civilian clothes rather than his SS uniform, and slipped into the Vatican at night, with the help of a priest who knew his way around the complex of buildings. Wolff began by assuring Pope Pius that no kidnapping was going to take place, but went on to warn him that the Führer looked on him as 'a friend of the Jews' and a barrier to his plans for world domination. Apart from warning the pope to be on his guard, General Wolff could do little more and he departed Rome with his forces shortly before the Allied army arrived and occupied the city.

German soldiers patrol within sight of St Peter's Basilica in the Vatican. They are under strict orders not to cross the painted white line that indicates the frontier between the Vatican and the rest of Rome.

A carefully worded protest, using general terms, was sent from the Vatican, deploring 'these measures which gravely hurt the natural human rights of persons, merely because of their race'.

Any words of Pius XII directed against a madman like Hitler, would have brought on an even worse catastrophe… (and) accelerated the massacre of Jews and priests.

HORRIFIC NAZI RETALIATIONS

This was a lesson the Jews had learnt the hard way, from the violent sequel to the killing at the German embassy in Paris of Ernst von Rath, a junior diplomat. The culprit was a young German Jew, Herschel Grynspan, who was protesting against the expulsion of his family from Germany. This murder alone led to the death and destruction wrought by Nazi gangs on *Krystallnacht.*

Later, as World War II continued, there were more demonstrations of the horrific heights that Nazi retaliation could reach. They let pass minor infringements of their draconian rules, but any sense of security this invoked was sadly misplaced. When

they considered the challenge serious enough, the Nazis hit back hard.

Faced with an enemy of implacable character, capable of any cruelty and any atrocity that human wickedness could devise, Pope Pius came to the conclusion that impartiality, or at least the appearance of impartiality, was the only way to ensure that the Vatican could remain neutral and therefore relatively free to act. As a neutral state, and one that even the Nazis might think twice about attacking, the Vatican City, its buildings and its facilities could be used to implement clandestine rescue work on a scale that only a pope could achieve.

Pope Pius XII greets members of the Press, soldiers and other military personnel in his apartments at the Vatican on 7 June 1944, three days after the Allied liberation of Rome.

A DIFFICULT STRATEGY

This was by no means an easy stance to maintain. Inevitably, the pope's strategy had to be kept secret. But just as inevitably, the secret led to assumptions about the 'indifference' shown by a 'heartless' Pius XII towards atrocities that deeply shocked others with less

A panoramic view of the Castel Gandolfo, the summer residence of the popes overlooking Lake Albano, about 30 kilometres (19 miles) southeast of Rome in the Alban Hills.

need to sit on the fence, or rather, give the impression of doing so. As early as September 1940, a full year after the start of World War II, the neutrality of the Vatican and its pope was being invoked to fend off sometimes strongly worded pleas for positive action.

In October 1941, for instance, the American delegate to the Vatican, Harold H. Tittmann, pressed Pope Pius to speak out against the atrocities being committed against the Jews. Tittmann was told that Pius wished to remain 'neutral'. This, though, was before the 'Final Solution to the Jewish Question', the euphemistic title used by the Nazis to describe the extermination of the Jews, which had been planned in detail at a conference of high-ranking Nazis held at Wannsee, a suburb of Berlin, in January 1942.

The effect of the Wannsee Conference, and the decisions taken there, was soon evident. In March 1942, 80,000 Slovakian Jews were earmarked for transportation to Poland. This move, according to the Vatican *chargé d'affaires* in Bratislava, the Slovakian capital, 'condemned a great number of them to certain death'. A carefully worded protest, using general terms, was sent from the Vatican, deploring 'these measures

which gravely hurt the natural human rights of persons, merely because of their race'. The message was coded in so far as the Nazis were not specifically mentioned. This was a tactic Pius used more than once to keep the Nazis, and especially the Gestapo, the dreaded secret police, from interfering in Vatican affairs.

Although critics of Pope Pius regarded his failure to call the Nazis to account as the coward's way out, the underlying message still got through when he made his Christmas broadcast on Vatican Radio. In 1941, Catholic and other families across the United States were moved to tune in. Just over two weeks earlier, on 7 December, a day that President Roosevelt said would 'live in infamy', the Americans had themselves been forced into the war by the Japanese attack on the US Pacific Fleet at Pearl Harbor, in Hawaii.

On this occasion, the editors of the *New York Times* certainly got the true measure of Pius when he called for 'a real new order' based on 'liberty, justice and love' and then dismissed the chance of any agreement between combatants 'whose reciprocal war aims and programmes seem to be irreconcilable'. A *New York Times* article indicated that, even though it was in coded form, the Pope's message was a clear condemnation of the Nazis' persecution of European Jews. The article stated:

> *The voice of Pius XII is a lonely voice in the silence and darkness enveloping Europe this Christmas... Nazi aims [are] also irreconcilable with Pius' own concept of a Christian peace.*

Around 3000 were smuggled into the Castel Gandolfo, the pope's summer residence 30 kilometres southeast of Rome.

At Christmas 1942, Pope Pius was a little more specific, although he still did not directly name any culprits when he broadcast his

> *... passionate concern for those hundreds of thousands who, without any fault of their own, sometimes only by reason of their nationality or race, are marked down for death or progressive extinction.*

The reference was unmistakable.

AVOIDING THE ISSUE

Towards the end of 1942, the massacres of Jews had reached 'frightening proportions and forms', as Monsignor Giovanni Montini, the future Pope Paul VI, informed Pius in a letter that reached the Vatican in September 1942. The horror stories escalated from there. In the same month, the American envoy to the Vatican, Myron Taylor, told Pope Pius that he was damaging his 'moral prestige' by remaining silent over the rapidly escalating Nazi atrocities. Representatives from several countries, including Britain, Brazil, Uruguay, Belgium and Poland, delivered the same warning only to be told, as was Myron Taylor, that the truth of rumours about the genocide of the Jews could not be properly established.

> One Irish priest, Monsignor Hugh O'Flaherty, who worked as a diplomat at the Vatican, was in particular danger.

At this stage, the Nazis seemed to have a clear idea of what the pope was doing and readily recognized that it was not in their favour. The German Foreign Office analyzed the Christmas message of 1942 and interpreted it for what it really was. He described it as

> *One long attack on everything we stand for. He is clearly speaking on behalf of the Jews... he is virtually accusing the German people of injustice toward the Jews and makes himself the mouthpiece of the Jewish war criminals.*

The Allied occupation of Rome finally thwarted Hitler's plan to kidnap Pope Pius. But what the Allied forces found in Rome was something that could hardly have been expected of the pro-Nazi pope of so many accusations. There was an extraordinary network of 'safe houses' and other refuges, forged by Pope Pius, his cardinals and priests, to serve as hiding places for thousands of fugitives. Most of them were Italian Jews but the refugees also included prisoners of war who were released from prison camps after Italy (formerly an ally of Nazi Germany) changed sides and joined the Allies late in 1943. Included, too, were members of the Italian resistance on the run from Nazi pursuers. When the Allied Fifth Army entered Rome on 4 June 1944, it was the first time for a very long while that these fugitives had been able to go out into the streets without fear of being killed or caught and punished.

Buildings both inside and beyond the Vatican had been commandeered for a wide-ranging rescue mission. On the orders of Pope Pius, almost the entire Italian National Committee of Liberation, which directed the activities of some 20,000 partisans across Italy, was concealed in the Roman Seminary at St John Lateran, only a few metres from the headquarters of the Gestapo. The Vatican buildings hid 477 Jews while another 4238 were distributed around the 155 monasteries and nunneries in Rome. In normal times, the sexes were strictly separated so that nuns were not allowed to host males, neither could the monks take in fugitive females. Pope Pius, however, lifted these restrictions, so that families sheltering in religious houses would not be separated.

Other fugitive Jews were installed in the Jesuit Gregorian University or slept in the basement of the Pontifical Bible Institute. Around 3000 were smuggled into the Castel Gandolfo, the pope's summer residence 30 kilometres southeast of Rome. Several others were cunningly disguised to escape detection. Some 3700 were dressed in the uniform of the Palatine Guard, whose task it was to protect Vatican City. Others were smeared with cosmetic creams to make them look like patients hospitalized with skin diseases in the Dermatological Institute of the Immaculate Conception. The Vatican even commissioned a film to be made in which some 300 of the 'extras' were really fugitives. Scores of cassocks were issued to Jews so that they would be mistaken for Catholic priests.

Some Jews went all the way and converted to Catholicism. For most of them, it was a temporary

> O'Flaherty and his team built up a stock of hideouts, using private homes and flats, convents or farms.

measure and once World War II was over the 'converts' returned to their own faith. But for as long as a Catholic identity was required, they were protected by an agreement with the Nazis that baptized Jews would not be persecuted. The converts were equipped with false baptismal certificates, Vatican passports and bogus papers. Thousands of these fake documents were produced inside the Vatican, some 80,000 being handed out to Jews in Hungary alone.

HELPING THE JEWS

The risks involved in aiding Jews and other fugitives on the run from the Nazis were enormous and even Pope Pius could not guarantee that his cardinals, bishops or

Gregory Peck (centre) played Monsignor Hugh O'Flaherty in *The Scarlet and the Black* (1983) a made-for-TV film about O'Flaherty's exploits in Rome during World War II.

priests could escape execution by Nazi firing squad if they were caught.

One Irish priest, Monsignor Hugh O'Flaherty, who worked as a diplomat at the Vatican, was in particular danger. Before he embarked on rescues in Rome, in 1943, the Nazis knew him as a visitor to prisoner of war camps in Italy, which could make it easy for him to be recognized. In the camps, O'Flaherty searched for prisoners who, though reported missing in action, might have survived. As and when O'Flaherty found them alive, he sent the news to their families via Vatican Radio. But this was innocent stuff, even to the Nazis who occupied Italy after the Italian surrender of 1943.

PRISONERS OF WAR ON THE LOOSE

With Italy on the side of the Allies after its surrender in September 1943, there was no reason for the Italians to keep Allied prisoners of war confined. The camps were opened, the guards fled and the prisoners were free to go. Many of them remembered their visits from O'Flaherty and despite the dangers of a journey through Nazi-occupied territory they headed for Rome to seek his help. Before long, O'Flaherty had some 4000 POWs and Jews on his hands and needed a rescue network of his own to deal with them. For this work, he recruited fellow priests, a couple of Free French agents, several communists and a British Army colonel called Samuel Derry.

O'Flaherty and his team built up a stock of hideouts, using private homes and flats, convents or farms. One of them was right next to the headquarters of the SS. He concealed Jews in the Castel Gandolfo or in the German College where he had once been a student. Before long, Hugh O'Flaherty was being called 'The Pimpernel of the Vatican' after the fictional Scarlet Pimpernel, Sir Percy Blakeney, who rescued aristocrats and others from the guillotine during the French Revolution of 1789.

DIPLOMATIC IMMUNITY

As long as O'Flaherty remained within the confines of the Vatican and behind the thick white line that separated the papal enclave from the rest of Rome, diplomatic immunity preserved him from arrest. But he was obliged to venture out into the city on several occasions to organize his network, shepherd fugitives from place to place and check out the safety potential of new venues. All the while, the Nazi SS were watching for the elusive 'Pimpernel' and it was not long before they discovered first, that he was a priest and next, that he was the one-time prison visitor, Monsignor Hugh O'Flaherty.

Kappler hatched a plot to send two Gestapo thugs into the Vatican to seize O'Flaherty and drag him beyond its precincts and kill him there and then.

Safe inside Vatican territory, O'Flaherty took to loitering in the porch at St Peter's Basilica, waiting for Jews, prisoners of war and other fugitives to approach him. He was in full view of the German soldiers across the piazza but more important, easily visible to those who needed his help. When they arrived, O'Flaherty took them across the piazza and out of sight of the Nazis, through a cemetery and into the German College.

One evening, a Jewish man came up to O'Flaherty and gave him a solid gold chain. He and his wife, he said, expected to be arrested and taken to a concentration camp at any moment, but wanted to save their seven-year-old son from death in the gas chambers. The gold chain, the priest learnt, was intended to pay for the boy's upkeep. O'Flaherty took the chain, located the boy and kept him in hiding. He also provided false papers for the boy's parents, which kept them safe in Rome. After the end of World War II, O'Flaherty returned the boy – and the long golden chain.

PLOTTING TO TRAP O'FLAHERTY

Naturally, the Nazis were always waiting for the moment when O'Flaherty stepped outside the confines of the Vatican, ready to arrest or assassinate him. But they reckoned without the Monsignor's skill at disguise, which he wore whenever he ventured out into Rome. One day, he was a road sweeper, the next a butcher and the day after that a deliveryman. All this was extremely frustrating for Colonel Herbert Kappler, Chief of the Gestapo in Rome, a dangerous opponent who regularly ordered his troops to torture and execute partisans. O'Flaherty was proving a very elusive customer and Kappler resorted to having him continually watched.

O'Flaherty was easy to spot. Tall, well built and broad shouldered, the Irish monsignor was a successful amateur boxer and looked every inch the part. Once, Kappler thought he had O'Flaherty trapped when he confronted him with a group of Gestapo troops who were all set to arrest him. But O'Flaherty was fast on his feet and before they could get hold of him, he barged through the doors of Santa Maria Maggiore, which was Catholic Church property and out of bounds to the military. On another occasion, O'Flaherty was visiting the palace owned by Prince Filippo Doria Pamphili, who financed his rescue operations, when the building was surrounded by SS troops. O'Flaherty ran down into the basement, where a truck was unloading the Prince's winter supply of coal through a trapdoor.

ESCAPE VIA THE TRAPDOOR

The SS were only moments away from catching up with him and he had to act fast. He stuffed his monsignor's hat and robe into a coal sack, rubbed coal dust all over himself until he was unrecognizable, slung the sack over his shoulder and climbed out of the trapdoor. Two lines of SS men standing nearby stepped back, not wanting to get their uniforms dirty by close proximity to the tall, blackened figure who strolled past them nonchalantly and headed for the coal truck waiting at the palace gates. The truck drove to a nearby church where O'Flaherty cleaned himself up, dressed in his hat and robe and returned to the Vatican. Later, he telephoned the Prince to make sure that he and his family were all right. They were and, the Prince told the monsignor, Colonel Kappler was incandescent with fury.

Growing truly desperate, Kappler hatched a plot to send two Gestapo thugs into the Vatican to seize O'Flaherty and drag him beyond its precincts and kill him there and then. Fortunately, O'Flaherty's helpers learnt of the plan. The would-be assassins were intercepted and given a sound beating by four of the Vatican's Swiss Guards. Kappler never managed to catch O'Flaherty, who survived World War II.
So did Kappler, but he did so in Gaeta jail, between

Hugh O'Flaherty's arch-enemy, Hubert Kappler, head of the German security police in Rome, arrives for his trial in 1948. He was sentenced to life imprisonment but escaped from jail in 1978.

Rome and Naples, as a war criminal sentenced to life in prison. Once a month for year after year, Kappler received a single visitor – Monsignor Hugh O'Flaherty. Finally, in 1959, O'Flaherty baptized Kappler into the Roman Catholic Church. In 1977, Kappler, who was suffering from cancer and weighed only 48 kilograms (105 pounds) was hidden in a large suitcase and smuggled out of Gaeta and into Germany by his wife, Anneliese. He died the following year.

The State of Israel recognized O'Flaherty as one of the Righteous Among the Nations, a title given to non-Jews who helped Jews during World War II.

After the war ended in 1945, Monsignor O'Flaherty received many awards for his rescue work, including the U.S. Medal of Freedom with Silver Palm. King George VI also made him a Commander of the British Empire (CBE). The State of Israel, too, recognized O'Flaherty as one of the Righteous Among the Nations, a title given to non-Jews who helped Jews during World War II. After suffering a serious stroke, O'Flaherty retired in 1960 to his sister's home in County Kerry, Ireland, where he died in 1963.

In Italy, cardinals were also hard at work preserving lives. For instance, Cardinal Pietro Boetto of Genoa saved at least 800 refugees. Bishop Giuseppi Nicolini of Assisi hid some 300 Jews for two years. Two future popes, the successors of Pius XII, also took risks to help Jews and others escape the clutches of the Nazis. One was Cardinal Angelo Roncalli, later Pope John XXIII, the other was Cardinal Giovanni Montini (afterwards Pope Paul VI). Both of them were offered awards for their rescue work among the Jews, but both declined. Montini outlined their reasons. He said:

> *All I did was my duty. And besides, I only acted upon orders from the Holy Father* [Pius XII]. *Nobody deserves a medal for that.*

Troops of the multinational Allied Fifth Army arrive to liberate Rome on 4 June 1944.

In 1985, another Catholic churchman, Cardinal Pietro Palazzini, accepted recognition from the State of Israel as Righteous among the Nations for his own contribution to the succour and rescue of Jews in war-torn Europe. But he emphasized during the ceremony at *Yad Vashem,* the Holocaust Memorial in Jerusalem, that 'the merit is entirely Pius XII's who ordered us to do whatever we could to preserve the Jews from persecution'. In the event, an estimated 860,000 Jews were saved through the many initiatives promoted by Pope Pius XII.

Pius' seminal role in this far-reaching rescue mission has been stressed over and over again in the countless tributes paid to him by Jewish leaders and by presidents, prime ministers, other popes and scores of grateful individuals, or in books and articles on the subject. The pope's rescue of thousands of Jewish and other fugitives made Albert Einstein, the world-renowned Jewish scientist and an agnostic, change his mind about the Catholic Church and the papacy. He was moved from indifference to 'great affection and admiration because the Church alone had the courage and persistence to stand for intellectual truth and moral freedom'. But arguably the greatest compliment Pius XII received came from Israel Zolli, Chief Rabbi of Rome, who was so impressed by the Pope's compassion and courage that he became a Roman Catholic in 1945.

In the event, an estimated 860,000 Jews were saved through the many initiatives promoted by Pope Pius XII.

THE MUD STILL STICKS

And yet, despite all evidence to the contrary, and the moves made in recent years to canonize him, the list of accusations against Pius XII still proliferates, still questioning his courage, moral fibre and compassion. The Internet is full of such charges, many of them worded in the language of hate. One critic has labelled the 'misdeeds' of the pope as so fearful that he should have been in the dock at the Nuremberg trials of 1945–46, alongside 21 major Nazi war criminals. Another considered Pope Pius equally responsible with Adolf Hitler and other Nazis for the wartime slaughter of six million Jews together with four million gypsies, three million Catholics and countless other victims. In 2008, 50 years after the pope's death, a new book about his conduct during World War II, entitled *The Hound of Hitler,* called the pontiff too 'weak' to stand up to the Führer and a 'disaster for the Jews'. The mud, being flung to this very day, still sticks.

Israel Zolli, Chief Rabbi of Rome (left) delivers a special message to the Jews of the world in a broadcast from the Great Synagogue in the city on 31 July 1944.

Pope Pius XII lies in state following his death at Castel Gandolfo on 9 October 1958. He was buried in the Vatican grottoes under St Peter's Basilica, among the tombs of the popes.

INDEX

Page numbers in *italics* refer to illustrations

PICTURE CREDITS

AKG Images: 21, 31, 43, 44 (T. Lafranchis), 48, 56 (British Library), 62 (E. Lessing), 64, 71, 72, 81 (British Library), 84/85 (H. Champollion), 91 (Schütze/Rodemann), 96b (J. Raible), 99, 125 (E. Lessing), 135r, 145 (E. Lessing), 150, 152/153, 154/155 (E. Lessing), 165, 168, 231 **Alamy:** 39 (London Art Archive), 179 (EmmePi Europe) **Art Archive:** 57 (G. Dagli Orti/Bibliothèque de Carcassonne), 65 & 69 (G. Dagli Orti/Biblioteca Nazionale Marciana), 77 (G. Dagli Orti/Biblioteca Nazionale Marciana), 86 (G. Dagli Orti/Bibliothèque de Carcassonne), 88 (N. Setchfield) **Art-Tech/John Batchelor:** 55 **Bridgeman Art Library:** 14/15 (Giraudon), 76 (Musee des Augustins), 96t & 102 (Lauros/Giraudon), 109 (Archives Charmet), 115 & 119 (Bibliotheque Nationale, Paris), 121 (Corsham Court, Wiltshire), 140/141 (Museo Civico Rivoltello), 147 both (Look & Learn), 151 (Palazzo Vecchio, Florence), 156 (Regional M. Vrubel Art Museum, Omsk), 164 (E. Harvey-Lee), 171 (P. Willi), 214/215 (Lauros/Giraudon), 235 (Peter Newark Military Pictures) **Cody Images:** 54 **Corbis:** 95 (Stapleton Collection), 105 (C. Gerstenberg), 122 (S. Bianchetti), 149 (T. Spiegel), 161 (Bettmann), 167 (A. De Luca), 173 (M. Jodice), 211 (Bettmann), 224 (Hulton-Deutsch Collection), 229 & 233 (Bettmann), 234 & 236 (Bettmann), 240/241 (Bettmann), 247 (DPA), 250 (Bettmann), 251 (D. Lees) **De Agostini Picture Library:** 13 (A. Dagli Orti), 18, 23, 35 (G. Carfagna), 37 (G. Nimatallah), 38 & 49 (G. Dagli Orti), 53 & 61 (G. Dagli Orti), 63, 67 & 73 (G. Dagli Orti), 74 (G. Cigolini), 89, 93, 100 (A. Dagli Orti), 106, 112, 124, 126 (G. Dagli Orti), 128, 129, 130 (A. Dagli Orti), 132 (C. Dani), 134/135 (C. Pozzoni), 138, 158, 169, 185t (A. De Gregorio), 185b, 188 (A. Dagli Orti), 191 (M. Seemuller), 192/193 (A. De Gregorio), 194, 197 (G. Nimatallah), 200, 205, 218/219 both, 221, 222 (A. Dagli Orti), 225, 232, 238, 240l, 242/243 (U. Colnago), 248/249 **Getty Images:** 9 & 10 (Hulton Archive), 19 & 160 (Hulton Archive), 162 (Hulton Archive), 166 (AFP), 210, 226 (Time & Life Pictures), 228 & 230 (Hulton Archive) **Heritage Image Partnership:** 40 (British Library) **iStockphoto:** 6 (R. A. Sanchez), 28/29 (A. Kolundzija), 50/51 & 58 (J. Fernández) **Library of Congress:** 66, 181, 182/183, 187, 196, 204t, 207, 216, 227 **Mary Evans Picture Library:** 11, 12 (Tallandier/Rue des Archives), 16, 22, 24/25, 26, 33, 34, 45, 68, 78, 82, 94, 108, 110, 111, 113, 116, 131, 137, 139 (AISA Media), 146, 163b, 176/177, 184 (ILN Pictures), 186, 199, 202 (ILN Pictures), 209 both (Tallandier/Rue des Archives), 212, 213 **Photos12.com:** 59 (ARJ), 83 (G. Rivet), 120 (ARJ), 223 **Photos.com:** 7, 8, 157, 170, 180, 203, 204b, 206, 217 **Public Domain:** 30, 42, 46/47, 97, 104, 114, 142, 143 **Ronald Grant Archive:** 245 **Science Photo Library:** 163t, 174 (Royal Astronomical Society) **TopFoto:** 36 (J.P. Laurens/HIP), 87 (F. Taylor/Fortean), 101 (Topham Picturepoint), 144 (Alinari), 237 (Topham Picturepoint), 239 (AP)